Threat Modeling
A Practical Guide for Development Teams

Izar Tarandach and Matthew J. Coles

Beijing · Boston · Farnham · Sebastopol · Tokyo

Threat Modeling

by Izar Tarandach and Matthew J. Coles

Published by O'Reilly Media, Inc., 1005 Gravenstein Highway North, Sebastopol, CA 95472.

O'Reilly books may be purchased for educational, business, or sales promotional use. Online editions are also available for most titles (*http://oreilly.com*). For more information, contact our corporate/institutional sales department: 800-998-9938 or *corporate@oreilly.com*.

Acquisitions Editor: John Devins	**Indexer:** Sue Klefstad
Development Editor: Virginia Wilson	**Interior Designer:** David Futato
Production Editor: Deborah Baker	**Cover Designer:** Karen Montgomery
Copyeditor: Sharon Wilkey	**Illustrator:** Kate Dullea
Proofreader: Kim Cofer	

December 2020:   First Edition

Revision History for the First Edition

2019-11-12:   First Release

See *http://oreilly.com/catalog/errata.csp?isbn=9781492056553* for release details.

978-1-492-05655-3

[LSI]

Table of Contents

Foreword

For the past 15 years, when I've talked to engineers about security in the development life cycle, they've asked one question again and again: "Out of everything you security professionals prescribe, what is the one most critical activity we should do?" I have been amused, frustrated, and often jaded by this question because, frankly, no one critical activity will guarantee security in the development life cycle. It is a process—and, many times, even when every part of the process is followed, the application still can be vulnerable and get exploited in production. There is no silver bullet to security done right, just as there is no perfect bug-free software.

But one activity continues to deliver tremendous value, when done right, and that is *threat modeling*. Threat modeling is certainly not a replacement for all the other security activities we prescribe, and it comes with some baggage over what is meant by "doing it right." It has a reputation for being onerous, never-ending, and dependent on the security expertise of the individual or teams doing the exercise. But, let me share with you my experience of why this is a high-value activity every development team should incorporate.

When I was leading Security at EMC and we had a few years of data from having our secure software development program in place, we decided to do a deep dive into the vulnerabilities that external researchers reported to our Product Security Response Center (PSRC). The objective of this exercise was simple: figure out how many of these reported vulnerabilities could have been identified by threat modeling. The data overwhelmingly told us that a large majority (upwards of 80%) of these issues were design-level issues that would have been found during a threat model.

We then did a similar exercise on penetration testing results to compare whether a threat model could have identified what our external testing vendors identified in their reports. The results were similar. Taking a data-driven approach led us to focus on more actively developing and executing our internal threat modeling practice.

This is something I have carried forward in my current role at Autodesk. I find threat modeling not just more effective, but also much less noisy than, say, running source code analysis tools on our applications. This is not a judgment on the capability of these tools to find security vulnerabilities, but, in my experience, less noise equates to more satisfied engineers with less skepticism over incorporating security practices in the development life cycle.

Developers are busy. They have full work plates and so either don't want to change the way they work or don't want to slow down to incorporate what the security teams want them to. Izar and Matt have years of experience working with developers, and have gathered a host of practical tips for how to make threat modeling accessible to all developers and how to apply the results from threat modeling toward effective risk management. What Matt and Izar are proposing in this book takes us one step closer to identifying the most egregious security flaws earlier in the life cycle so that development teams can follow risk management practices when there is still time—before the software goes into production.

Threat modeling may seem out of place in the cloud world, where it is critical to adopt techniques for continuous integration and continuous deployment. This book shows you what continuous modeling looks like so you can identify design risks without spending hours whiteboarding. More work is needed on this front, and I have continued to challenge Matt and Izar to come up with new techniques for incorporating continuous modeling and developing automation around it. At Autodesk, we follow a simple mantra: automate everything. A few years back, automating threat modeling would have seemed like a pipe dream. Today, with some of the concepts laid out in this book, it seems like we are getting closer to this dream.

Now, when I am asked the question, "Out of everything you security professionals prescribe, what is the one most critical activity we should do?" I answer, "Let's start with threat modeling and then we will tell you more." This book shows you how to do it right and how to incorporate it seamlessly into your product development life cycle.

— Reeny Sondhi
Vice President and Chief Security Officer, Autodesk

Preface

Welcome to our practical guide to real-world threat modeling. This book is the result of 10 years of research, development, and practice in threat modeling and in secure systems design over the course of our respective careers. We worked hard to make sure the content is well supported, not only by our own observation, but also by the experiences of our colleagues and associates in the application security community.

While we have tried to present a collection of methods and techniques that are current and forward-looking, we know that changes will outpace the book over the coming months and years. Threat modeling is ever evolving. At the time of this writing (in 2020), close to two dozen distinct approaches to performing security modeling and analysis are available. Active forums within security-focused organizations and development communities worldwide are inventing new techniques or updating existing ones all the time. With this in mind, our goal with this book is to provide you information that is both actionable and accessible, with enough theory and guidance for you to reach your own conclusions and to adapt these techniques for your team and your systems.

Why We Wrote This Book

There's a perception that you have to be part of the exclusive club of security experts to perform threat modeling. But it shouldn't be that way. It should be a function and discipline of development. So our ultimate goal in this book is to change the perception of threat modeling so it is an accessible discipline that anyone can learn and perform.

So why us? Years ago, we were where many of you are right now: feeling confused about this whole "threat modeling" thing.

Over time, we came to know some of the methodologies out there, many of the pain points, and much of the joy a good threat model can bring. Along the way, we met many interesting, smart people who take threat modeling (and the meta knowledge that goes with it) to a whole new level, and we learned from them. We have developed our own ideas, and realized we could help others along the journey, give them a leg up, and relieve them from much of the fear, uncertainty, and doubt (FUD) around threat modeling. In short: we want people to be as excited about it as we are.

Who This Book Is For

We wrote this book for members of the system development team (developers, architects, designers, testers, DevSecOps) who are (or want to be) responsible for raising the security posture of their designs, their development processes, and their released systems. This includes people who are designing, building, or maintaining product or IT systems.

Traditional security practitioners will also find value in this book—especially those who aren't yet experienced in threat modeling—but we wrote this material specifically with the system development team in mind. Product managers, program managers, and other less technical functions should also be able to find value here—at least to understand their own value in the process!

What Is (and Isn't!) in This Book

Our main focus is on how to use threat modeling to analyze system design so you can identify the risk inherent in the system's implementation and deployment and can avoid that risk in the first place. We do not provide how-to recipes for secure design or analysis of specific topologies, systems, or algorithms; we cite other books throughout that do a fine job of these. Instead, we aim to equip you with the tools you need to recognize risk conditions when they exist, give you concrete methodology options for addressing those risk conditions, and point you to sources for further information to help you broaden your threat modeling skills.

In the Introduction, we provide a background of security principles and secure design techniques, and discuss fundamental properties and mechanisms for securing your data and your system's functionality. We examine the relationships among security, privacy, and safety, and define *risk*. We also identify factors that determine risk to your system. The security fundamentals covered in the Introduction are especially important for those who are new to application security, and those looking for a refresher on principles and objectives, to read.

In Chapter 1, we look at system modeling techniques and show you how to identify key characteristics that are crucial for assessing the security of your system. We identify exploitable weaknesses and the methods by which these weaknesses negatively impact your system's security.

In Chapters 2 and 3, we present an overview of threat modeling as an activity during your system's development life cycle, and provide an in-depth review of popular threat modeling techniques to consider using when you model and analyze your systems. We also discuss newer methodologies and touch on gamification of threat modeling.

Chapter 2 and beyond should be valuable to all readers, including the seasoned security practitioner who already understands why threat modeling is a crucial activity and has command of the principles of secure design.

In Chapters 4 and 5, we discuss the future of threat modeling methodologies, automation, and Agile development methodologies (including DevOps automation). We also cover specialized techniques to perform threat modeling in new and interesting ways. These chapters should be especially interesting to the more advanced reader.

Chapter 6 presents frequently asked questions we often hear from development teams embarking on a journey to adopt threat modeling in their organizations. We offer advice and guidance to help users make progress and avoid common pitfalls and roadblocks to success.

Appendix A contains a complete example of the use of pytm to construct and analyze a system model for threats. Appendix B contains the Threat Modeling Manifesto—a statement of direction on what makes threat modeling valuable and necessary in system deployment today.

These Techniques Apply Across Various Systems

Throughout this book, we feature software-based systems because of their commonality in all scenarios and because we didn't want knowledge of, for example, the Internet of Things (IoT) or cloud technologies to be a prerequisite for understanding the examples. But the techniques we discuss are applicable to all system types, whether hardware based, cloud based, or almost any combination of systems and software responsible for moving data from one end to another and storing it securely. We even provide guidance for analyzing business processes to help you understand their impact on the system.

Your Contribution Matters

If you have read other texts on how to conduct a threat model, you will probably notice slight differences of opinion on the techniques, constructs, and approaches we offer. This is by design (no pun intended!). If our work here instigates constructive debate within the community over how to understand security and its effects on system design, threat modeling will improve, and the individuals who rely on it will benefit. As we've stated, threat modeling is ever evolving, and we encourage you to contribute to its evolution. Perhaps some day we will meet you at a conference or work with you on a development project, discuss our experiences, and learn from each other.

You can reach us by opening a ticket at *https://threatmodeling.dev*.

Conventions Used in This Book

The following typographical conventions are used in this book:

Italic
> Indicates new terms, URLs, email addresses, filenames, and file extensions.

`Constant width`
> Used for program listings, as well as within paragraphs to refer to program elements such as variable or function names, databases, data types, environment variables, statements, and keywords.

`Constant width bold`
> Shows commands or other text that should be typed literally by the user.

`Constant width italic`
> Shows text that should be replaced with user-supplied values or by values determined by context.

> This element signifies a tip or suggestion.

> This element signifies a general note.

This element indicates a warning or caution.

O'Reilly Online Learning

 For more than 40 years, *O'Reilly Media* has provided technology and business training, knowledge, and insight to help companies succeed.

Our unique network of experts and innovators share their knowledge and expertise through books, articles, and our online learning platform. O'Reilly's online learning platform gives you on-demand access to live training courses, in-depth learning paths, interactive coding environments, and a vast collection of text and video from O'Reilly and 200+ other publishers. For more information, visit *http://oreilly.com*.

How to Contact Us

Please address comments and questions concerning this book to the publisher:

O'Reilly Media, Inc.
1005 Gravenstein Highway North
Sebastopol, CA 95472
800-998-9938 (in the United States or Canada)
707-829-0515 (international or local)
707-829-0104 (fax)

We have a web page for this book, where we list errata and any additional information. You can access this page at *https://oreil.ly/Threat_Modeling*.

Email *bookquestions@oreilly.com* to comment or ask technical questions about this book.

For news and information about our books and courses, visit *http://oreilly.com*.

Find us on Facebook: *http://facebook.com/oreilly*

Follow us on Twitter: *http://twitter.com/oreillymedia*

Watch us on YouTube: *http://www.youtube.com/oreillymedia*

Acknowledgments

We would like to thank the following individuals for their experience, knowledge, and time invested in the form of reviews, discussions, opinions, technical details, and their prior work in the field. This text would have looked completely different without their gracious input:

Aaron Lint, Adam Shostack, Akhil Behl, Alexander Bicalho, Andrew Kalat, Alyssa Miller, Brook S. E. Schoenfield, Chris Romeo, Christian Schneider, Fraser Scott, Jonathan Marcil, John Paramadilok, Kim Wuyts, Laurens Sion, Mike Hepple, Robert Hurlbut, Sebastien Deleersnyder, Seth Lakowske, and Tony UcedaVélez.

Special thanks go to Sheila Kamath for lending her technical writing skills to help us improve the quality and clarity of this book. As first-time authors, we learned through her valuable comments that there is a big difference between dumping thoughts on the page, writing whitepapers, and writing for the broad audience we hope finds this book useful.

To our editor, Virginia Wilson, for your patience, dedication, professionalism, and for pushing us forward.

 If you are curious about the Security Toolbox mentioned in the Dedication, check out the first work we co-presented (*https:// oreil.ly/Ps9uw*), at SOURCE Boston 2011.

Some of the concepts from Security Toolbox found their way into our pytm (*https://owasp.org/www-project-pytm*) project, which is still an area of active research for us.

Introduction

How you get to know is what I want to know.
—Richard Feynman, American physicist

In this introduction, we'll explain the very basics of threat modeling. We'll also cover the most crucial security principles you need to know as the foundation for assessing the security of the systems you are analyzing.

The Basics of Threat Modeling

Let's begin by taking a bird's-eye view of what threat modeling is, why it's useful, and how it fits into the development life cycle and overall security plan.

What Is Threat Modeling?

Threat modeling is the process of analyzing a system to look for weaknesses that come from less-desirable design choices. The goal of the activity is to identify these weaknesses before they are baked into the system (as a result of implementation or deployment) so you can take corrective action as early as possible. The activity of threat modeling is a conceptual exercise that aims to help you understand which characteristics of a system's design should be modified to reduce risk in the system to an acceptable level for its owners, users, and operators.

When performing threat modeling, you look at a system as a collection of its components and their interactions with the world outside the system (like other systems it interacts with) and the actors that may perform actions on these systems. Then you try to imagine how these components and interactions may fail or be made to fail. From this process, you'll identify threats to the system, which will in turn lead to changes and modifications to the system. The result is a system that can resist the threats you imagined.

But let's make clear right from the beginning: threat modeling is a cyclic activity. It starts with a clear objective, continues with analysis and actions, and then it repeats. It is not a silver bullet—by itself it does not solve all your security issues. It is also not a push-button tool, like a scanner that you point at your website or your code repository that generates a punch list of items to be ticked off. Threat modeling is a logical, intellectual process that will be most effective if you involve most, if not all, of your team. It will generate discussion and create clarity of your design and execution. All of this requires work and a certain amount of specialized knowledge.

The first rule of threat modeling might be the old maxim *garbage in, garbage out* (GIGO).[1] If you make threat modeling part of your team's toolbox and get everyone to participate in a positive manner, you will reap its many benefits, but if you enter into it half-heartedly, without a complete understanding of its strengths and shortcomings or as a compliance "check the box" item, you'll see it only as a time sink. Once you find a methodology that works for you and your team and put in the effort needed to make it work, your overall security posture will grow substantially.

Why You Need Threat Modeling

You need threat modeling because it will make your work easier and better in the long term. It will lead to cleaner architectures, well-defined trust boundaries (you don't know what those are yet and why they are important, but soon you will!), focused security testing, and better documentation. And most of all, it will instill in you and your team the superpower of security mindedness in an organized, orchestrated way, leading to better security standards and guidelines across your development effort.

As important as all those side benefits are, they are not the most important. Understanding what could possibly go wrong in your system and what you can do about it will increase your trust in what you're delivering, leaving you free to concentrate on other facets of the system. And that is what's really behind the need for threat modeling.

Also important is to point out why you *don't* need threat modeling. It is not going to solve all your security problems by itself; it will also not transform your team into security experts immediately. Most of all, you don't need it for compliance. An empty exercise that aims only at putting the check mark in the compliance list will lead you to more frustration than knowing you do not have that specific requirement covered.

---

1 This phrase is accredited to Wilf Hey and to Army Specialist William D. Mellin.

Obstacles

The trouble with programmers is that you can never tell what a programmer is doing until it's too late.

—Seymour R. Cray, creator of the Cray line of supercomputers (*https://oreil.ly/vg51w*)

This maxim holds true to this day. Give a developer a specification or a reasonably well-documented set of requirements, and stand back, and many interesting things may happen.

Honestly, we know that development teams can be stressed-out overachievers who work under heavy demands and heavy responsibility. You have to deal with an almost constantly changing landscape of learning, becoming proficient, and then forgetting whole subdisciplines. It is unfair to pressure you on "not knowing some security thing that's really basic and important." Consider that the entire training content industry is mostly focused on delivering business-oriented objectives such as compliance and meeting training goals and other assorted metrics. There is significant room for improvement in actually delivering effective, useful content that development teams can translate into knowledge and practical use.

One of the tasks of security professionals is to further the security education of development communities. This includes how to implement *secure* systems and how to *assess* the security of code and systems, post facto. It may seem easier to rely on an expensive set of tools to supplement (and to a large extent, hide from view) the organization's security expertise. The challenge is that the expertise built into the tools is often hidden from the user; development teams would benefit greatly if the methods of detection were transparent to them. Here are some examples:

- Computer-based training (CBT) is the scourge of every new worker. Sets of 45 minutes of boring voices reading tired-looking slides, in the usual standard fonts, with the same stock pictures and images? And worse still, the innocuous, "solve by exclusion," teach-nothing multiple-choice questions?

- Overreliance on "silver bullet" scanners and static code analyzers that promise to use artificial intelligence, machine learning, taint analysis, attack trees, and the *Powers of Grayskull*, but fail to consistently produce the same results, or give more false positives than actual useful answers. Or the analysis tools expect the whole system to exist before they can run a scan, not to mention inserting long times in the build process that are anathema to the continuous integration/continuous development (CI/CD) values.

- Consulting services where, upon request, a security practitioner will swoop in, execute remediation work (or "directed training"), and disappear (we call this *seagull consulting*; they swoop in, poop on you, and then fly off), leaving the team to deal with the consequences. Relying on a just-in-time security consultant carries significant downsides: they have no vested interest in the outcome of their actions, they are external to the team (if not to the enterprise), they bring a personal bias, and they perform "magic," leaving the team feeling that something happened but without a sense of what transpired. Cargo cult[2] behavior follows, as the team tries to constantly replicate that subset of results the consultant left behind.

We security professionals have also created a false sense of developer expectations within organizations:

- An organization can buy its way to a strong security posture. If it invests enough money in tools, it will solve all of its security problems.

- Thirty minutes of mandatory training a quarter is sufficient for the organization to pass the audit. These 30 minutes should be sufficient for development teams to learn what is expected of them. Since development teams have access to top-notch training content, the expensive tools they use will only "look over their shoulders" and validate that they have, indeed, done their job in a perfectly secure manner.

Lately (since mid-2019) the industry of security has been consumed by the idea of *shifting left* (*https://oreil.ly/DWAiY*). Imagine a workflow that you read from left to right. The start of the workflow is on the left. When we say "shifting left," we mean that we want the security processes to move as far "left," to the beginning of the development workflow (of whatever development methodology is in use) as possible. This allows security events to happen and be dealt with as early as possible. An activity such as threat modeling, which is closely associated with design, should happen as early as possible in the lifetime of a system. And, if it didn't happen then, it should happen *right now*.

 We don't subscribe to the "shift left" phenomenon, preferring instead to *start left* by using methodologies that begin with design, or sooner—with requirements—as the foundation for the security of a system.

---

2 "A cargo cult is a millenarian belief system in which adherents practice rituals which they believe will cause a more technologically advanced society to deliver goods." Wikipedia, accessed 10/24/2020.

With changes to the process resulting in a less linear "left-to-right" development cycle, shifting left may not be capable of addressing all security needs in a system. Instead, the security community will need to shift even further left into the lives of developers and designers as individuals, *before* a system is being considered. There we will need to focus on training development teams to make secure choices, and bring capabilities along with them, to avoid threats at a much more fundamental level.

Then, there is the implementation, where security is supposedly shifted left by the industry's collective training efforts, and is expressed semantically and logically by secure code. But if training has failed to deliver on the promised expectations, what possible corrective measures are available to correct for the failed assumptions?

Let's look at another angle of the problem and then connect the pieces into a coherent response to this rant (an invitation to a crusade!). Some speak about "a place at the table" when discussing security strategy. Security teams and executives want the "stakeholders" to hold "a place" for security in the "ongoing discussion." This allows them to justify their need to take that slice of the resources pie. But there's another important resource that is not as recognized, because it is obfuscated by "extensive training" and "silver bullet tools." And that resource is the developer's time and focus.

Let's consider a web developer. Infinite numbers of memes reflect the fact that if today a web developer learns everything they can about the LAMP stack[3] before breakfast, that knowledge becomes useless right after lunch because the whole industry will have moved to the MEAN stack.[4] And the MEAN stack will be superseded two grande lattes later by yet another shiny new thing until it comes right around again to the new, improved (and totally non-backward-compatible!) version of where we just started. Each one of these new stacks brings about a new set of security challenges *and* security-related idioms and mechanisms that must be understood and incorporated to effectively protect the system they are developing. And of course, each stack requires a distinct security contract that the web developer must learn and become fluent in quickly.

But the website can't be down, and its administration is supposed to happen *at the same time* the developer is learning their new ~~toy~~ tool. How can security possibly expect to share the same pie (i.e., the developer's time and attention) and receive anything but a sliver of a slice?

---

3 The LAMP stack consists of the collection of Linux OS, Apache web server, MySQL database, and PHP scripting language.

4 The MEAN stack consists of MongoDB, Express.js, Angular.js, and Node.js.

And this is where the crusade begins—as Richard Feynman tells us: "Teach principles, not formulas." In this book, we will focus on *principles* to help you understand and think through what threat modeling is for you, how it can help in your specific case, and how you can best apply it to your project and your team.

Threat Modeling in the System Development Life Cycle

Threat modeling is an activity performed during the system development life cycle that is critical to the security of the system. If threat modeling is not performed in some fashion, security faults will likely be introduced through design choices that are possibly easily exploited, and most definitely will be hard (and costly[5]) to fix later. In keeping with the "build in, not bolt on" principle of security, threat modeling should not be considered a compliance milestone; real-world consequences exist for failing to perform this activity when it matters most.

Most successful companies today don't execute projects the way they did even a couple of years ago. For example, development paradigms like serverless computing,[6] or some of the latest trends and tools in CI/CD,[7] have made a deep impact on how development teams design, implement, and deploy today's systems.

Because of market demand and the race to be first, you rarely have the opportunity nowadays to sit down prior to the development of a system and see a fully fleshed-out design. Product teams rely on "minimum viable product" versions to introduce their new ideas to the public and to start building a brand and a following. They then rely on incremental releases to add functionality and make changes as issues arise. This practice results in *significant* changes to design occurring later in the development cycle.

Modern systems are of a complexity not seen before. You might use many third-party components, libraries, and frameworks (which may be open or closed source) to build your new software, but the components are many times poorly documented, poorly understood, and poorly secured. To create "simple" systems, you rely on intricate layers of software, services, and capabilities. Again, using serverless deployments as an example, to say "I don't care about the environment, libraries, machines, or network, I only care about my functions" is shortsighted. How much machinery is hidden behind the curtain? How much control do you have over what's happening

---

5 Arvinder Saini, "How Much Do Bugs Cost to Fix During Each Phase of the SDLC?," Software Integrity Blog, Synopsis, January 2017, *https://oreil.ly/NVuSf*; Sanket, "Exponential Cost of Fixing Bugs," DeepSource, January 2019, *https://oreil.ly/ZrLvg*.

6 "What Is Serverless Computing?," Cloudflare, accessed November 2020, *https://oreil.ly/7L4AJ*.

7 Isaac Sacolick, "What Is CI/CD? Continuous Integration and Continuous Delivery Explained," InfoWorld, January 2020, *https://oreil.ly/tDc-X*.

"under" your functions? How do these things impact the overall security of your system? How do you validate that you are using the most appropriate roles and access rules?

To answer those questions reliably and obtain immediate results, you might be tempted to use an external security expert. But expertise in security can vary, and experts can be expensive to hire. Some experts focus on specific technologies or areas, and others' focus is broad but shallow. Of course, this by no means describes every consultant, and we will be the first to attest to having had some great experiences with threat modeling consultants. However, you can see that there is a huge incentive to develop in-house knowledge of threat modeling and try to adapt it as much as possible to your team's development methodology.

Developing secure systems

Regardless of the development methodology you use, the way your system develops must pass through some very specific phases (see Figure I-1).

- Idea inception
- Design
- Implementation
- Testing
- Deployment

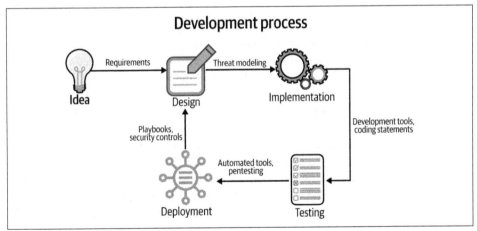

Figure I-1. Development loop and related security activities

In the waterfall methodology, for example, these phases naturally follow each other. Note that documentation plays an ongoing role—it must happen in parallel with the other phases to be truly efficient. When using this methodology, it is easy to see that a threat model provides the most benefit at design time.

This is an affirmation you will see many times in this book. We meticulously link threat modeling with design. Why is that?

A much-quoted[8] concept indicates that the cost of solving an issue rises significantly the closer it happens to or after deployment. This is quite obvious for people familiar with making and marketing software; it is much cheaper to apply solutions to a system in development than the one already deployed at thousands or, in some extreme cases, millions of places.[9] You don't have to deal with the liability of some users not applying a patch, or the possible failures in backward compatibility introduced by patching a system. You don't have to deal with users who cannot for one reason or another move forward with the patch. And you don't have to incur the cost of supporting a lengthy and sometimes unstable upgrade process.

So, threat modeling by its nature looks at a *design*, and tries to identify *security flaws*. For example, if your analysis shows that a certain mode of access uses a hardcoded password, it gets identified as a *finding* to be addressed. If a finding goes unaddressed, you are probably dealing with an issue that will be exploited later in the life of the system. This is also known as a *vulnerability*, which has a *probability of exploitation* and an associated *cost* if exploited. You might also fail to identify an issue, or fail to make a correct determination of something that can be exploited. Perfection and completeness are not goals of this exercise.

The key objective of threat modeling is to identify flaws so they become *findings* (issues that you can address) and not *vulnerabilities* (issues that can be exploited). You can then apply mitigations that reduce both the probability of exploitation and the cost of being exploited (that is, the damage, or impact).

Once you identify a finding, you move to *mitigate*, or rectify, it. You do this by applying appropriate controls; for example, you might create a dynamic, user-defined password instead of a hardcoded one. Or, if the case warrants, you might run multiple tests against that password to ensure its strength. Or you might let the user decide on a password policy. Or, you might change your approach altogether and entirely remove the flaw by removing the password use and offer support for WebAuthn[10] instead. In some cases, you might just assume the risk—you decide that for the

---

8 Barry Boehm, *Software Engineering Economics* (Prentice Hall, 1981).

9 Kayla Matthews, "What Do IoT Hacks Cost the Economy?," IoT For All, October 2018, *https://oreil.ly/EyT6e*.

10 "What is WebAuthn?," Yubico, *https://oreil.ly/xmmL9*.

manner in which the system will be deployed, it could be OK to use a hardcoded password. (Hint: It is not. Really. Think about it.) Sometimes you have to determine that a risk is acceptable. In those cases, you need to document the finding, identify and describe the rationale for not addressing it, and make that part of your threat model.

It is important to emphasize (and we will return to this throughout the book) that threat modeling is an evolutionary process. You may not find all the flaws in your system the first time it is analyzed. For example, perhaps you didn't have the appropriate resources or the correct stakeholders examining the system. But having an initial threat model is much better than having no threat model at all. And the next iteration, when the threat model is updated, will be better, identify other flaws, and carry a higher level of assurance that no flaws were found. You and your team will acquire the experience and confidence that will lead you to consider new and more complex or subtle attacks and vectors, and your system will constantly improve.

No more waterfalling

Let's move forward to the more modern Agile and CI/CD approaches.

Because these are faster ways of developing and deploying software, you may find it impossible to stop everything, initiate a proper design session, and agree on what needs to happen. Sometimes your design evolves with requirements from customers, and other times your design *emerges* from the ongoing development of your system. In these situations, it can be hard to predict the overall design of the complete system (or even to know what the complete system is), and you may not be able to make wide-ranging design modifications beforehand.

Many design proposals outline how to perform threat modeling under these circumstances—from Microsoft's proposal of "security sprints" (*https://oreil.ly/LWesA*) to applying threat modeling against smaller system units, iteratively, at every sprint. And, unfortunately, claims have been made that threat modeling "reduces the velocity" of an Agile team. Is it better to reduce the velocity of an Agile team, or that of a team of hackers who are trying to access your data? For right now, the important thing is to recognize the issue; we will point at possible solutions later.

Once you address security in the design process, you will see how security impacts all other phases of development. This will help you recognize how threat modeling can have an even bigger impact on the overall *security posture* of the system, which is a collective measure of:

- The current state of security within the system
- Attack vectors, or intrusion points, or opportunities to change the system behavior, available for an actor to explore and exploit (also known as the *attack surface*)

- The existing vulnerabilities and weaknesses within the system (also known as the *security debt*) and the combined risk to the system and/or the business resulting from these factors

Implementation and testing

It is hard not to consider implementation and testing as the most important aspect of security in development. At the end of the day, security problems come (mostly!) from issues or mistakes made when putting lines of code into place. Some of the most infamous security issues—Heartbleed (*https://heartbleed.com*), anyone?—and most buffer overflow issues stem not from bad design, but from lines of code that didn't do what they were supposed to do, or did it in an unexpected way.

When you look at classes of vulnerabilities (for example buffer overflows and injection issues), it is easy to see how a developer may inadvertently introduce them. It is easy to cut and paste a previously used stanza, or fall into the "who would possibly do that?" belief when considering bad input. Or the developer may simply introduce errors due to ignorance, time constraints, or other factors without any consideration of security.

Many tools out there identify vulnerabilities in written code by performing static analysis. Some tools do this by analyzing the source code; others do it by running code through simulations of input and identifying bad outcomes (this technique is known as *fuzzing*). Machine learning has recently emerged as another alternative for identifying "bad code."

But does threat modeling influence these code-related issues? That depends. If you look at a system as a whole and decide you are able to completely remove an entire class of vulnerabilities by addressing the root flaw, then you have an opportunity at design time to address code-related issues. Google did this with cross-site scripting (and other vulnerability classes) by instituting libraries and patterns to be used in all products that deal with the issue.[11] Unfortunately, choices made to address some types of issues may cut off any avenue to address other concerns. For example, let's say you are working on a system with primary requirements for high performance and high reliability. You may choose to use a language that offers direct memory control and less execution overhead, such as C, instead of languages like Go or Java that offer better memory management capabilities. In this case, you may have limited options to influence the breadth of potential security concerns that need to be addressed by changing the technology stack. This means that you have to use development-time and testing-time tools to police the outcome.

---

11 Christoph Kern, "Preventing Security Bugs through Software Design," USENIX, August 2015, *https://oreil.ly/rcKL_*.

Documentation and deployment

As systems are developed, the teams responsible for them may go through a self-development process. *Tribal knowledge*, or institutional knowledge, exists when a set of individuals comes to learn or understand something and retains that knowledge without documenting it. However, as team membership changes over time, with individuals leaving the team and new ones joining, this tribal knowledge can be lost.

Luckily, a well-documented threat model is a great vehicle to provide new team members with this formal and proprietary knowledge. Many obscure data points, justifications, and general thought processes (e.g., "Why did you folks do it like *this* here?!") are well suited for being captured as documentation in a threat model. Any decisions made to overcome constraints, and their resulting security impacts, are also good candidates for documentation. The same goes with deployment—a threat model is a great place to reference an inventory of third-party components, how they are kept up-to-date, the efforts required to harden them, and the assumptions made when configuring them. Something as simple as an inventory of network ports and their protocols explains not only the way data flows in the system, but also deployment decisions concerning authentication of hosts, configuration of firewalls, etc. All these kinds of information fit well into a threat model, and if you need to respond to compliance audits and third-party audits, locating and providing relevant details becomes much easier.

Essential Security Principles

The remainder of this Introduction gives a brief overview of the foundational security concepts and terminology that are critically important for both development teams and security practitioners to have at least some familiarity with. If you wish to learn more about any of these principles, check out the many excellent references we provide throughout this chapter and the book.

Familiarity with these principles and terminology is key as a foundation for additional learning—as an individual or as a team, learning as you go through your security travels.

Basic Concepts and Terminology

Figure I-2 highlights crucial concepts in system security. Understanding these relationships and the nomenclature of security are key to understanding why threat modeling is critically important to a secure system design.

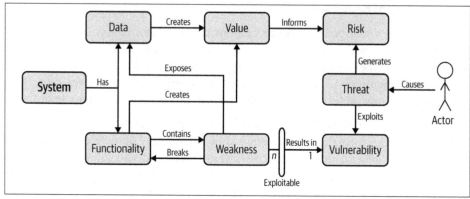

Figure I-2. Relationships of security terminology

A *system* contains assets—*functionality* its users depend upon, and *data* accepted, stored, manipulated, or transmitted by the system. The system's functionality may contain defects, which are also known as *weaknesses*. If these weaknesses are exploitable, meaning if they are vulnerable to external influence, they are known as *vulnerabilities*, and exploitation of them may put the operations and data of the system at risk of exposure. An *actor* (an individual or a process external to the system) may have malicious intent and may try to exploit a vulnerability, if the conditions exist to make that possible; some skilled attackers are capable of altering conditions to create opportunities to attempt exploitation. An actor creates a *threat* event in this case, and through this event threatens the system with a particular effect (such as stealing data or causing functionality to misbehave).

The combination of functionality and data creates *value* in the system, and an adversary causing a threat negates that value, which forms the basis for *risk*. Risk is offset by controls, which cover functional capabilities of a system as well as operational and organizational behaviors of the teams that design and build the system, and is modified by probabilities—the expectations of an attacker wishing to cause harm and the likelihood they will be successful should they attempt to do so.

Each concept and term requires additional explanation to be meaningful:

Weakness
> A weakness is an underlying defect that modifies behavior or functionality (resulting in incorrect behavior) or allows unverified or incorrect access to data. Weaknesses in system design result from failure to follow best practices, or standards, or convention, and lead to some undesirable effect on the system. Luckily for threat modelers (and development teams), a community initiative—Common Weakness Enumeration (CWE) (*http://cwe.mitre.org*)—has created an open taxonomy of security weaknesses that can be referenced when investigating system design for concerns.

Exploitability

Exploitability is a measure of how easily an attacker can make use of a weakness to cause harm. Put another way, exploitability is the amount of exposure that the weakness has to external influence.[12]

Vulnerability

When a weakness is exploitable (exploitability outside the local authorization context is nonzero),it is known as a vulnerability. Vulnerabilities provide a means for an adversary with malicious intent to cause some sort of damage to a system. Vulnerabilities that exist in a system but that are previously undiscovered are known as *zero-day vulnerabilities*. Zero days are no more or less dangerous than other vulnerabilities of a similar nature but are special because they are likely to be unresolved, and therefore the potential for exploitation may be elevated. As with weaknesses, community efforts have created a taxonomy of vulnerabilities, encoded in the CVE (*https://cve.mitre.org*) database.

Severity

Weaknesses lead to an impact on a system and its assets (functionality and/or data); the damage potential and "blast radius" from such an issue is described as the defect's severity. For those whose primary profession is or has been in any field of engineering, severity may be a familiar term. Vulnerabilities—exploitable weaknesses—are by definition at least as severe as the underlying defect, and more often the severity of a defect is increased because it is open to being exploited. Methods for calculating severity are described in "Calculating Severity or Risk" on page xxx.

 Unfortunately, the process of determining the severity of a weakness is not always so cut and dried. If the ability to leverage the defect to cause an impact is unrecognized at the time of discovery of the weakness, how severe is the issue? What happens if the defect is later determined to be exposed, or worse *becomes* exposed as a result of a change in the system design or implementation? These are hard questions to answer. We'll touch on this later when we introduce risk concepts.

Impact

If a weakness or vulnerability is exploited, it will result in some sort of impact to the system,such as breaking functionality or exposing data. When rating the severity of an issue, you will want to assess the level of impact as a measure of potential loss of functionality and/or data as the result of successful exploitation.

---

12 "External" is relative when used here, and is specific to what is known as the *authorization context*; for example, the operating system, application, databases, etc.

Actor

When describing a system, an actor is any individual associated with the system, such as a user or an attacker. An actor with malicious intent, either internal or external to the organization, creating or using the system, is sometimes referred to as an *adversary*.

Threat

A threat is the result of a nonzero probability of an attacker taking advantage of a vulnerability to negatively impact the system in a particular way (commonly phrased in terms of "threat to…" or "threat of…").

Threat event

When an adversary makes an attempt (successful or not) to exploit a vulnerability with an intended objective or outcome, this becomes known as a threat event.

Loss

For the purpose of this book and the topic of threat modeling, loss occurs when one (or more) impacts affect functionality and/or data as a result of an adversary causing a threat event:

- The actor is able to subvert the confidentiality of a system's data to reveal sensitive or private information.

- The actor can modify the interface to functionality, change the behavior of functionality, or change the contents or provenance of data.

- The actor can prevent authorized entities from accessing functionality or data, either temporarily or permanently.

  Loss is described in terms of an asset or an amount of value.

Risk

Risk combines the value of the potentially exploited target with the likelihood an impact may be realized. Value is relative to the system or information owner, as well as to the attacker. You should use risk to inform priority of an issue, and to decide whether to address the issue. Severe vulnerabilities that are easy to exploit, and those that lead to significant damages through loss, should be given a high priority to mitigate.

Calculating Severity or Risk

Severity (the amount of damage that can be caused by successful exploitation of a vulnerability), and risk (the combination of the likelihood of initiation of a threat event and the likelihood of success to generate a negative impact as a result of exploitation)—can be determined formulaically. The formulas are not perfect but using them provides *consistency*. Many methods exist today for determining severity or risk, and some threat modeling methodologies use alternative risk-scoring methods (not described in this book). A sample of three popular methods in general use (one for measuring severity, two for risk) are presented here.

CVSS (severity)

The Common Vulnerability Scoring System (CVSS) (*https://www.first.org/cvss*) is now in version 3.1, and is a product of the Forum of Incident Response and Security Teams (FIRST).

CVSS is a method for establishing a value from 0.0 to 10.0, that allows you to identify the components of *severity*. The calculation is based upon the likelihood of a successful exploitation of a vulnerability, and a measurement of potential impact (or damage). Eight metrics, or values, are set in the calculator to derive a severity rating, as shown in Figure I-3.

Exploitability metrics			Impact metric		
Attack vector	AV	Network (N) Adjacent (A) Local (L) Physical (P)	Scope changed	SC	Changed (C) Unchanged (U)
Attack complexity	AC	Low (L) High (H)	Confidentiality	C	None (N) Low (L) High (H)
Privileges required	PR	None (N) Low (L) High (H)	Integrity	I	None (N) Low (L) High (H)
User interaction	UI	None (N) Required (R)	Availability	A	None (N) Low (L) High (H)

Figure I-3. Common Vulnerability Scoring System metrics, vector, and score

Likelihood of success is measured on specific metrics that are given a numeric rating. This results in a value known as the *exploitability subscore*. Impact is measured similarly (with different metrics) and is known as the *impact subscore*. Added together, the two subscores result in an overall *base score*.

Remember, CVSS does not measure *risk* but *severity*. CVSS can tell you the likelihood that an attacker will succeed in exploiting the vulnerability of an impacted system, and the amount of damage they can do. But it *cannot* indicate *when* or *if* an attacker will attempt to exploit the vulnerability. Nor can it tell you how much the impacted resource is *worth* or how expensive it will be to address the vulnerability. It is the likelihood of the *initiation* of an attack, the value of the system or functionality, and the cost to mitigate it that drives the risk calculation. Relying on raw severity is a good way to communicate information about a defect, but is a very imperfect way to manage risk.

DREAD (risk)

DREAD is an older,[13] yet foundationally important, method for understanding the risk from security concerns. DREAD is the partner to the STRIDE threat modeling methodology; STRIDE is discussed in depth in Chapter 3.

DREAD is an acronym for:

Damage
　　If an adversary conducted an attack, how much destruction could they cause?

Reproducibility
　　Is a potential attack easily reproduced (in method and effect)?

Exploitability
　　How easy is conducting a successful attack?

Affected users
　　What percentage of the user population might be impacted?

Discoverability
　　If the adversary does not already know of the potential for an attack, what is the likelihood they can discover it?

DREAD is a process for documenting characteristics of a potential for an attack against a system (via a vector by an adversary) and coming up with a value that can be compared to other such values for other attack scenarios and/or threat vectors. The risk score for any given attack scenario (combination of a security vulnerability and adversary) is calculated by considering the characteristics of exploitation of a vulnerability by an attacker and assigning them a score in each dimension (i.e., D, R, E, A, D), for low-, medium-, and high-impact issues, respectively.

---

13 Some say DREAD has outlived its usefulness; see Irene Michlin, "Threat Prioritisation: DREAD Is Dead, Baby?," NCC Group, March 2016, *https://oreil.ly/SJnsR*.

The total of the scores for each dimension determine the overall risk value. For example, an arbitrary security issue in a particular system may have scores of [D = 3, R = 1, E = 1, A = 3, D = 2] for a total risk value of 10. To have meaning, this risk value can be compared to other risks that are identified against this particular system; it is less useful to attempt to compare this value with values from other systems, however.

FAIR Method for risk quantification (risk). The Factor Analysis of Information Risk (FAIR) (*https://oreil.ly/hkpLy*) method is gaining popularity among executive types because it offers the right level of granularity with more specificity to enable more effective decision making. FAIR is published by the Open Group (*https://www.open group.org*) and is included in ISO/IEC 27005:2018 (*https://oreil.ly/IZF9v*).

DREAD is an example of a *qualitative* risk calculation. FAIR is an international standard for *quantitative* risk modeling and for understanding the impact to *assets* from threats using measurements of value (hard and soft currency costs) and probability of realization (occurrences, or threat events) of a threat by an actor. Use these quantitative values to describe to your management and business leaders the financial impact to the business from risks identified in your systems, and compare them against the cost to defend against threat events. Proper risk management practices (*https://oreil.ly/eVWyp*) suggest the cost to defend should not exceed the value of the asset, or the potential loss of an asset. This is also known as the *$50 lock on a $5 pen* paradigm.

 FAIR is thorough and accurate, but also complex, and requires specialized knowledge to perform the calculations and simulations correctly. This is not something you want to do live in a threat modeling review session, nor something you want to hoist on your security subject matter experts (SMEs), if you have them. Security experts have expertise in finding weaknesses and threats, not modeling financial impact valuations. Hiring individuals with skills in computational methods and financial modeling, or finding a tool that does the hard math for you, is a better course of action if you plan to adopt FAIR.

Core Properties

Three core properties—confidentiality, integrity, and availability—form the foundation on which all other things in security are built. When someone wants to know if something is secure, these properties and whether they are intact determine a response. These properties support a key goal: trustworthiness. In addition, fourth and fifth properties (privacy and safety), are related to the first three but have slightly different focuses.

Confidentiality

A system has the property of *confidentiality* only if it guarantees access to the data entrusted to it exclusively to those who have the appropriate rights, based on their need to know the protected information. A system that does not have a barrier stopping unauthorized access fails to safeguard confidentiality.[14]

Integrity

Integrity exists when the authenticity of data or operations can be verified and the data or functionality has not been modified or made unauthentic through unauthorized activity.[15]

Availability

Availability means authorized actors are able to access system functionality and/or data whenever they have the need or desire to do so. In certain circumstances, a system's data or operations may not be available as a result of a contract or agreement between users and system operators (such as a website being down for regular maintenance); if the system is unavailable because of a malicious action by an adversary, availability will have been compromised.[16]

Privacy

While *confidentiality* refers to the controlled access to private information shared with others, *privacy* refers to the right of not having that information exposed to unauthorized third parties. Many times when people talk about confidentiality, they really expect privacy, but although the terms are often used interchangeably, they are *not* the same concept. You could argue that confidentiality is a prerequisite to privacy. For example, if a system cannot guarantee the confidentiality of the data it stores, that system can never provide privacy to its users.

---

14 NIST 800-53 Revision 4, "Security and Privacy Controls for Federal Information Systems and Organizations": B-5.

15 NIST 800-53 Revision 4, "Security and Privacy Controls for Federal Information Systems and Organizations": B-12.

16 NIST 800-160 vol 1, "Systems Security Engineering: Considerations for a Multidisciplinary Approach in the Engineering of Trustworthy Secure Systems": 166.

Safety

Safety is "freedom from unacceptable risk of physical injury or of damage to the health of people, either directly, or indirectly as a result of damage to property or to the Environment."[17] Naturally, for something to meet safety requirements, it has to operate in a predictable manner. This means that it must at least maintain the security properties of integrity and availability.

Fundamental Controls

The following *controls*, or functional behaviors and capabilities, support the development of highly secure systems.

Identification

Actors in a system must be assigned a unique identifier meaningful to the system. Identifiers should also be meaningful to the individuals or processes that will consume the identity (e.g., the authentication subsystem; authentication is described next).

An actor is anything in a system (including human users, system accounts, and processes) that has influence over the system and its functions, or that wishes to gain access to the system's data. To support many security objectives, an actor must be granted an identity before it can operate on that system. This identity must come with information that allows a system to positively identify the actor—or in other words, to allow the actor to show proof of identity to the system. In some public systems, unnamed actors or users are also identified, indicating that their specific identity is not important but is still represented in the system.

Guest is an acceptable identity on many systems as a shared account. Other shared accounts may exist, although use of shared accounts should be carefully considered as they lack the ability to trace and control actor behavior on an individual basis.

Authentication

Actors with identities need to prove their identity to the system. Identity is usually proven by the use of a credential (such as a password or security token).

All actors who wish to use the system must be able to satisfactorily provide proof of their identity so that the target system can verify that it is communicating with the right actor. Authentication is a prerequisite for additional security capabilities.

---

17 "Functional Safety and IEC 61508," International Electrotechnical Commission, *https://oreil.ly/SUC-E*.

Authorization

Once an actor has been authenticated—that is, their identity has been proven satisfactorily—the actor can be granted privileges within the system to perform operations or access functionality or data. Authorization is contextual, and *may* be, but is not required to be, transitive, bidirectional, or reciprocal in nature.

With authentication comes the ability for a system, based on the offered proof of identification provided by an actor, to specify the rights of that actor. For example, once a user has authenticated into a system and is allowed to perform operations in a database, *access* to that database is granted based only on the actor's rights. Access is usually granted in terms of primitive operations such as read, write, or execute. Access-control schemes that govern an actor's behavior within a system include the following:

Mandatory access control (MAC)
> The system constrains the authorizations for actors.

Discretionary access control (DAC)
> Actors can define privileges for operations.

Role-based access control (RBAC)
> Actors are grouped by meaningful "roles," and where roles define privilege assignments.

Capability-based access control
> An authorization subsystem assigns rights through tokens that actors must request (and be granted) in order to perform operations.

> Guest accounts are usually not authenticated (there is no identity to prove), but these accounts may be *authorized* explicitly with a minimal level of capability.

Logging

When an actor (human or process) performs a system operation, such as executing a feature or accessing data stores, a record of that event should be recorded. This supports traceability. Traceability is important when trying to debug a system; when the recorded events are considered security relevant, the traceability also supports the ability for critical tasks such as intrusion detection and prevention, forensics, and evidence collection (in the case of a malicious actor intruding upon a system).

Auditing

Logging creates records; audit records are well-defined (in format and content), ordered in time, and usually tamper resistant (or at least tamper evident). The capability of "looking back in time" and understanding the order in which events occurred, who performed which operations, and when, and optionally to determine whether the operations were correct and authorized, is critical for security operations and incident response activities.

Basic Design Patterns for Secure Systems

When you are designing a system, you should keep certain security principles and methodologies in mind. Not all principles may apply to your system. But it is important for you to consider them to ensure that they hold true if they apply to you.

In 1975, a seminal article by Jerome Saltzer and Michael Schroeder, "The Protection of Information in Computer Systems,"[18] was published. Although much has changed since its publication, the basic tenets are still applicable. Some of the fundamentals we discuss in this book are based on the principles laid out by Saltzer and Schroeder. We also want to show you how some of those principles have become relevant in different ways than originally intended.

Zero trust

A common approach to system design, and security compliance, is "trust, but verify," or *zero trust*, which is to assume the best outcome for an operation (such as a device joining a network, or a client calling an API) and then perform a verification of the trust relationship secondarily. In a zero trust environment, the system ignores (or never establishes) any prior trust relationship and instead verifies everything before deciding to establish a trust relationship (which may then be temporary).[19]

Also known as *complete mediation*, this concept looks amazingly simple on paper: ensure that the rights to access an operation are checked every time an object is accessed, and that the rights for that access operation are checked beforehand. In other words, you must verify that an actor has the proper rights to access an object every time that access is requested.

---

18 J. Saltzer and M. Schroeder, "The Protection of Information in Computer Systems," University of Virginia Department of Computer Science, *https://oreil.ly/MSJim*.

19 "Zero Trust Architecture," National Cybersecurity Center of Excellence, *https://oreil.ly/P4EJs*.

John Kindervag created the concept of zero trust in 2010,[20] and it has been commonly applied to network perimeter architecture discussions. The authors decided to import the concept into the security principles, and believe it also applies with no modifications to the security decisions that need to happen at the application level.

Design by contract

Design by contract is related to zero trust, and assumes that whenever a client calls a server, the input coming from that client will be of a certain fixed format and will not deviate from that contract.

It is similar to a lock-and-key paradigm. Your lock accepts only the correct key and trusts nothing else. In "Securing the Tangled Web,"[21] Christoph Kern explains how Google has significantly reduced the amount of cross-site scripting (XSS) flaws in applications by using a library of inherently safe API calls—by design. Design by contract addresses zero trust by ensuring that every interaction follows a fixed protocol.

Least privilege

This principle means that an operation should run using only the most restrictive privilege level that still enables the operation to succeed. In other words, in all layers and in all mechanisms, make sure that your design constricts the operator to the minimum level of access required to accomplish an individual operation, and nothing more.

If least privilege is not followed, a vulnerability in an application might offer full access to the underlying operating system, and with it all the consequences of a privileged user having unfettered access to your system and your assets. This principle applies for every system that maintains an authorization context (e.g., an operating system, an application, databases, etc.).

Defense in depth

Defense in depth uses a multifaceted and layered approach to defend a system and its assets.

When thinking about defense of your system, think about the things you want to protect—assets—and how an attacker might try to access them. Consider what controls you might put in place to limit or prevent access by an adversary (but allow

---

20 Brook S. E. Schoenfield, expert threat modeling practitioner and prolific author, reminds us that the idea of "observe mutual distrust" was already posited by Microsoft in 2003–04, but unfortunately we were unable to locate a reference. We trust Brook!

21 Christoph Kern, "Securing the Tangled Web," *acmqueue*, August 2014, *https://oreil.ly/ZHVrI*.

access by a properly authorized actor). You might consider parallel or overlapping layers of controls to slow down the attacker; alternatively you might consider implementing features that confuse or actively deter an adversary.

Examples of defense in depth applied to computer systems include the following:

- Defending a specific workstation with locks, guards, cameras, and air-gapping
- Introducing a bastion host (or firewall) between the system and the public internet, then an endpoint agent in the system itself
- Using multifactor authentication to supplement a password system for authentication, with a time delay that raises exponentially between unsuccessful attempts
- Deploying a honeypot and fake database layer with intentionally priority-limited authentication validation functions

Any additional factor that acts as a "bump in the road" and makes an attack costlier in terms of complexity, money, and/or time is a successful layer in your defense in depth. This way of evaluating defense-in-depth measures is related to risk management—defense in depth does not always mean defense at all costs. A balancing act occurs between deciding how much to spend to secure assets versus the perceived value of those assets, which falls into scope of risk management.

Keeping things simple

Keeping things simple is about avoiding overengineering your system. With complexity comes the increased potential for instability, challenges in maintenance, and other aspects of system operation, and a potential for ineffectual security controls.[22]

Care must be taken to avoid oversimplification as well (as in dropping or overlooking important details). Often that happens in input validation, as we assume (correctly or not) that an upstream data generator will always supply valid and safe data, and avoid (incorrectly) our own input validation in an effort to simplify things. For a more extensive discussion of these expectations, see Brook S. E. Schoenfield's work on security contracts.[23] At the end of the day, a clean, simple design over an overengineered one will often provide security advantages over time, and should be given preference.

---

22 Eric Bonabeau, "Understanding and Managing Complexity Risk," *MIT Sloan Management Review*, July 2007, *https://oreil.ly/CfHAc*.

23 Brook S. E. Schoenfield, *Secrets of a Cyber Security Architect* (Boca Raton, FL: CRC Press, 2019).

No secret sauce

Do not rely on obscurity as a means of security. Your system design should be resilient to attack even if every single detail of its implementation is known and published. Notice, this doesn't mean you *need* to publish it,[24] and the data on which the implementation operates *must* remain protected—it just means you should assume that every detail is known, and not rely on any of it being kept secret as a way to protect your assets. If you intend to protect an asset, use the correct control—encryption or hashing; do not hope an actor will fail to identify or discover your secrets!

Separation of privilege

Also referred to as *separation of duties*, this principle means segregating access to functionality or data within your system so one actor does not hold all rights. Related concepts include *maker/checker*, where one user (or process) may request an operation to occur and set the parameters, but another user or process is required to authorize the transaction to proceed. This means a single entity cannot perform malicious activities unimpeded or without the opportunity for oversight, and raises the bar for nefarious actions to occur.

Consider the human factor

Human users have been referred to as the weakest link in any system,[25] so the concept of *psychological acceptability* must be a basic design constraint. Users who are frustrated by strong security measures will inevitably try to find ways around them.

When developing a secure system, it is crucial to decide just how much security will be acceptable to the user. There's a reason we have two-factor authentication and not sixteen-factor authentication. Put too many hurdles between a user and the system, and one of these situations will occur:

- The user stops using the system.
- The user finds workarounds to bypass the security measures.
- The powers that be stop supporting the decision for security because it impairs productivity.

---

24 Except when using copyleft licenses and open source projects, of course.

25 "Humans Are the Weakest Link in the Information Security Chain," Kratikal Tech Pvt Ltd, February 2018, *https://oreil.ly/INf8d*.

Effective logging

Security is not only preventing bad things from happening, but also about being aware that something happened and, to the extent possible, what happened. The capability to see what happened comes from being able to *effectively* log events.

But what constitutes effective logging? From a security point of view, a security analyst needs to be able to answer three questions:

- Who performed a specific action to cause an event to be recorded?
- When was the action performed or event recorded?
- What functionality or data was accessed by the process or user?

Nonrepudiation, which is closely related to integrity, means having a set of transactions indicating who did what, with the record of each transaction maintaining integrity as a property. With this concept, it is impossible for an actor to claim they did not perform a specific action.

As important as it is to know what to log and how to protect it, knowing what *not* to log is also crucial. In particular:

- Personally identifiable information (PII) should never be logged in plain text, in order to protect the privacy of user data.
- Sensitive content that is part of API or function calls should never be logged.
- Clear-text versions of encrypted content likewise should not be logged.
- Cryptographic secrets, such as a password to a system or a key used to decrypt data, should not be logged.

Using common sense is important here, but note that keeping these logs from being integrated into code is an ongoing battle against the needs of development (mostly debugging). It is important to make it clear to development teams that it is unacceptable to have switches in code that control whether sensitive content should be logged for debugging purposes. Deployable, production-ready code should *not* contain logging capabilities for sensitive information.

Fail secure

When a system encounters an error condition, this principle means not revealing too much information to a potential adversary (such as in logs or user error messages) and not simply granting access incorrectly, such as when the failure is in the authentication subsystem.

But it is important to understand that there is a significant difference between *fail secure* and *fail safe*. Failing while maintaining *safety* may contradict the condition of failing *securely*, and will need to be reconciled in the system design. Which one is appropriate in a given situation, of course, depends on the particulars of the situation. At the end of the day, failing secure means that if a component or logic in the system falters, the result is still a secure one.

Build in, not bolt on

Security, privacy, and safety should be fundamental properties of the system, and any security features should be included in the system from the beginning.[26]

Security, like privacy or safety, should not be considered an afterthought or rely solely or primarily on external system components to be present. A good example of this pattern is the implementation of secure communications; the system must support this natively—i.e., should be designed to support Transport Layer Security (TLS) or a similar method for preserving confidentiality of data in transit. Relying on the user to install specialized hardware systems to enable end-to-end communications security means that if the user *does not do so*, the communications will be unprotected and potentially accessible to malicious actors. Do not assume that users will take action on your behalf when it comes to the security of your system.

Summary

After reading this Introduction, you should have all the foundational knowledge you need to get the most out of the chapters that follow: the basics of threat modeling and how it fits into the system development life cycle, and all the most important security concepts, terminology, and principles that are fundamental to understanding the security of your system. When you perform threat modeling, you will be looking for these security principles in your system's design to ensure your system is properly protected from intrusion or compromise.

In Chapter 1 we discuss how to construct abstract representations of a system's design to identify security or privacy concerns. In later chapters, we will introduce specific threat modeling methodologies that build on the concepts in this Introduction and the modeling techniques in Chapter 1 to perform complete security threat assessments using the threat modeling activity.

Welcome aboard the security train!

---

26 Some security features or functionality may have negative effects on usability, so it may be acceptable to disable some security capabilities by default if users can enable them when deploying the system.

Modeling Systems

All models are wrong, but some are useful.
> —G. E. P. Box, "Science and Statistics," *Journal of the American Statistical Association,*
> 71 (356), 791–799, doi:10.1080/01621459.1976.10480949.

System modeling (creating abstractions or representations of a system) is an important first step in the threat modeling process. The information you gather from the system model provides the input for analysis during the threat modeling activity.

In this chapter we'll cover different types of system models, the reasons why you might choose to use one model type over another, and guidance for creating the most effective system models. Expert proficiency of system model construction will inform your threat models and lead to more precise and effective analysis and threat identification.

Throughout this chapter, we use the words *model* or *modeling* to mean an abstraction or representation of a system, its components, and interactions.

Why We Create System Models

Imagine, if you will, a group of Benedictine monks looking at the monastic church of St. Gall and then at a manuscript, back and forth. At some point, one turns to the others and says, "Well, listen, it was not a plan per se. It was more like a 'two-dimensional meditation on the ideal early medieval monastic community.'"[1] Such is the purpose associated with the Plan of St. Gall, currently recognized as the oldest preserved 2D visualization and plan of a building complex. The church looks very different from the plan.

Humans create models to plan ahead or to decide what resources might be needed, what frameworks need to be put in place, what hills need moving, what valleys need filling, and how independent pieces will interact once put together. Humans create models because it is easier to visualize changes on a schematic, smaller scale than to embark on construction right away. It is easier and cheaper to make changes to that schematic, and change the ways these pieces interact, than to move walls, frames, screws, engines, floors, wings, firewalls, servers, functions, or lines of code, after the fact.

We also recognize that while the model and the final outcome may differ, having a model will always help understanding nuances and details relevant to the process of making and building. For security purposes, we model software and hardware systems, in particular, because it enables us to subject the systems to theoretical stress, understand how that stress will impact the systems before they are implemented, and see the systems holistically so we can focus on vulnerability details as needed.

In the rest of this chapter, we'll show you the various visual forms your threat model can take and explain how to gather requisite information to support system analysis. The specific actions you take after you have constructed your model will depend on the methodology you choose to follow; we'll get to the methodologies in the next couple of chapters.

System Modeling Types

As you know, systems can be complex, with many moving parts and interactions occurring among components. Humans are not born with extensive security knowledge (although we know a few who may well have been), and most system designers and developers are not intimately familiar with how functionality can be abused or misused. So those who want to make sure their system analysis is both practical and effective need to reduce the complexity and amount of *data* to consider for analysis and maintain the right amount of *information*.

---

1 "The Plan of St. Gall," Carolingian Culture at Reichenau and St. Gall, *https://oreil.ly/-NoHD*.

This is where system modeling, or an abstraction of a system describing its salient parts and attributes, comes to the rescue. Having a good abstraction of the system you want to analyze will give you enough of the right information to make informed security and design decisions.

Models have been used to express ideas or deliver knowledge to others for centuries. The tomb builders of ancient China would create models of buildings,[2] and architects since the Ancient Egyptians have routinely created scale models to demonstrate the feasibility and intentions of a design.[3]

Creating a system model—an abstraction or representation of a system to be analyzed for threats—can make use of one or more model types:[4]

Data flow diagrams

Data flow diagrams (DFDs) describe the flow of data among components in a system and the properties of each component and flow. DFDs are the most used form of system models in threat modeling and are supported natively by many drawing packages; shapes in DFDs are also easy for humans to draw by hand.

Sequence diagrams

These are activity diagrams in Unified Modeling Language (UML) that describe the interactions of system components in an ordered fashion. Sequence diagrams can help identify threats against a system because they allow a designer to understand the *state* of the system over time. This allows you to see how the system's properties, and any assumptions or expectations about them, change over the course of its operation.

Process flow diagrams

Process flow diagrams (PFDs) highlight the operational flow through actions among components in a system.

Attack trees

Attack trees depict the steps along a path that an attacker might try as part of reaching their goal to perform actions with nefarious intent.

---

2 A. E. Dien, *Six Dynasties Civilization* (New Haven: Yale University Press, 2007), 214.

3 A. Smith, *Architectural Model as Machine* (Burlington, MA: Architectural Press, 2004).

4 There are other methods of producing graphical models suitable for analysis, such as using other UML model types, or the System Modeling Language (SysML), and other model types that may be useful for performing an effective analysis, such as control flow graphs and state machines. But those methodologies are beyond the scope of this book.

Fishbone diagrams

> Also known as *cause-and-effect* or *Ishikawa* diagrams, these show the relationships between an outcome and the root cause(s) that enabled such an effect to occur.

Separately or together, you can use these system-modeling techniques to effectively see the changes in security posture that make an attacker's job easier. This is important to help designers recognize and eliminate potential issues by changing their designs or assumptions of the system. Use different model types for the purposes for which they are best suited. For example, use DFDs to describe *relationships* between objects, and use sequence diagrams to describe *ordering* of operations. We'll explore each of these in some detail, so you can understand the benefits of each.

Data Flow Diagrams

When modeling a system to perform security analysis, experts identified DFDs as a useful way to visually describe a system. DFDs were developed with a symbology that expresses the complexity of systems.

Using models to understand the components of a system and how they relate to each other came about in the 1950s with the functional flow block diagram (*https://oreil.ly/A8fms*). Later, in the 1970s, the structured analysis and design technique (*https://oreil.ly/Umez5*) introduced the concept of a DFD.[5] DFDs have become a standard way to describe a system when performing threat analysis.

DFDs Have Levels

Data flow diagrams often result in multiple drawings, each of which indicate a layer or level of abstraction. The top layer is sometimes referred to as the *context layer*, or *layer 0* or simply *L0*, and contains the system from a high-level view and its interactions with external entities such as remote systems or users. Subsequent layers, referred to as *L1*, *L2*, and so on, drill down into more detail on individual system components and interactions, until the intended level of detail has been reached or no additional value can be achieved from further decomposition of system elements.

While there is no formal standard that defines the shapes used when modeling the data flow of a system, many drawing packages use a *convention* to associate shapes and their meaning and use.

When constructing DFDs, we find it useful to highlight particular architectural elements alongside the data flows. This additional information can be helpful when

---

5 "Data Flow Diagrams (DFDs): An Agile Introduction," Agile Modeling Site, *https://oreil.ly/h7Uls*.

trying to make accurate decisions while analyzing the model for security concerns, or while using the model to educate people new to the project. We include three non-standard *extension* shapes for your consideration; they function as shortcuts that can make your models easier to create and understand.

An *element* (shown in Figure 1-1) is a standard shape that represents a process or operating unit within the system under consideration. You should always label your element, so it can be referred to easily in the future. Elements are the source and/or target for data flows (described later) to and from other units in the model. To identify human actors, use the actor symbol (refer to Figure 1-4 for a sample).

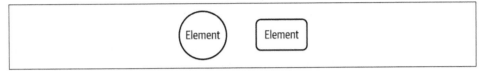

Figure 1-1. Element symbols for drawing data flow diagrams

You should also *annotate* each object with a description of its basic properties and metadata. You can put the annotation on the diagram itself, or in a separate document and then use the label to associate the annotation to the object.

The following is a list of potential information that you might want to capture in annotations for objects in the model:

 This list of potential metadata to obtain regarding an element, as annotations to the model, is not comprehensive. The information you need to know about the elements in your system depends on the methodology you eventually decide to use (see Chapters 3 through 5) as well as the threats you are trying to identify. This list presents a few of the options you may encounter.

- Name of the unit. If it is an executable, what is it called when built or installed on a disk?
- Who owns it within your organization (the development team, usually)?
- If this is a process, at what privilege level is it running (e.g., always root, or setuid'd, or some nonprivileged user)?
- If this is a binary object, is it expected to be digitally signed, and if so, by what method and/or which certificate or key?
- What programming language(s) are used for the element?
- For managed or interpreted code, what runtime or bytecode processor is in use?

People often overlook the influence of their choice of programming language. For example, C and C++ are more prone to memory-based errors than an interpreted language, and a script will more easily lend itself to reverse engineering than a (possibly obfuscated) binary. These are important characteristics that you should understand during the design of the system, especially if you identify them while you are threat modeling, to avoid common and serious security concerns. If you don't know this information early enough in the system development process to include it in the threat model (because, as you may know by now, threat modeling should be done early and often), this is a perfect example of why threat models should be kept up to date as the system evolves.[6]

There is some additional metadata, which provides context and opportunities for deeper assessment, as well as the discussion between development teams and system stakeholders, you may want to consider:

- Is the unit production ready or a development unit *or* does the element only exist part-time? For example, does the unit exist only in production systems but not in development mode? This may mean that the process represented by the element may not execute or be initialized in certain environments. Or it may not be present, for example, because it is compiled out when certain compile flags are set. A good example of this is a test module or a component that only applies in a staging environment to facilitate testing. Calling it out in the threat model would be important. If the module operates through particular interfaces or APIs that are open in staging to facilitate testing, but remain open in production even though the test module has been removed, then this is a weakness that needs to be addressed.

- Does information on its expected execution flow exist, and can it be described by a state machine or sequence diagram? Sequence diagrams can aid in identifying weaknesses, as we will discuss later in this chapter.

- Optionally, does it use or have enabled specific flags from compilation, linking, or installation,[7] or is it covered by an SELinux policy distinct from the system default? As mentioned earlier, you may not know this when you construct the first threat model, but it provides you with another opportunity to add value by keeping the threat model up to date over the course of the project.

---

6 For an extensive discussion of the subject, see Brook S.E. Schoenfield, *Securing Systems: Applied Security Architecture and Threat Models* (Boca Raton, FL: CRC Press, 2015).

7 Common flags include for ASLR or DEP support or stack canaries.

Use the element symbol to show a self-contained unit of processing, such as an executable or a process (depending on the level of abstraction), where subdividing the element into representative components is unlikely to help people understand how the unit operates and to which threats it may be susceptible. This may take some practice—sometimes you may need to describe the subelements of the processing unit to better understand the interactions it contains. To describe subelements, you use a container symbol.

A *container*, or containing element, shown in Figure 1-2, is another standard shape that represents a unit within the system under consideration that contains additional elements and flows. This shape is usually used in the context layer (see "DFDs Have Levels" on page 4) of a model, highlighting the major units within the system. When you create container elements, you are signaling a need to understand the contained elements, and that the container represents the combined interactions and assumptions of all the included elements. It is also a good way to reduce the busyness of a model when drawn. Containers can be the source and/or target for data that flows to and from other model entities when present in any given level of abstraction.

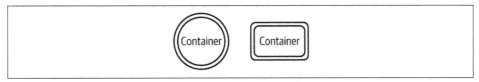

Figure 1-2. Container symbols for drawing data flow diagrams

As with the element described earlier, you should assign a label to your container objects, and include metadata for the object in its annotations. Metadata should include (at least) any of the metadata items from the element as described earlier, plus a brief summary of what is contained within (i.e., the major subsystems or subprocesses that might be found inside).

Unlike an element, which represents a unit within the system under consideration, an *external entity* shape, shown in Figure 1-3, represents a process or system that is involved in the operation or function of the system but is not in scope for the analysis. An external entity is a standard shape. At the very least external entities offer a source for data flows coming into the system from a remote process or mechanism. Examples of external entities often include web browsers used to access web servers or similar services, but may include any type of component or processing unit.

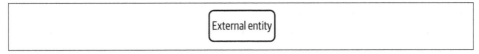

Figure 1-3. External entity symbol for drawing data flow diagrams

Actors (see Figure 1-4), which represent primarily human users of the system, are standard shapes that have connections to interfaces offered by the system (directly, or through an intermediate external entity such as a web browser) and are often used at the context layer of the drawing.

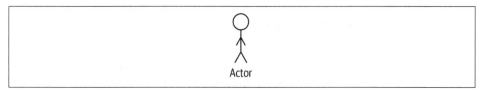

Figure 1-4. Actor symbol for drawing data flow diagrams

The data store symbol, shown in Figure 1-5, is a standard shape representing a functional unit that indicates where "bulk" data is held, such as a database (but not always the database *server*). You could also use the data store symbol to indicate a file or buffer holding small amounts of security-relevant data, such as a file containing the private key to your web server's TLS certificate,[8] or for an object data store such as an Amazon Simple Storage Service (S3) bucket holding your application's logfile output. Data store symbols can also represent a message bus, or a shared memory region.

Figure 1-5. Data store symbols for drawing data flow diagrams

Data stores should be labeled and have metadata such as the following:

Type of storage
  Is this a file, an S3 bucket, a service mesh or a shared memory region?

Type and classification of data held
  Is the data that is being sent to or read from this module structured or unstructured? Is it in any particular format; for example, XML or JSON?

Sensitivity or value of data
  Is the managed data personal information, security relevant, or otherwise sensitive in nature?

Protections on the data store itself
  For example, does the root storage mechanism offer drive-level encryption?

---

8 As in Apache Tomcat's use of this mechanism.

Replication

Is the data replicated on a different data store?

Backup

Is the data copied to another place for safety, but with potentially reduced security and access controls?

 If you are modeling a system that contains a database server (such as MySQL or MongoDB), you have two choices when it comes to rendering it in a model: (a) use the data store to represent both the DBMS process *and* the data storage location, or (b) an element for the DBMS and a connected data store for the actual data storage unit.

Each option carries benefits and trade-offs. Most people would choose option (a), but option (b) is especially useful with effective threat analysis for cloud and embedded system models in which data may live on shared data channels or temporal storage nodes.

If an element is self-contained and has no connection to external entities, the element describes a secure, but probably pretty useless, piece of functionality within the system (hopefully, this is not your only unit within the system!). For an entity to have *value*, it should at least provide data or create a transformative function. Most entities also communicate with external units in some fashion. Within a system model, use the data flow symbols to describe where and how interactions are made among entities. The data flow is actually a set of symbols that represent the multiple ways system components can interact.

Figure 1-6 shows a basic line, which indicates a connection between two elements in the system. It does not, and cannot, convey any additional information, making this symbol an excellent choice when that information is not available to you at the time of the modeling exercise.

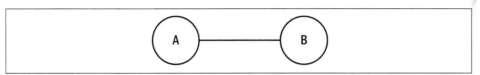

Figure 1-6. A line symbol for basic undirected data flow

Figure 1-7 shows a basic line with an arrow on one end, which is used to represent a unidirectional flow of information or action.

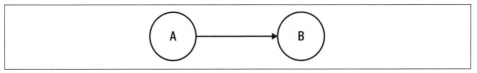

Figure 1-7. An arrow symbol for basic directed data flow

In Figure 1-8, the lefthand side of the image shows a basic line with arrows at both ends that represents a bidirectional communication flow. The righthand side of the image shows an alternate symbol for bidirectional communication flow. Either is acceptable, although the version on the right is more traditional and easier to recognize in a busy diagram (at the risk of making the diagram too busy as a result).

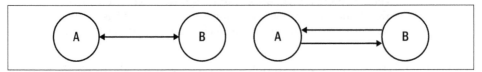

Figure 1-8. Two-headed arrows for bidirectional data flow

Figures 1-6, 1-7, and 1-8 are standard shapes in data flow diagram construction.

 Keep in mind that we are presenting *conventions*, not rules. These shapes and what they represent or how they are used in a diagram come from collective practice, not an official standard document.[9] In our practice of threat modeling, we sometimes find it useful to extend the conventional shapes and metadata to better suit our requirements. You will see some of these extensions in this chapter and throughout the book. But you should be comfortable, once you are familiar with the objectives and expected outcomes of the activity, to make modifications as you see fit. Customization can make the activity, the experience, and the information gained through this activity valuable to you and the team members involved.

Figure 1-9 shows a nonstandard *extension* shape (see prior note) that we propose above and beyond the normal set of DFD shapes. This shape is a single-headed arrow that indicates where the communication originated. We have circled it to highlight the mark. The mark is available in engineering stencils for transmission flows in the major graphics packages.

---

9 Adam Shostack, "DFD3," GitHub, *https://oreil.ly/OMVKu*.

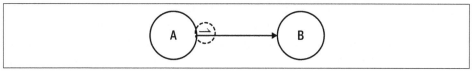

Figure 1-9. Optional initiator mark

Data flows should have a label for reference, and you should provide the following critical metadata:

Type or nature of communication channel
Is this a network-based communication flow or a local interprocess communication (IPC) connection?

Protocol(s) in use
For example, is the data transiting over HTTP or HTTPS? If it uses HTTPS, does it rely on client-side certificates to authenticate an endpoint, or mutual TLS? Is the data itself protected in some way independently of the channel (i.e., with encryption or signing)?

Data being communicated
What type of data is being sent over the channel? What is its sensitivity and/or classification?

Order of operations (if applicable or useful for your purposes)
If flows are limited in quantity within the model, or the interactions are not very complex, it may be possible to indicate the order of operations or flow order as part of the annotations on each data flow, rather than creating a separate sequence diagram.

 Be careful expressing authentication or other security controls on the data flow itself. Endpoints (servers or clients) are responsible for, and/or "offer," access controls independent of any potential data flows between them. Consider using the interface extended modeling element, described later in this section, as a "port" to simplify your drawing and facilitate a more effective analysis for threats.

Keep the following considerations in mind when using data flows in your models.

First, use arrows to indicate the direction of data flows in your diagram and in your analysis. If you have a line that starts at element A and goes to element B where it terminates in an arrow (as shown in Figure 1-7), it indicates the flow of meaningful communications goes from A to B. This is the exchange of data that is of value to the application, or to an attacker, but not necessarily individual packets and frames and acknowledgments (ACKs). Likewise, a line starting at B and ending in an arrow at A would mean communication flows from B to A.

Second, you can choose from two basic approaches to show bidirectional communication flows in your model: use a single line with an arrow at each end, as shown in Figure 1-8 (left), or use two lines, one for each direction, as shown in Figure 1-8 (right). The two-line method is more traditional, but they are functionally equivalent. The other benefit of using the two-line method is that each communication flow may have different properties, so your annotations may be cleaner in the model using two lines instead of one. You can choose to use either method, but be consistent throughout your model.

Lastly, the purpose of a data flow in a model is to describe the primary direction of travel of communications *that is relevant for the purposes of analysis*. If a communication path represents any standard protocol based on Transmission Control Protocol (TCP) or User Datagram Protocol (UDP), packets and frames pass back and forth along the channel from source to destination. But this level of detail is usually not important for threat identification.

Instead, it *is* important to describe that application-level data or control messages are being passed on the established channel; this is what the data flow is meant to convey. However, it is often important to understand for analysis which element *initiates* the communication flow. Figure 1-9 shows a mark you can use to indicate the initiator of the data flow.

The following scenario highlights the usefulness of this mark in understanding the model and analyzing the system.

Element A and element B are connected by a unidirectional data flow symbol, with data flowing from A to B, as shown in Figure 1-10.

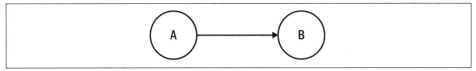

Figure 1-10. Sample elements A and B

Element A is annotated as *service A*, while element B is the *logger client*. You might come to the conclusion that B, as the recipient of data, initiated the communication flow. Or, you may alternatively conclude that A initiated the data flow, basing your analysis on the label for each endpoint. In either case, you may be correct, because the model is ambiguous.

Now, what if the model contains the additional initiator mark, attached to the endpoint at element A? This clearly indicates that element A, not element B, initiates the communication flow and that it pushes data to B. This may happen in cases you are modeling; for example, if you were modeling a microservice pushing log information to a logger client. It is a common architectural pattern, shown in Figure 1-11.

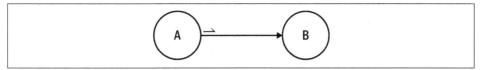

Figure 1-11. Sample elements A and B, with initiator mark at element A

However, if the initiator mark is placed on B rather than A, you would reach a different conclusion on the potential threats with this model segment. This design would reflect an alternate pattern in which the logger client, being perhaps behind a firewall, needs to communicate outbound to the microservice instead of the other way around (see Figure 1-12).

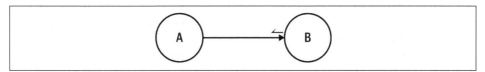

Figure 1-12. Sample elements A and B, with initiator mark at element B

The symbol shown in Figure 1-13 is traditionally used to delineate a *trust boundary*: any elements behind the line (the curvature of the line determines what is behind the line versus in front) trust one another. Basically, he dotted line identifies a boundary where all of the entities are trusted at the same level. For example, you might trust all processes that run in behind your firewall or VPN. This does not mean flows are automatically unauthenticated; instead a trust boundary means that objects and entities operating within the boundary operate at the same trust level (e.g., Ring 0).

This symbol should be used when modeling a system in which you wish to assume symmetric trust among system components. In a system that has asymmetric component trust (that is, component A may trust component B, but component B doesn't trust component A), the trust boundary mark would be inappropriate, and you should use an annotation on the data flow with information describing the trust relationship.

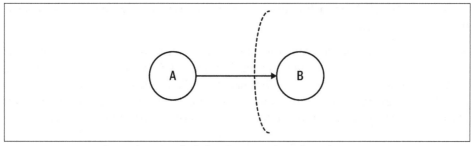

Figure 1-13. Trust boundary symbols for drawing data flow diagrams

The same symbol is also sometimes used, as shown in Figure 1-14, to indicate the security protection scheme on a particular data flow, such as marking the data flow as having confidentiality and integrity through the use of HTTPS. An alternative to this symbol and annotation, which could lead to a lot of clutter in models with a significant number of components and/or data flows, is to provide an annotation to the data flow itself.

The necessary metadata for a trust boundary, if used in the traditional sense (to denote a boundary beyond which all entities are of the same trust level), is a description of the symmetrical trust relationship of the entities. If this symbol is used to indicate a control on a channel or flow, the metadata should include the protocol(s) in use (e.g., HTTP or HTTPS, mutual TLS or not), the port number if not the default, and any additional security control information you wish to express.

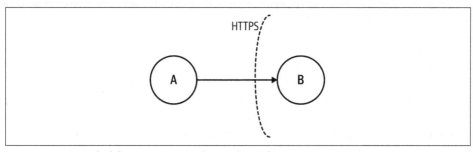

Figure 1-14. Symbol for an annotated trust boundary

An *interface element*, circled in Figure 1-15, is another nonstandard extension shape that indicates a defined connection point for an element or container. This is useful for showing ports or service endpoints exposed by the element. This is especially helpful when the specific use of the endpoint is undefined or indeterminate at design time, or in other words, when the clients of the endpoint are unknown ahead of time, which means drawing a particular data flow is difficult. While this may seem a trivial concern, an open listening endpoint on a service can be a major source of architectural risk, so having the ability to recognize this from the model is key.

Figure 1-15. Interface element symbol

Each interface should have a label and metadata describing its core characteristics:

- If the interface represents a known port, indicate the port number.
- Identify the communications channel or mechanism—e.g., PHY or Layer 1/Layer 2: Ethernet, VLAN, USB human interface device (HID), or a software-defined network—and whether the interface is exposed externally to the element.
- Communication protocol(s) offered by the interface (e.g., protocols at Layer 4 and above; or TCP, IP, HTTP).
- Access controls on incoming connections (or potentially outbound data flows), such as any type of authentication (passwords, or SSH keys, etc.) or if the interface is impacted by an external device such as a firewall.

Knowing this information can make analysis easier, in that all data flows connecting to the interface can inherit these characteristics. Your drawing will also be simpler and easier to understand as a result. If you don't want to use this optional element, create a dummy entity and data flow to the open service endpoint, which can make the drawing appear more complex.

 The shape in Figure 1-16—the block—is not part of the accepted collection of DFD shapes. It is included here because Matt finds this useful and wanted to demonstrate that threat modeling need not be bound solely to the traditional stencil when there is an opportunity to add value and/or clarity to one's models.

A *block* element, shown in Figure 1-16, represents an architectural element that selectively alters the data flow on which it is attached. Blocks can also modify a port at the connection of a data flow or process boundary. This shape highlights when a host firewall, another physical device, or a logical mechanism as a function of the architecture, and important for analysis, exists. Block elements can also show optional or add-on equipment that may impact the system in a way outside the control of the project team, yet are not external entities in the traditional sense.

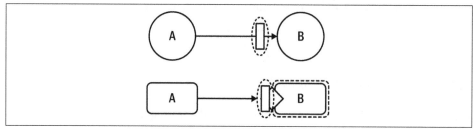

Figure 1-16. Block symbols

Metadata that you should collect for blocks include the usual labels as well as the following:

The type of block
    A physical device or logical unit, and whether the unit is an optional component for the system.

Behavior
    What the block does and how it may modify the flow or access to the port or process. Use a sequence diagram or state machine to provide additional detail on the behavior modification supported by the unit the block represents.

 When developing a model of your system, always be sure to decide whether you and the project team will use a particular symbol, and whether you decide to alter its meaning (effectively making your own house rules for threat modeling, which is perfectly acceptable!). Be consistent with the symbol's use, which will result in the activity being effective and showing value.

Sequence Diagrams

While DFDs show interactions and interconnections among system components and how data moves between them, *sequence diagrams* show a time or event-based sequence of actions. Sequence diagrams come from the UML (*https://oreil.ly/U_9q-*), and are a specialization of the interaction diagram type in UML. Supplementing DFDs with sequence diagrams as part of modeling in preparation for threat analysis can be instrumental in providing necessary context about the way your system behaves and any temporal aspects required for proper analysis. For example, DFDs can show you that a client communicates with a server and passes some form of data to the server. A sequence diagram will show you the order of operations used in that communication flow. This may reveal important information, such as who initiates the communication and any steps in the process that may introduce security or privacy risk, such as a failure to implement a protocol correctly or some other weakness.

There has been some discussion in the security community as to whether the sequence diagram is actually more important for performing this activity than development of DFDs. This is because a properly constructed sequence diagram can provide significantly more useful data than DFDs. The sequence diagram not only shows what data is involved in a flow and which entities are involved, but also explains *how* the data flows through the system, and in what order. Flaws in business logic and protocol handling are therefore easier to find (and in some cases are the only possible way to find) with a sequence diagram.

Sequence diagrams also highlight critical design failures such as areas that lack exception handling, or failure points or other areas where security controls are not consistently applied. It can also expose controls that are suppressed or inadvertently defeated, or potential instances of race conditions—including the dreaded time of check time of use (TOCTOU) (*https://oreil.ly/G1E8o*) weakness—where simply knowing that data flows, but not the order in which it flows, does not identify these weaknesses. Only time will tell if using sequence diagrams as an equal partner in threat modeling becomes popular.

The formal definition of a sequence diagram in UML includes a significant number of modeling elements, but for the purposes of creating a model suitable for threat analysis, you should be concerned only with the following subset.

Figure 1-17 shows a sample sequence diagram simulating a potential communication and call flow of a mythical system.

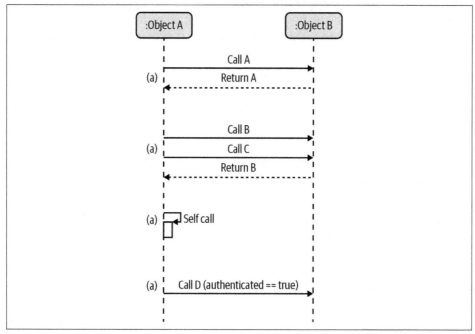

Figure 1-17. Sequence diagram shapes

The modeling elements shown in Figure 1-17 include the following:

Entities (objects A and B)
Within the scope of the system being considered, and their "lifeline" for connecting to interactions with other entities.

Actors (humans)
Not represented here, but they reside externally to the system components and interact with the various entities within the system.

Messages
Messages containing data ("Call A", "Return B") being passed from one entity to another. Messages may be synchronous or asynchronous between entities; synchronous messages (represented by solid arrowheads) block until the response is ready, while asynchronous messages (represented by open arrowheads, not shown) are nonblocking. Dashed lines ending in arrow heads represent return messages. Messages may also initiate and terminate from an entity without passing to another entity, which is represented by an arrow that circles back on the lifeline for the entity from which it initiated.

Conditional logic

This may be placed on message flows to provide constraints or preconditions, which help identify problems introduced by business logic flaws and their impact on data flows. This conditional logic (not shown in Figure 1-17) would have the form of [condition] and would be placed inline with the message label.

Time

In a sequence diagram, time flows from top to bottom: a message higher up in the diagram occurs sooner in time than the messages that follow.

Constructing a sequence diagram is fairly easy. The hard part is deciding *how* to draw one. We recommend that you find a good drawing tool that can handle straight lines (both solid and dashed), basic shapes, and arrows that can curve or bend. Microsoft Visio (and any of the Libre or open alternatives such as draw.io or Lucidchart) or a UML modeling tool like PlantUML should do fine.

You will also need to decide what actions you plan to model as a sequence. Good choices include authentication or authorization flows, as these involve multiple entities (at least an actor and a process, or multiple processes) exchanging critical data in a predefined manner. You can successfully model interactions involving a data store or asynchronous processing module as well as any standard operating procedure involving multiple entities.

Once you have decided on the actions you want to model, identify the interaction and operation of elements within your system. Add each element to the diagram as a rectangle toward the top of the diagram (shown in Figure 1-17), and draw a long line straight downward from the lower center of the element's rectangle. Finally, starting toward the top of the diagram (along the long vertical lines), use lines ending in arrows in one direction or another to show how the elements interact.

Continue to describe interactions, moving further down the model, until you reach the natural conclusion of interactions at the expected level of granularity. If you are using a physical whiteboard or similar medium to draw your model and take notes, you may need to continue your model across multiple boards, or take a picture of the incomplete model and erase it to continue going broader and deeper in your modeling. You would then need to stitch the pieces together later to form a complete model.

Process Flow Diagrams

Traditionally used in process design and chemical engineering, *process flow diagrams* (PFDs) show the sequence and directionality offlow of operations through a system (*https://oreil.ly/5AWOZ*). PFDs are similar to sequence diagrams, but are generally at a higher level, showing the activity chain of events in the system rather than the flow of specific messages and component state transitions.

We mention process flows here for completeness, but the use of PFDs in threat modeling is not common. The ThreatModeler tool (*https://oreil.ly/ifk00*) uses PFDs as its primary model type, however, so some may find it of value.

PFDs may be complementary in nature to sequence diagrams. You can sometimes describe the activity chain from a PFD with a sequence diagram using labels that indicate which segments of message flow are bound to a specific activity or event. Figure 1-18 shows a PFD for the events of a simple web application.

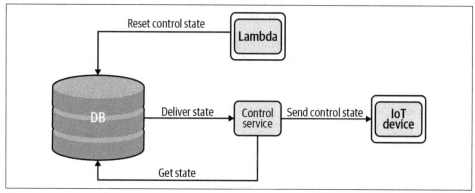

Figure 1-18. Sample process flow diagram

Figure 1-19 shows the same PFD redrawn as a sequence diagram with activity frames added.

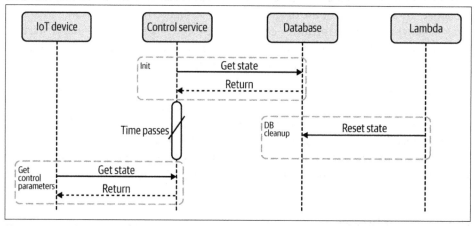

Figure 1-19. Sequence diagram as PFD

Attack Trees

Attack trees have been used in the field of computer science for more than 20 years (*https://oreil.ly/3PDpY*). They are useful for understanding how a system is vulnerable by modeling how an attacker may influence a system. Attack trees are the primary model type in threat analysis when using an attacker-centric approach.

This type of model starts at the root node that represents the goal or desired outcome. Remember, in this model type the result is a negative outcome for the system owners, but a positive outcome for the attackers! The intermediate and leaf nodes represent possible ways of achieving the goal of the parent node. Each node is labeled with an action to be taken, and should include information such as the following:

- The difficulty in performing the action to accomplish the parent node's goal
- The cost involved to do so
- Any special knowledge or conditions required to allow the attacker to succeed
- Any other relevant information to determine overall capability for success or failure

Figure 1-20 shows a generic attack tree with a goal and two actions and two subactions an attacker uses to reach the goal.

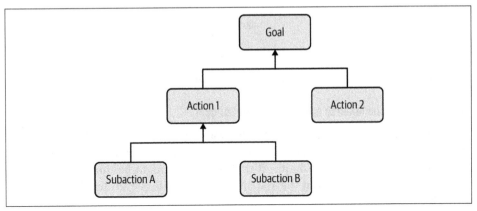

Figure 1-20. A generic attack tree diagram

Attack trees, which can be valuable for threat analysis, and for understanding the actual level and degree of risk to a system from attackers, need a couple of things to be well constructed and to provide the correct analysis of impact:

- Complete knowledge of how something can be compromised—favoring completeness and "what is possible" over "what is practical"

- An understanding of the motivations, skills, and resources available to different types and groups of attackers

You can construct an attack tree relatively easily, using the following steps:

1. Identify a target or goal for an attack.

2. Identify actions to be taken to achieve the target or goal.

3. Rinse and repeat.

Identify a target or goal for an attack

For this example, let's say that an attacker wants to establish a persistent presence on a system via remote code execution (RCE) on an embedded device. Figure 1-21 shows what this might look like in an evolving attack tree.

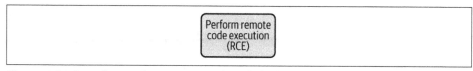

Figure 1-21. Sample attack tree, step 1: identify high-level target or goal

Identify actions to be taken to achieve the target or goal

How do you get to RCE on this system? One way is to find an exploitable stack buffer overflow and use it to deliver an executable payload. Or you could find a heap overflow and use it in a similar fashion. At this point, you might be thinking, "But wait, we don't know anything about the system to know if this is even feasible!" And you are right.

When performing this exercise in real life, you want to be realistic and make sure you identify only targets and actions that make sense to the system under evaluation. So for this example, let's assume that this embedded device is running code written in C. Let's also make the assumption that this device is running an embedded Linux-like operating system—either a real-time operating system (RTOS) or some other resource-constrained Linux variant.

So what might be another action needed to gain RCE capability? Does the system allow a remote shell? If we assume this device has flash memory and/or bootable media of some kind, and can accept over-the-air updates (OTAs), we can add file manipulation and OTA firmware spoofing or modification as actions to achieve RCE as well. Any possible actions you can identify should be added as elements to the attack tree, as shown in Figure 1-22.

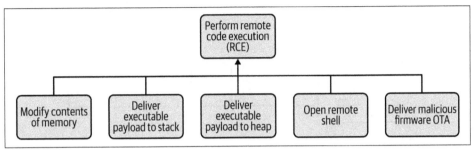

Figure 1-22. Sample attack tree, step 2: identify actions required to achieve the goal

Rinse and repeat

Here is where it really gets interesting! Try to think of ways to achieve the next order of outcomes. Don't worry about feasibility or likelihood; analysis and decisions made from such analysis will happen later. Think outside the box. Remember, you're putting on your hacker hat, so think like they would. No matter how crazy your ideas are, someone might try something similar. At this stage, an exhaustive list of possibilities is better than a partial list of feasibilities.

Your tree is done when no additional substeps are needed to complete an action. Don't worry if your tree looks lopsided; not all actions need the same level of complexity to achieve results. Also don't worry if you have dangling nodes—it may not be easy to identify all possible scenarios for an attacker to achieve a goal (it's good to think of as many scenarios as you can, but you might not be able to identify all of them). Figure 1-23 shows an evolved (and possibly complete) attack tree indicating the methods by which an attacker may reach their goal.

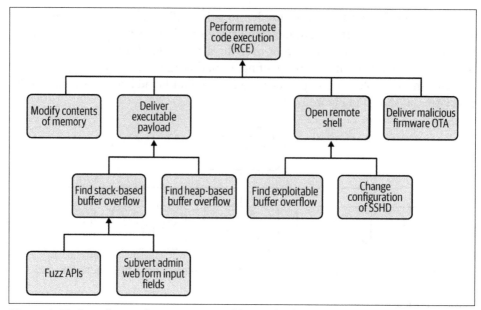

Figure 1-23. Sample attack tree, step 3 and beyond: identify subactions to achieve subtargets

Learning how to break something or accomplish prerequisite goals is easier as a group brainstorming exercise. This lets individuals with technical and security knowledge add their expertise to the group so that you can identify all the attack tree's possible nodes and leaves. Understanding your organization's *risk appetite*, or the amount of risk your organization is willing to accept, will clarify how much time you should spend on the exercise and if the organization is willing to take the necessary actions to address any concerns identified.

Knowing how attackers behave is a significant challenge for most businesses and security practitioners, but community resources such as the MITRE ATT&CK framework (*https://attack.mitre.org*) make identification and characterization of threat actors' techniques, skills, and motivations much easier. It is certainly not a panacea, as it is only as good as the community that supports it, but if you are unfamiliar with how attacker groups behave in the real world, this blog entry by Adam Shostack, summarizing a talk by Jonathan Marcil, is an excellent resource (*https://oreil.ly/ xizOp*) for you to consider.

Fishbone Diagrams

Fishbone diagrams (*https://oreil.ly/B8Xbe*), also known as *cause-and-effect*, or *Ishikawa*, diagrams, are used primarily for root cause analysis of a problem statement. Figure 1-24 shows an example of a fishbone diagram.

Similar to attack trees, the fishbone diagrams can help you identify weaknesses in the system for any given area. These diagrams are also useful for identifying pitfalls or weaknesses in processes such as those found in the supply chain for a system where you may need to analyze component delivery or manufacturing, configuration management, or protection of critical assets. This modeling process can also help you understand the chain of events that lead to exploitation of a weakness. Knowing this information allows you to construct better DFDs (by knowing what questions to ask or what data you seek), and identify new types of threats as well as security test cases.

Constructing a fishbone diagram is similar to creating attack trees, except instead of identifying a target goal and the actions to achieve the goal, you identify the effect you want to model. This example models the causes of data exposure.

First, define the effect you want to model; Figure 1-24 demonstrates the technique with data exposure as the effect to model.

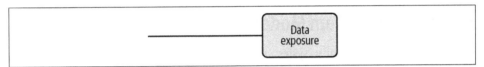

Figure 1-24. Sample fishbone diagram, step 1: main effect

Then you want to identify a set of primary causes that lead to the effect. We've identified three: overly verbose logs, covert channels, and user error, as shown in Figure 1-25.

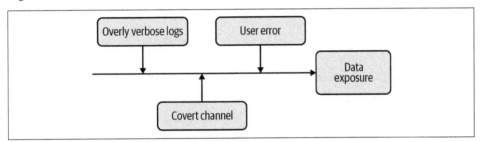

Figure 1-25. Sample fishbone diagram, step 2: primary causes

Finally, you identify the set of causes that drive the primary causes (and so on). We have identified that a primary cause for user error is a confusing UI. This example recognizes only three threats, but you will want to create larger and more expansive models, depending on how much time and effort you wish to expend versus the granularity of your results. Figure 1-26 shows the fishbone diagram in a complete state, with the expected effect, primary, and secondary causes.

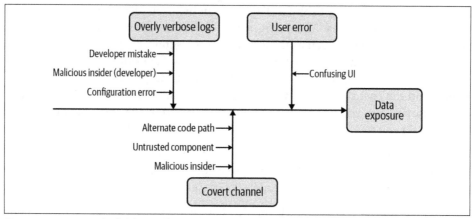

Figure 1-26. Sample fishbone diagram, step 3: secondary causes

How to Build System Models

The basic process for creating system models starts by identifying the major building blocks in the system—these could be applications, servers, databases, or data stores. Then identify the connections to each major building block:

- Does the application support an API or a user interface?
- Does the server listen on any ports? If so, over what protocol?
- What talks to the database, and whatever communicates to it, does it only read data, or does it write data too?
- How does the database control access?

Keep following threads of conversation and iterate through every entity at this context layer in the model until you have completed all necessary connections, interfaces, protocols, and data streams.

Next, choose one of the entities—usually an application or server element—that may contain additional details you need to uncover in order to identify areas for concern, and break it down further. Focus on the entry and exit points to/from the application, and where these channels connect, when looking at the subparts that make up the application or server.

Also consider how the individual subparts may communicate with each other, including communication channels, protocols, and the type of data passed across the channels. You will want to add any relevant information based on the type of shape added to the model (later in the chapter you will learn about annotating the model with metadata).

When building models, you will need to leverage your judgment and knowledge of security principles and technology to gather information to enable a threat assessment. Ideally, you would perform this threat assessment immediately after your model is built.

Before you begin, decide which model types you may need and the symbol set for each model type you intend to use. For example, you may decide to use the DFD as your primary model type but use the default symbol set defined by whatever drawing package you are using. Or you may decide to also include sequence diagrams, which would be appropriate if your system uses nonstandard interactions between components where exploitable weaknesses can hide.

As the leader of a modeling exercise (which, for the purposes of this chapter, we assume is you—lucky you), you need to make sure you include the right stakeholders. Invite the lead architect, the other designers, and the development lead(s) to the modeling session. You should also consider inviting the quality assurance (QA) lead. Encourage all members of the project team to provide their input to the construction of the model, although as a practical matter, we recommend keeping the attendee list to a manageable set to maximize the time and attention of those who do attend.

If this is the first time you or your development team are creating a system model, start slowly. Explain the goals or expected outcomes of the exercise to the team. You should also indicate how long you expect the exercise to take, and the process that you will follow, as well as your role in the exercise and the role of each stakeholder. In the unlikely event that team members are not all familiar with each other, go around the room to make introductions before you begin the session.

You should also decide who is responsible for any drawing and note-taking required during the session. We recommend you do the drawing yourself because it puts you in the center of the conversation at all times and provides attendees an opportunity to focus on the task at hand.

A few points are worth mentioning as you explore the system:

Timing of the exercise is important
> If you meet too early, the design will not be formed sufficiently, and a lot of churn will occur as designers with differing viewpoints challenge each other and take the discussion off on tangents. But if you meet too late, the design will be fixed, and any issues identified during threat analysis may not be resolved in a timely fashion, making your meeting a documentation exercise rather than an analysis for threats.

Different stakeholders will see things differently

We have found it common, especially as the attendee count increases, that stakeholders are not always on the same page when it comes to how the system was designed or implemented; you need to guide the conversation to identify the correct path for the design. You may also need to moderate the discussion to avoid rabbit holes and circling conversation threads, and be wary of sidebar conversations, as they provide an unnecessary and time-consuming distraction. A well-moderated conversation among stakeholders in the system-modeling process often leads to "eureka!" moments, as the discussion reveals that the expectation from the design and the reality of the implementation clash, and the team can identify the spots where constraints modified the initial design without control.

Loose ends are OK

As we mentioned previously, while you may strive for perfection, be comfortable with missing information. Just make sure to avoid or minimize knowingly *incorrect* information. It is better to have a data flow or element in the model that is filled with question marks than it is to have everything complete but some known inaccuracies. Garbage in, garbage out; in this case, the inaccuracies will result in poor analysis, which may mean multiple false findings, or worse, a lack of findings in a potentially critical region of the system.

We recommend that you present system modeling as a *guided exercise*. This is especially important if the project team is unfamiliar with the model construction process. It is often beneficial for someone external to the product development team to facilitate the modeling exercise because this avoids a conflict of interest with respect to the system design and its potential impact on delivery requirements.

This is not to say that someone facilitating the construction of a model should be totally impartial. The leader will be responsible for gathering the necessary participants and working with this team to define the system the team intends to build with sufficient detail to support later analysis. As such, the leader should be an enabler of outcomes, not a disinterested third party. They do need to be removed enough from the design (and assumptions or shortcuts made or risks ignored) to provide a critical look at the system and be able to tease out tidbits of information that will be useful for the threat analysis.

As a leader, it's important that you have accurate and complete information, as much as possible, when analyzing your model; your analysis may lead to changes to the system design, and the more accurate the information you start with, the better analysis and recommendations you can make. Keep an eye on the detail and be willing and able to overturn "rocks" to find the right information at the right time. You should also be familiar with the technologies under consideration, the purpose of the system being designed, and the people involved in the exercise.

While you don't need to be a security expert to build a good system model, model building is usually conducted as a prerequisite to the threat analysis phase. This usually happens in rapid succession, which suggests you should probably be the security leader for that part of the project as well. The reality is that, with modern development projects, you may not be an expert in everything involved with a system. You have to rely on your teammates to shore up your knowledge gaps, and act more as a facilitator to ensure that the team efficiently develops a representative and accurate model. Remember, you don't need to be an auto mechanic to drive a car, but you do need to know how to drive your car and the rules of the road.

If you are the leader charged with delivering a system model for analysis, you should be OK with imperfection, especially when starting a new model of a system. You will have an opportunity to improve the model over successive iterations.

No matter how skilled you are at drawing models, or interrogating designers about the systems they present to you, it is highly likely that the information you need in its entirety will be missing or unavailable, at least initially. And that is fine. System models represent the system under consideration and do not need to be 100% accurate to be of value. You must know some basic facts about the system and each element in the system for you to be effective in your analysis, but do not try for perfection or you will be discouraged (unfortunately, we know this from experience).

You can improve your chances of success in leading this activity by keeping in mind a few simple things:

Establish a blame-free zone
> Individuals with a strong attachment to a system being analyzed will have opinions and feelings. While you should expect professionalism from attendees, contention and heated arguments may create sour working relationships if you don't avoid getting personal in a system-modeling session. Be prepared to moderate the discussion to prevent singling out individuals for mistakes, and redirect the conversation to recognizing the great learning opportunity you now have.

No surprises
> Be up front about what you intend to accomplish, document your process, and give your development teams plenty of notice.

Training
> Help your team help you by showing them what needs to be done and what information will be required of them so that they can be successful. Hands-on training is especially effective (e.g., "show one, do one"), but in this age of video logs (vlogs) and live-streaming, you may also consider recording a live modeling session Critical Role-style (*https://critrole.com/videos*) and making the video

available for your development teams to review. This could be the best two to three hours of time spent in training.

Be prepared

Ask for information about the target system ahead of your system-modeling exercise, such as system requirements, functional specifications, or user stories. This will give you a sense of where the designers might go when considering a set of modules, and help you to frame questions that can help obtain the necessary level of information for a *good* model.

Motivate attendees with food and drink

Bring donuts or pizza (depending on the time of day) and coffee or other snacks. Food and drink goes a long way toward building trust and getting attendees to discuss hard topics (like that big security hole that was introduced by accident!).

Gain buy-in from leadership

Attendees will feel more comfortable being present and sharing their thoughts and ideas (and uncovering skeletons in the closet, so to speak) if they know their management team is on-board with this activity.

 At the time of this writing, the COVID-19 pandemic is making us think creatively about how to meet safely and build virtual comradery with shipped (or locally sourced) snacks and group video calls. These are lessons you can apply to distributed team collaboration any time.

When you create a system model, regardless of the type, you may choose to draw it out on a whiteboard or in a virtual whiteboard application and translate it into your favorite drawing package. But you don't have to always do it by hand. Know that online and offline utilities are available today[10] that enable you to create models without manually drawing them first.

If you use any of these drawing packages, you should come up with your own method of adding metadata annotations for each element as described earlier. You can do this within the diagram itself as a textbox or callout, which might clutter the diagram. Some drawing applications perform automatic layout of objects and connections, which on complex diagrams can look like spaghetti. You can also create a separate document, in your favorite text editor, and provide the necessary metadata for each element shown in the diagram. The combination of diagram(s) and text documents becomes the "model" that allows a human to perform analysis that can identify threats and weaknesses.

---

10 draw.io, Lucidchart, Microsoft Visio, OWASP Threat Dragon, and Dia, to name a few.

What Does a Good System Model Look Like?

Despite your best efforts, complexity may occur because you have too much information, or worse, incorrect information. Sometimes, the potential level of detail in the model itself and subsequent amount of effort you need to perform analysis on the model is a welcome diversion from all the fires you're fighting. Alternatively, an extreme level of detail might be a requirement of your environment or market segment. For example, some industries, such as transportation or medical devices, require a higher degree of analysis to address a higher degree of assurance. For most of us, however, threat modeling is often seen as unfamiliar, unnerving, or an unwelcome "distraction" from other seemingly more critical tasks. But by now you already know: a good threat model will pay for itself.

But what makes a *good* model? It depends on various factors, including the methodology you use, your goals, and how much time and energy you can to devote to building out the model. While a good model is difficult to describe, we can highlight key points that form a good system model. Good models at a minimum have the following properties:

Accurate

> Keep your models free of inaccurate or misleading information that will result in an imperfect threat analysis. This is hard to do alone, so it is critical to have support from the system designers, developers, and others on the project. If the project team wonders aloud "What is *that*?" when everything is said and done, something bad happened during the system model's construction and should be revisited.

Meaningful

> Models should contain *information*, not just data. Remember that you are trying to capture information that points to "conditions for potential compromise" within your system. Identifying those conditions depends on the threat modeling methodology that you ultimately select. The methodology you use identifies whether you are looking for only exploitable weaknesses (aka vulnerabilities) or want to identify different parts of the system that have the *potential* to contain weaknesses, exploitable or not (because in theory they will likely become exploitable in practice while not so on paper).

> Sometimes people want to capture as much metadata about the system as possible. But the point of modeling is to create a representation of the system without re-creating it, providing sufficient data to make inferences and direct judgments on the characteristics of the system.

Representative

> The model should attempt to be representative of *either* the design intentions of the architect *or* the realized implementation by the development teams. The model can tell us what to expect from the system's security posture as designed or as implemented, but usually not both. Either way, the conversation around the conference room table will be the corporate equivalent of "he said, she said." The team should clearly recognize their system in the model created.

Living

> Your system isn't static. Your development team is always making changes, upgrades, and fixes. Because your systems are always changing, your models need to be living documents. Revisit the model on a regular basis to ensure it remains accurate. It should reflect the currently expected system design or the current system implementation. Model "what is" instead of "what should be."

Deciding when your model is "good" is not easy. To determine the quality and "goodness" of a system model, you should develop guidelines and make them available to all participants. These guidelines should spell out which modeling constructs (i.e., shapes, methods) to use and for what purposes. They should also identify the granularity level to strive for and how much information is too much. Include stylistic guidance such as how to record annotations or use color in the model diagram.

The guidelines are not rules, per se. They are there to provide consistency in the modeling exercise. However, if team members deviate from the guidelines but are effective in developing a quality model, take them all out for a drink. Declare success for the first model created by a team when the participants—the designers and other stakeholders of the system, and yourself—agree that the model is a good representation of what you want to build. Challenges may remain, and the stakeholders may have reservations about their creation (the system, not the model), but the team has cleared the first hurdle and should be congratulated.

Summary

In this chapter, you learned a brief history of creating models of complex systems and the types of models commonly used in threat modeling. We also highlighted techniques that will help you and your team get the right amount of information into your models. This will help you find the needles (data) in the haystack of information while also avoiding analysis paralysis.

Up next, in Chapter 2, we present a generalized approach to threat modeling. In Chapter 3, we'll cover a collection of industry-accepted methodologies for identifying and prioritizing threats.

## CHAPTER 2

A Generalized Approach to Threat Modeling

If you always do what you've always done, you'll always get what you've always got.
—Henry Ford

Threat modeling as an exercise in analyzing a system design for threats follows a consistent approach that can be generalized into a few basic steps; this chapter presents that general flow. This chapter also provides information on what to look for in your system models, and what you may never be able to discover as a result of threat modeling.

Basic Steps

This section shows the basic steps that outline the general flow of threat modeling. Experienced modelers perform these steps in parallel and, for the most part, automatically; they are continuously assessing the state of the system as the model is being formed, and they may be able to call out areas for concern well before the model has reached an expected level of maturity.

It may take you some time to achieve that level of comfort and familiarity, but with practice these steps will become second nature:

1. *Identify objects in the system under consideration.*

   Identify the elements, data stores, external entities, and actors, present in and associated with the system you are modeling, and gather characteristics or attributes as metadata about these things (later in the chapter we provide some sample questions you can use to ease metadata collection). Make note of the security capabilities and controls each object supports or provides, and any clear deficiencies (such as an element exposing a web server on HTTP, or a database that does not require authentication to access).

2. *Identify flows between those objects.*

Identify how data flows between the objects described in step 1. Then record metadata about those flows, such as protocols, data classification and sensitivity, and directionality.

3. *Identify assets of interest.*

Detail relevant or interesting assets that are held by the objects or communicated by the flows identified in step 2. Remember that assets may include data—either internal to the application (such as control flags or configuration settings) or related to the function of the application (i.e., user data).

4. *Identify system weaknesses and vulnerabilities.*

Understand how the confidentiality, integrity, availability, privacy, and safety of the assets identified in step 3 may be impacted, based on the characteristics of the system objects and flows. In particular, you are looking for violations of the security principles described in the Introduction. For example, if an asset were to include a security token or key, and the key may be accessed incorrectly (resulting in loss of confidentiality) in certain conditions, then you have identified a weakness. If that weakness is exploitable, you have a vulnerability that may be under threat.

5. *Identify threats.*

You will need to associate vulnerabilities against the system's assets with threat actors to determine how likely each vulnerability is going to be exploited, which drives risk to the system.

6. *Determine exploitability.*

Lastly, identify paths through the system an attacker may take to cause an impact against one or more assets; in other words, identify how an attacker may exploit a weakness identified in step 4.

What You Are Looking for in a System Model

Once you have a model to work from, in any state of completeness (or accuracy), you can begin to review the model for vulnerabilities and threats. This is where you move from system modeling to threat modeling. At this point, you might be asking yourself: "What exactly should I be looking for among this mess of boxes and lines and text?"

The short answer is: you are looking for the *means* and *opportunity* an attacker would need,[1] should they also have the *motive*, to conduct an attack against your system. What does this mean?

Means
> Does the system present a vector for attack?

Opportunity
> Does the use or deployment of the system (or on a more granular level, an individual component) result in a path or access that a suitably motivated attacker may use to conduct an exploit?

Motive
> Does an attacker have a reason to conduct an attack against your system? A sufficiently motivated attacker may also create opportunities for exploitation beyond your expectations.

Means and opportunity form the basis of a threat. Motivation of an adversary is the most difficult to know precisely, which is why risk exists as a concept—motivation can be known only with some level of confidence, and actual exploitation attempts can be rated reliably only by probability. Risk, by definition, is a measure of likelihood (what are the chances an adversary has a motive, opportunity, *and* means?) and impact. In addition to motivation, you also have to assess a potential attacker's capability to cause a threat event.

Because so many factors contribute to the likelihood of an attack and the likelihood of its success, it's not possible to accurately quantify risk except under specific (and potentially unique) circumstances.

The Usual Suspects

The following is a nonexhaustive checklist of terms to look out for as you learn to recognize areas for concern in the models you produce:

Any nonsecure protocol
> Some protocols come in two flavors, one with security and one without (and those with security often have names that end in "s"). Alternatively, protocols may be known to be weak through changes in security knowledge, attack or analysis techniques, or flaws in the design or popular implementations. For example:
>
> ```
> http
> ftp
> telnet
> ntp
> ```

---

1 Peter J. Dostal, "Circumstantial Evidence," The Criminal Law Notebook, *https://oreil.ly/3yyB4*.

```
snmpv1
wep
sslv3
```

If you see any of these or similar insecure (nonsecure, impossible to secure, or no longer capable of meeting security expectations) or weak protocols *and* your assets of interest are being communicated or accessed through one of them, flag this as a potential vulnerability and loss of confidentiality (primarily) and integrity (secondarily).

Any process or data store without authentication

Processes that expose critical services, such as a database server or web server, and that do not require authentication are an immediate red flag, especially if one of these components houses, transmits, or receives your critical assets (data). Lack of authentication exposes your data just as easily as an insecure protocol.

It is important to look for compensating controls in this case that can help mitigate the impact from threats. These controls usually rely on identification of an attacker, but in this case, you would not have an identity assigned by your system. You may, though, have identification in the form of a source IP address (which, of course, any smart attacker would spoof to throw your Security Operations Center off their scent). Be sure to highlight any capabilities to detect malicious access; if no controls are available, lack of authentication will be one of your highest priorities to address (good find!).

Any process that fails to authorize access to critical assets or functionality

Similar to lack of authentication, processes that expose critical services that fail to properly authorize access—either by granting the same privileges to all users regardless of identity, or granting excessive privileges to individual actors—is a hot spot attackers will try to leverage to compromise your sensitive assets. Credential stuffing, brute-forcing, and social engineering can deliver credentials to malicious actors who will then use them to access key functionality with access to your system's "crown jewels," and having a weak authorization model means effectively any account will do.

Instead, if your system erected virtual walls and enforced an authorization model based on least privilege and separation of duties, then an attacker's path to the target assets would be much more challenging. Using effective access-control schemes (such as RBAC for users and MAC for processes) makes administration easier and less error prone, and provides visibility that enables security verification more effectively than a piecemeal approach.

Any process with missing logging

While the primary goal for any developer or system designer who is trying to enforce security principles is to prevent an attacker from getting into the system in the first place, a secondary goal is to make it hard for an attacker to move around in a system (causing them to spend more effort and time, and maybe take their attacks elsewhere). Traceability is a key capability that a system should have, so any attempts by attackers to take advantage of system vulnerabilities can be identified, and proper behavior can be audited after the fact. A process that is missing logging of critical system events, especially security-relevant events, should be a cause for concern. Without the visibility into the behaviors of the system and actions of actors within it (or attempts at actions), the operators of the system will suffer from the "fog of war" (*https://oreil.ly/UIF6Y*), which puts them at a severe disadvantage against skilled adversaries.

Sensitive assets in plain text

If you consider an asset such as data to be sensitive, would you write it down on a piece of paper and tape it to your computer monitor?[2] So why would you want to let it reside "in the clear" on a computer disk or nonvolatile storage? Instead, it should be protected in some fashion—encrypted or hashed, depending on its usage.

Sensitive data assets without integrity controls

Even if you cryptographically secure your assets, protecting them from being accessed (read), you need to protect them from being tampered with. If tamper evidence or tamper resistance is not a feature of your system when it comes to your sensitive assets, this should be a red flag. *Tamper evidence* can mean having sufficient logging when modifications are made to an asset, but we also recommend performing an integrity check in addition. Digital signatures and cryptographic hash algorithms use keys to generate information that can be used to verify the integrity of data, and this information can be verified for integrity and authenticity as well. *Tamper resistance* is a harder feature to support. And, in software, usually involves the use of a security reference monitor—a specially protected process that can enforce integrity verification on all assets and operations—to guard against malicious modification. Physical security options for tamper-evidence and tamper-resistance capabilities exist as well.[3]

---

2 This is a common way computer users store their passwords!

3 Such as defined in the US NIST FIPS 140-2, *https://oreil.ly/N_pfq*.

In some systems, like embedded devices, you can store certain assets in memory locations in plain text as long as access to the location is severely restrictive. For example, a key stored in one-time programmable (OTP) memory is in clear text, but access is often available to only a segregated security processor such as a cryptographic accelerator, and an attacker would almost certainly need to completely destroy the device to gain access to the key, which may make the risk "acceptable" to you and your leadership.

Incorrect use of cryptography

Cryptography is critical to protecting sensitive assets, but using it incorrectly is so very easy. It may be difficult to know when cryptography is not being used correctly, but looking out for the following will tell you if there is a potential for concern:

- Hashing information that needs to be read or used in its original form (such as when authenticating to a remote system)

- Encrypting using a symmetric cryptographic algorithm (such as Advanced Encyption Standard, or AES) when the key resides on the same component as the data

- Not using a cryptographically secure random number generator (*https://oreil.ly/Ld4wm*)

- Using your own homegrown cryptographic algorithm[4]

Communication paths transiting a trust boundary

Any time data moves from one system component to another, an attacker could possibly intercept it to steal it, tamper with it, or prevent it from reaching its destination. This is especially true if the communication path leaves the confines of a trust relationship between components (where each component is considered trustworthy among the collection of components); this is what is meant by *transiting a trust boundary*. As an example, consider corporate communications—if the messages are passed between individuals within the company, each individual is generally trusted, and the trust boundary has not been crossed. But if the message leaves the organization, such as through email to an outside actor, the message is no longer protected by trusted actors or systems, and requires protective measures to ensure that the trustworthiness, integrity, and confidentiality of the messages are maintained.

The previous checklist is weighted toward looking for security concerns, but could easily be expanded to include privacy or safety hazards as well; some of the security

---

4 Please, unless you are a cryptographer or math savant, just don't do it!

red flags to look out for may directly lead to privacy or other issues, depending on the assets and goals of the system in its design and operation.

Some system model types, such as sequence diagrams, make it easy to spot insecurities. For example, to identify a TOCTOU (*https://oreil.ly/l3Jaq*) security concern, look for a sequence of interactions between two or more entities and data (either a store or a buffer). Specifically, you want to locate where a single process interacts with the data twice, but a separate entity interacts with the data *in between* the two interactions. If the intervening access results in a change of state to the data, such as locking memory or changing the value of the buffer or deleting the data store contents, this may result in bad behavior from the other entity.

Figure 2-1 shows a sample sequence diagram that highlights a common scenario for TOCTOU weaknesses to exist.

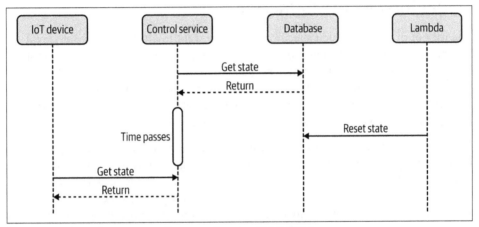

Figure 2-1. Sample sequence diagram showing TOCTOU

Can you spot the issue?[5]

What You Should Not Expect to Discover

System models are abstractions or approximations of a system and its properties. Threat modeling is best done "early and often," and will mostly focus on architecture and design aspects of the system. As a result, the key thing you will *not* be able to find through this exercise are flaws based on the implementation, due to language constraints, embedded components, or developer choices.

---

5 Answer: the control service gets the control state variable from the database too early, and does not update its local copy, which results in an incorrect value being returned to the device when it asks for the state variable.

For example, while it is possible to know you are using the correct form of cryptography for protecting a sensitive asset, it is difficult to know at design time whether during key generation the random number generator is being seeded correctly. You can *predict* there *may* be a cause for concern, and may simulate the impact from poor seeding should it occur in practice, but your finding would be theoretical, and therefore nonactionable, at this point.[6] Likewise, you may know from the model that a particular piece of functionality is written in a language that makes memory safety difficult (e.g., by the use of the C programming language), but it will be difficult to know that of your two hundred APIs, three of them have remotely exploitable stack-based buffer overflows. You should take care to not be the person in your organization that "cries wolf" (*https://oreil.ly/fVc3L*) and instead focus on actionable and defensible results.

Threat Intelligence Gathering

The idea of predicting which specific actors may want to attack your system, exploiting the vulnerabilities you have identified to gain access to the assets in your system, may seem daunting—but fear not. Yes, you could do the research to identify specific hacking groups, learn about their modus operandi, and convince yourself and your team that doom is coming for your assets. The MITRE ATT&CK framework (*https://attack.mitre.org*) makes that research project easier.

But before you go that far, consider threats in terms of what someone might do and then what *type* of attacker might do that something. In a sense, you might almost think of it like the high-tech version of the *Field of Dreams* idea (*https://oreil.ly/hN2tW*), in that simply having a vulnerability is not a perfect predictor of exploitation. But you can almost certainly determine how someone *might* go about exploiting your system, and you can just as likely determine the qualifications, motivations, and level of interest that an attacker may have and how that translates to a potential impact against your system.

In Chapter 3, you will learn more about the threat modeling methodologies that do exactly this. These methodologies formalize these things as tactics, techniques, and procedures (TTPs).

---

6 Continuous threat modeling (CTM), presented in Chapter 5, offers a potential solution to this conundrum.

Summary

In this chapter, you learned about a generalized flow to threat modeling. You also learned how to look for data from the information gathered as a result of creating a system model. Finally, you learned what can and cannot be determined from threat modeling, and sources of threat information.

In the next chapter, you will learn about specific threat modeling approaches in common practices, pros and cons of each methodology, and how to choose one specific to your needs.

## CHAPTER 3

Threat Modeling Methodologies

So since all models are wrong, it is very important to know what to worry about; or, to put it in another way, what models are likely to produce procedures that work in practice (where exact assumptions are never true).

—G. E. P. Box and A. Luceño, *Statistical Control: By Monitoring and Feedback Adjustment* (John Wiley and Sons)

This chapter introduces some of the many available threat modeling methodologies, highlighting the many facets of the discipline. We discuss our personal views and experiences (and where appropriate, borrow opinions from trusted sources) on these methodologies' advantages and drawbacks, so you can identify a methodology that may work for you.

Before We Go Too Deep...

It is important to make one point clear from the start: there isn't a *best* methodology. A particular methodology will work successfully in some organizations and teams, or for specific technologies or compliance requirements, and yet will completely fail in others. The reasons are as varied as the team's organizational culture, the people involved in the threat model exercise, and the constraints put upon the team by the current state of the project (which will vary over time).

Consider, for example, a team that begins without security-oriented goals, then evolves to appointing a *security champion* (*https://oreil.ly/KQfS3*) representing security interests for the whole team, and finally achieves the state in which every developer, architect, and tester has enough security knowledge to be individually responsible for the product's overall security.[1] In each of the three stages, this team faces a distinct set of issues that affect the choice of threat modeling methodology differently:

Stage 1, no previous security goals (and little knowledge)
The team should opt for a methodology that offers educational values and focuses on low-hanging fruit. This allows the team to incorporate security fundamentals into its routines and initial decisions, and bakes in security knowledge so that it becomes an intrinsic part of the overall development methodology.

Stage 2, a security champion is appointed
The team may be more successful using a more structured threat modeling methodology that requires a more experienced security practitioner to guide the team to achieve more granular and action-oriented results.

Stage 3, all individuals own product security equally
The team can move to a more documentation-oriented approach: identified risks are immediately mitigated and documented as a "we thought this bad thing might happen, so here is what we did about it" way. Or the organization may come up with a handcrafted methodology that can be used across the various product teams, and that is fine-tuned to the organization's needs.

Whichever stage you and your team find yourselves in right now, you want to consider a threat modeling methodology that helps take your current security posture to the next level. Your methodology should be compatible with any development methodology currently in use and should also allow for any resources you may have at your disposal or be able to acquire.

Adam Shostack, threat modeling guru and one of the principal proponents of the field, has famously said that "a good threat model is one that produces valid findings."[2] The difference between a good threat model and a bad threat model is that the good one has valid findings. What is a *valid finding*? It is a conclusion, an observation, or a deduction about the security state of your system. The finding is timely and relevant, and can be translated into actions that allow you to mitigate a possible vulnerability, document a piece of system-specific knowledge, or verify that a potentially delicate aspect of the system was evaluated and found to be "OK to live with."

Yet another fundamental contribution by Shostack that is extremely helpful in determining how to threat model is the four-question framework (*https://oreil.ly/g0zx8*).

---

1 In our experience, this final state is the necessary end goal for making threat modeling an accessible *discipline* that anyone can learn and apply.

2 Paraphrased: we (including Adam!) don't remember exactly where it was said first, but it bears repeating because it's true.

For the purpose of these questions, "we" refers to the team or organization performing the threat model:

What are we working on?

Understand what the system *is* right now and what it *needs to be*, meaning, where its development is leading.

What could go wrong?

In light of understanding the composition and the objectives of the system, come up with those things that might interfere with its purpose by altering its confidentiality, integrity, availability, and privacy properties, as well as any other security-related property the system has defined.

What are we going to do about it?

What are the mitigation steps that we can take to reduce the liability created by what we identified in the previous question? Can we change design, add new security controls, perhaps remove altogether the more vulnerable parts of the system? Or should we accept the risk in the context of where and how the system will operate, and chalk it up to the cost of doing business?

Did we do a good job?

Understanding this is less an aspect of threat modeling itself, but nonetheless important for the overall success of the practice. It is important to look back and understand how well the threat modeling exercise reflected the security posture of the system: did we identify "what could go wrong" and did we make good decisions regarding "what we did about it" (aka did we mitigate the threat effectively)? By closing the loop and understanding our performance in threat modeling, we are able to measure how we applied the methodology, identify whether we need to refine the approach, and which details we should pay more attention to in the future.

These four questions should be enough to help you decide whether your threat modeling effort will be successful. If the methodology you choose and the way it was used do not answer any of these questions to your satisfaction, then perhaps it is better to consider a different methodology.

So how do you go about finding a methodology that works in your situation? Do not hesitate in choosing one methodology and trying it out by yourself; if it doesn't work for you, choose a different one to try until you find one that works or that you can adapt to your needs. Once you have some personal experience under your belt, you easily can tailor or customize an existing method to make it more suitable for your team and organization.

Note that organizational culture and individuals' cross-cultural differences are important in the process of threat modeling. As we said earlier, what works for one team may not work for another for various reasons, and you should take that into consideration, especially in global enterprises. For some, asking "what could possibly go wrong" is a more comfortable process than for others, and this might be one of the deciding factors between using a more free-form methodology or one based on threat catalogs and long checklists of items. The availability of security experts (see the following note) that work hand in hand with the team can be a valuable mitigation for these issues, as security experts can significantly reduce any uncertainty created by the many possibilities in a "what could *possibly* go wrong" paradigm.

 When we say *security experts*, we mean those people who have the necessary training and experience and who can deliver that knowledge, guidance, and support when called upon. The range of capabilities a security expert may bring to bear will be context dependent, but may include playing the role of the adversary, or identifying additional areas of research for the team to follow and learn on their own, or to call on other experts to bring their expertise on board for specific problems. When threat modeling, experts should have the experience and knowledge to demonstrate credible threats to the system under analysis.

Ask two threat modeling experts what methodology they prefer and you will probably get three different answers. Once you get some threat models under your belt, especially if you stay in the same technology area for long enough, you will start to develop a sense of where things happen (or don't) and how things should look (or not), and be able to apply a "smell test" approach to your threat modeling. Even though their importance to the process is well understood, security experts, security architects, and others who can effectively perform threat modeling are still a rare breed. Not many organizations have access to these experts that allows a professional touch for every single threat model.[3]

Another important issue with threat modeling methodologies is that some apply the *threat modeling* term to more than actual start-to-end threat modeling methods. For example, many times methodologies that perform only threat elicitation are conflated with full threat modeling methodologies. Sometimes risk classification methodologies are also lumped into the threat identification category. A methodology that focuses solely on threat identification will build a catalog of possible threats and stop there. A full threat modeling methodology will rank those threats, understand which ones are relevant to the system at hand, and give a road map for which one should be solved first. In other words, a threat identification methodology plus a risk classification methodology equals a full threat modeling methodology. We tried to be mindful of this and present the methodologies from a real-work perspective, in the way they

---

3 Which is one more reason you should keep scaling in mind when deciding on your methodology!

are commonly adopted by practitioners even if a formal definition discrepancy is in place.

Looking Through Filters, Angles, and Prisms

You can translate a system into a representative model in many ways, decomposing the whole into parts according to the views that interest you. In threat modeling, three main approaches have been identified that help clearly highlight threats that may be present in your system. They do this primarily by asking a simple question: "What could possibly go wrong?"

System-centric approach

> The system-centric approach is arguably the most prevalent in threat modeling, especially when performing the activity manually. It is the approach you will see most distinctly used across this whole book, in part because it is the approach that is easiest to demonstrate. The approach considers the system and its decomposition into a set of its functional parts—software and hardware components— together with how those components interact. The approach also considers external actors and elements that interface with the system and its components. This approach is usually expressed with DFDs that show how data goes through the system during its operation (and using a modeling convention such as we highlighted in Chapter 1). This approach is also commonly referred to as *architecture-* or *design-centric.*

Attacker-centric approach

> In this approach, the modeler (you) adopts the point of view of the attacker to identify how vulnerabilities in the system enable an attacker to act on their motivation ("State actor wants to extract confidential information") to reach their goals ("State actor reads classified reports stored in the system"). This approach typically uses attack trees (also highlighted in Chapter 1), threat catalogs, and lists to identify entry points in the system based on the motivation and resources available to the attacker.

Asset-centric approach

> An asset-centric approach, as the name indicates, focuses on important assets that should be defended. After mapping and listing all involved assets, each one is examined in the context of its accessibility to an attacker (e.g., to read or tamper with the asset) to understand any threats that may be pertinent and how they affect the system as a whole.

Each methodology we illustrate in this chapter encompasses one or more of these approaches.

To the Methodologies, at Last!

To present a casual yet descriptive overview of these many methodologies, we decided to apply an unscientific metric to each one. We don't intend to pit one against the other, but simply to help you understand how these methodologies fare in categories that we recommend as useful. These values reflect our personal experience and our understanding of each methodology, and are not the result of any kind of survey or data collection. We will use a 0 to 5 (with 0 being "not really," and 5 being "close to an absolute yes") scale along the following attributes:

Accessible

Can development teams use this methodology independently, without significant security expertise? Can they do it correctly? Are resources available that they can refer to if they get stuck? For example, a methodology based on a threat library might be more accessible than one that is open-ended and expects the team to know all about attack vectors and techniques.

Scalable

Can the same methodology be applied to many teams and products in the same organization? In this context, scalability is a function of throughput—the more team members, security or otherwise, who are able to use this methodology, the more system models that can be analyzed. Scalability suffers when the methodology is accessible only to those who specialize in security, because it minimizes throughput and creates a bottleneck that depends on specialists. This also leads to increased security technical debt. If an organization is process-heavy and failure to conduct a threat model results in projects being held up, you might "miss the boat" for threat modeling to be part of the system development life cycle.

Educational

Is its focus on teaching rather than forcing a correction for a perceived violation (auditing)? Can the threat modeling exercise advance the overall security understanding and culture of the team?

Useful

Are the findings useful and applicable to both the system and security teams? Does the methodology reflect what is actually significant for the modeled system? In other words, does the methodology match the intent of the threat modeling process? In this context, *significant* and *intent* are subjective and depend on the specific situation:

- Can you derive value from the results of the threat modeling exercise—in terms of relevant findings, or from bringing multiple stakeholders (e.g., security, privacy, and engineering) together? Can you manage it through your DevOps pipeline—or all together, or even from the fact that a threat model now exists?

- Does the methodology make describing the system easier and clearer?

- Does it help the team identify weaknesses and/or threats?

- Does it generate good reports and help the team manage issues?

Agile

Does the methodology negatively impact the product team's velocity? Does it make the threat model a resource drain (when compared to the benefits it produces), or does it actually help with the ongoing secure development of the product? Does the methodology allow for changes during threat modeling?

Representative

How well does the abstraction of the system compare to the implementation of the system? Does the result truly reflect the system as implemented?

Unconstrained

Once the "known suspects" are evaluated, does the methodology support, or possibly lead to, further exploration or identification of other possible flaws?

We will provide a short explanation behind our grading for each category of each methodology. Again, this is not the result of scientific research (although where possible, academic studies were consulted and quoted). This is the result of our experience and understanding, and we welcome discussion of our views (open an issue at *https://www.threatmodeling.dev*).

This is by no means a catalog of all existing methodologies, but we tried to be all-encompassing in the ways we approach the problem. We also wanted to present methodologies that span various industries, including software development, government acquisitions, enterprise risk management, academia, and other sources where system risk needs to be evaluated and minimized. Some of these methodologies are current, and others border on being outdated, but each expresses important aspects of the science of threat modeling.[4] We tried to be representative and comprehensive in choosing the more popular methodologies, which are those that have been widely applied, and are generally recognized as effective in their proposed objectives. We apologize to the authors for any misconstruction when presenting these methodologies—any mistake is ours alone in our understanding of them.

We do not provide an in-depth exploration of each methodology, but we describe each methodology enough for you to get the gist of it. We also present supporting

---

4 You can see a different list, comparing 12 of the existing methodologies, by Natalya Shevchenco of the CMU Software Engineering Institute at *https://oreil.ly/j9orI*.

references that will give you a starting point to investigate any of the methodologies we go over. Where applicable, we call out the uniqueness of the methodology or give our personal interpretations. You should definitely question our interpretations and build your own opinions of the methodologies we discuss here.

STRIDE

It is safe to say that STRIDE has attained a somewhat unique place in the pantheon of threat modeling methodologies and tools, even though it is by itself more of a threat analysis and classification methodology than threat modeling per se. (In the past few years, it has become common to approach STRIDE as a *framework* rather than a full methodology.[5]) As such, it is fitting that we look at it first.

STRIDE was formalized at Microsoft in 1999, and the first published mention of it comes from a paper by Loren Kohnfelder and Praerit Garg, "The Threats To Our Products":[6]

> The STRIDE security threat model should be used by all [Microsoft] products to identify various types of threats the product is susceptible to during the design phase. Threats are identified based on the design of the product.

This is what *STRIDE* stands for:

S: Spoofing
> Spoofing threats imply that an attacker can mimic the identity of an element of the system, which could be another user, another system, or another process. Spoofing also assumes the element's privileges in the system.

T: Tampering
> Tampering threats directly impact the property of integrity by causing changes (arbitrarily, intentionally or not) to the data or functionality manipulated by the system.

R: Repudiation
> Another aspect of the trust imparted to a system is its ability to assert with full confidence that an operation was performed by the actor who declares having performed it, in the manner and time declared. Different from tampering, threats of this category give an attacker the ability to negate that certain operations took place and/or were initiated by the actor in question.

---

5 Adam Shostack, "The Threats to Our Products," Microsoft, *https://oreil.ly/n_GBD*.

6 Loren Kohnfelder and Praerit Garg, "The Threats to Our Products," April 1999 (.docx file), *https://oreil.ly/w6YKi*.

I: Information disclosure

Threats of this category are those that cause information that should remain restricted and controlled to leak outside its assigned trust boundaries, threatening the system's confidentiality property.

D: Denial of service

These threats, which go against the availability property of the system, consist of making the system unavailable or its performance degraded to a point where it interferes with its use.

E: Elevation of privilege

Well worthy of a category of their own, these threats involve the authorization mechanisms of the system and the attacker's goal of gaining a higher level of privilege than they may normally be granted (which may be none).

From a cursory reading of the categories listed, it is easy to see that while they offer good coverage of the types of threats a system may be subject to, they lack enough definition to perfectly force-fit all possible threats into a specific area. This is where STRIDE starts showing some of its deficiencies. In fact, if we step back and take a critical look, we see that as long as a specific threat has been identified and brought out, it is less important that it be classified in a perfectly labeled category—but on the other hand, that ambiguity can severely impact how we formally assess the risk associated with that threat.

Another, more pressing issue with STRIDE is that in order to make optimal use of it, a product team or practitioner needs to be aware of what can *actually* be a threat, and how that threat becomes a vulnerability by being exploited. For example, if a developer is not aware that leveraging a buffer overflow in a privileged process to run arbitrary code is possible, classifying "memory corruption" as one of these possible threats is difficult:

1. Elevation of privilege by running arbitrary code

2. Tampering if the attacker is able to change any arbitrary memory address that holds data

3. Denial of service if the memory corruption "merely" causes a crash instead of code execution

As a member of a development team, you are asked to "think like a hacker" when performing threat classification, but you may either lack the necessary knowledge or receive training that makes it difficult to think outside the box when it comes to security. This makes it understandably difficult for you to extrapolate examples into actual issues that are relevant to your own systems. Unfortunately, STRIDE does not offer a guiding framework.

STRIDE begins with a representation of the system that can help you examine its characteristics. The most common way to represent a system is by creating a DFD, which contains the parts of the system (elements) and their intercommunication (data flows), with trust boundaries that separate areas of the system with distinct trust values, as seen in Figures 3-1 and 3-2, and as explained in Chapter 1.

In the basic example in Figure 3-1, we see three trust boundaries, represented by the boxes around Alice, Bob, and the key repository. This representation is a pytm (see Chapter 4) artifact; trust boundaries are more commonly represented by a single line across the data flows that cross them. Effectively, the trust boundaries separate this system in three trust domains: Alice and Bob, as distinct users, and the key repository, which needs yet another level of trust to be accessed.

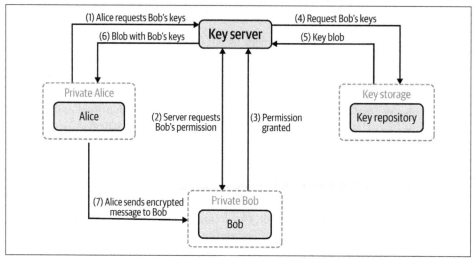

Figure 3-1. DFD representation of a simple system: naive message encryption

Because threat identification depends on the completeness of the DFD, it is important for you to create one that is simple yet as complete as possible. As you saw in Chapter 1, a simple symbology of squares for external elements, circles for processes (and double circles for complex processes), double lines for data stores, and arrow-headed lines to signify data flows is enough to express most of what's needed to understand the system. And this does not preclude the use of other symbols to make the diagram more representative. In fact, in pytm, we extended the symbology to include a dedicated lambda symbol, which added to the clarity of our diagrams. Annotations like the kind of protocol used by a data flow, or the underlying OS of a given set of processes, can help to further clarify aspects of the system. Unfortunately, they can also make the diagram overcrowded and harder to understand, so balance is important.

Extending STRIDE into a full threat modeling methodology then becomes an exercise in creating the threat classification (according to the acronym), ranking the risk of all identified threats (refer to the Introduction for options for rating severity and risk), and then suggesting mitigations that eliminate or reduce the risk for each threat (see Figure 3-2).

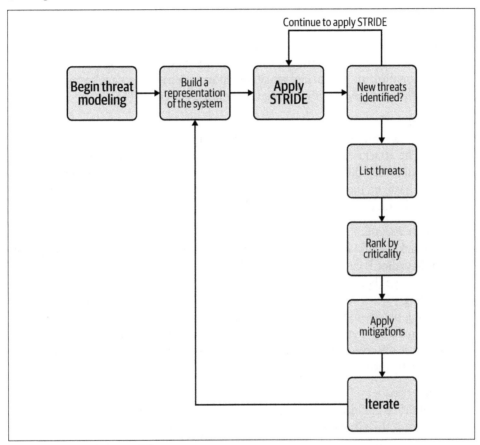

Figure 3-2. STRIDE workflow

For example, using the DFD in Figure 3-1 to represent a system of web comments in a forum, we could identify some basic threats (with some assumptions):

Spoofing

The user Alice can be spoofed when submitting a request, as there is no indication that the user is authenticated to the system at the time the request is submitted. This can be mitigated by creating a proper user authentication scheme.

Tampering

Tampering could occur between the key server and key repository. An attacker could intercept the communication and change the value of the key blob being transacted by impersonating one of the endpoints (which might lead to further impersonation or capturing sensitive information). This can be mitigated by establishing mutually authenticated communication over TLS.

Repudiation

An attacker could directly access the key repository database and add or alter keys. The attacker could also ascribe a key to a user who would have no way to prove that they did not alter it. This can be mitigated by logging the operation and a hash of the key at creation time on a separate system that cannot be accessed with the same trust level as that of the database.

Information disclosure

An attacker could observe the traffic between Alice and the key server and establish that Alice is communicating with Bob. Even without access to the contents of the message (because they do not traverse this system), there is potential value in knowing when two parties are communicating. A possible mitigation would be masking the identities of Alice and Bob in the identifiers that the system uses, so they would have ephemeral meaning and could not be derived in case the information is observed—together, of course, with encryption of the communication channel by means of TLS or IPsec.

Denial of service

An attacker could create an automated script to submit thousands of random requests at the same time, overloading the key server and denying proper service to other, legitimate users. This can be mitigated by flow-rate limitation at the session and network levels.

Elevation of privilege

An attacker might use the exec()-like functionality in the database to execute commands in the server under the database's level of privilege (which might potentially be higher than a common user). This can be mitigated by hardening the database and reducing the privileges it has when running, as well as validating all input and using prepared statements and an object-relational mapping (ORM) access mode in order to prevent SQL injection issues.

Brook S.E. Schoenfield makes this strong point about STRIDE: remember that a single technique can be used against multiple elements in a system. When performing STRIDE, it is important to stress that just because a single issue has been identified (for example, an instance of spoofing), it doesn't mean that the same issue will not be present in other parts of the system, either through the same attack vector or another one. To think otherwise would be a grave mistake.

How does STRIDE fare under our (unscientific) grading parameters? See Table 3-1.

Table 3-1. STRIDE and our grading parameters

Parameter	Score	Explanation
Accessible	2	Once presented with the framework, many teams are able to execute it with varying degrees of success, depending on their previous knowledge of security principles.
Scalable	3	While the framework can be used by many products and teams in the same organization, the efficacy of its use will vary wildly by team.
Educational	3	The framework provides many opportunities for you and your team to develop security education, but only if a security practitioner is available to help. The team will likely end the process with more security knowledge than when it started.
Useful	4	By definition of its categories STRIDE lends itself to working best on software systems; in that sense, the team will get useful results that apply to its system, and be focused on what the team *at that time* sees as relevant threats.
Agile	2	STRIDE is best performed when many team members can participate at the same time while using the same set of assumptions. It also helps to have a security practitioner present to direct the dialogue, while focusing on the system as a whole. In this sense, STRIDE does not lend itself well to Agile processes and is seen as a big resource drain by some organizations.
Representative	2	The framework "fires" when a truthful representation of the system is available, but as we have discussed under Agile, it does have issues when following the progress of the development process. An effort not unlike the initial threat model may be necessary to make sure that the resulting threat model correctly corresponds to the changes that the system went through during its development.
Unconstrained	5	By working on impacts, the framework puts no constraints on the source of a threat or which views of the system you must use to explore it. You can explore the system freely with no biases, generating threats based on your own experience and research. In this sense, STRIDE is unconstrained.

STRIDE per Element

One of the advantages of STRIDE is that it is unconstrained. Unfortunately, this is also one of its main disadvantages, especially when used by inexperienced teams or practitioners. It's easy to get bogged down in the "have I considered everything" and "what could possibly go wrong" possibilities and never reach an accepted state of "doneness."

STRIDE per Element is a variation of STRIDE, developed by Michael Howard and Shawn Hernan, that adds structure to address the lack of constraints by observing that some elements are more susceptible to specific threats than others. For example, consider an external entity (like a user, administrator, or an external system) that provides a different set of services to the system. This external entity is more susceptible to being spoofed (as in an attacker taking their identity) than a data flow. In fact, external entities can often be subject to completely different sets of security measures and might even have an elevated security posture. On the other hand, a data flow is more open to attacks that tamper with its contents than an external entity.

As seen in Figure 3-3, STRIDE per Element limits the set of attacks that target specific classes of elements and considerably focuses the analysis of possible threats. In this way, it is considerably less open-ended than the original STRIDE.

Different threats affect each type of element						
Element	S	T	R	I	D	E
External entity	X		X			X
Process	X	X	X	X	X	X
Data store		X	X	X	X	
Data flow		X		X	X	

Figure 3-3. STRIDE per Element chart (source: https://oreil.ly/3uZH2)

During related discussions with Brook S.E. Schoenfield, he drew from his experience to point out that STRIDE per Element has another disadvantage: threat models are not additive; you can't just smash two or more threat models together and consider it a threat model of the whole system. STRIDE per Element, in that sense, provides many benefits but might lead to ignoring the holistic approach to the system during the analysis, even if the system is completely represented.

STRIDE per Element allows your team to focus on individual elements more than on the overall system. A smaller portion of the team can focus solely on those members' elements as they develop, and have "mini-threat-modeling" sessions that focus on those threats. For that reason, scalable, Agile, and representative scores also go up, becoming 4, 3, and 4, respectively (see Table 3-2).

Table 3-2. STRIDE per Element

Parameter	Score	Explanation
Accessible	2	Once presented with the framework, many teams are able to execute it with varying degrees of success, depending on their previous knowledge of security principles.
Scalable	4	While many teams and products in the same organization can use the framework, the efficacy of STRIDE per Element will vary wildly by team.
Educational	3	The framework provides for a great deal of security education, but requires that a security practitioner is available to help the team through threat classification. A high probability exists that the team will complete the process with more security knowledge than when it started.
Useful	4	By definition of its categories STRIDE per Element lends itself to working best on software systems; in that sense, the team will get useful results, and will be focused on what the team identifies as current and relevant threats.
Agile	3	STRIDE per Element picks up one point over STRIDE because of the focus on the specific traits of elements, allowing the team to be more effective and, thus, cover more ground.
Representative	3	For the same reason as Agile, STRIDE per Element picks up one point over STRIDE. Focusing on specific elements allows truer representation of the system in its current form.
Unconstrained	3	STRIDE per Element modifies the STRIDE Unconstrained score to a 3, since it somewhat binds what each element will be subject to, giving you a smaller set of possibilities to focus on.

STRIDE per Interaction

When Microsoft made its Microsoft Threat Modeling Tool (*https://oreil.ly/sbhWK*) publicly available, it was based on a variation of STRIDE called STRIDE per Interaction. Developed by Larry Osterman and Douglas MacIver at Microsoft, this approach to STRIDE tries to identify threats as a function of the interaction between two elements in the model.

For example, in this framework, an external process (perhaps a client call to a server) has the interaction "sends data to server." In this case, the interaction "client sends data to server" may be subject to spoofing, repudiation, and information disclosure threats, but not an elevation of privilege. On the other hand, the server can take input from a process, in which case the interaction "client receives data from server" is subject only to spoofing threats. For example, the server could be an impersonator claiming to be the real server, in what's commonly known as a man-in-the-middle attack.

The chart containing all the possible threat classes per interaction is extensive, and beyond the scope of our needs here. For a full reference, please refer to *Threat Modeling: Designing for Security* by Adam Shostack (Wiley), page 81.

STRIDE per Interaction comparison results are equivalent to our STRIDE per Element results.

Process for Attack Simulation and Threat Analysis

Process for Attack Simulation and Threat Analysis (PASTA) is a "risk-centric threat modeling methodology aimed at identifying viable threat patterns against an application or system environment" coauthored by Tony UcedaVélez of VerSprite Security and Dr. Marco Morana of CitiGroup in 2012.[7] While a truly in-depth approach to this methodology is beyond the scope of this book, interested readers can refer to *Risk Centric Threat Modeling: Process for Attack Simulation and Threat Analysis* by UcedaVélez and Morana (Wiley), for more details.

PASTA is a risk-centric methodology. It quantifies risk that might impact a business or a system, by beginning with contextual references to the inherent importance that an application and its components, underlying infrastructure, and data have on businesses (stages 1, 2, and 7; see the stage definitions that follow). Stages 3–6 are more germane to architecture, development teams, and application security professionals who are seeking to understand inherent flaws in design, use cases, permissions, implicit trust models, and call flows.

PASTA reinterprets some of the terms we have been using so far, as shown in Table 3-3.

Table 3-3. PASTA terms

Term	Meaning in PASTA
Asset	A resource that has an intrinsic value to the business. This could include, among others: —Information the business uses, trades, or needs —Hardware, software, frameworks, libraries the business relies on for a subject application —The reputation of the business
Threat	Anything that can unfavorably impact an asset.
Weakness/vulnerability	What an attack (supporting a threat) leverages to make its way into the system, either a tangible issue (like a badly configured firewall, cloud component, third-party framework, or RBAC model) or a poor business logic or process (lack of financial oversight on expenses).
Use cases	Expected design behavior of the system.
Abuse cases	Manipulation of use cases in order to yield ulterior motives of the user (e.g., bypass, injection, information leakage, etc.).
Actor	Anything able to perform or use a use case or an abuse case.
Attack	Any action that supports a threat motive against a target asset by exploiting a vulnerability/weakness.
Attack vector	An interface through which an attack traverses.
Countermeasures	Mitigations of a weakness that reduce the probability an attack will be successful.
Attack surface	The set of all possible attack vectors, both logical and physical.

---

7 Tony UcedaVélez, "Risk-Centric Application Threat Models," VerSprite, accessed October 2020, *https://oreil.ly/w9-Lh*.

Term	Meaning in PASTA
Attack trees	A representation of the relationship between threats, target assets, associated vulnerabilities, correlating attack patterns, and countermeasures. Use cases can serve as metadata associated with assets, and abuse cases similarly can serve as metadata for attack patterns.
Impact	The direct or indirect financial value of the damage caused by an attack.

PASTA uses these "ingredients" (pun sort of intended) by implementing a seven-stage process that quantifies the impact to the application and enterprise:

1. Define business objectives.
2. Define technical scope.
3. Decompose the application.
4. Perform threat analysis.
5. Detect vulnerabilities.
6. Enumerate attacks.
7. Perform risk and impact analysis.

Let's take a brief look at these steps and see how they build the definitions into a process. Please note: these are by no means exhaustive explanations of the process, its artifacts, and their use. By the end of this explanation, you'll have a basic understanding of PASTA.

Define business objectives

The point of the *define business objectives* stage is to set the risk context for the threat modeling activity, since the understanding of the business objectives supported by the application or system leads to better understanding the risk variable of *impact*. When you define business objectives, you capture the requirements for the analysis and management of the risks in your scope. Formal documents like requirements, security policies, compliance standards, and guidelines help you to divide these actions into subactivities like these:

1. Define business requirements.
2. Define security and compliance requirements.
3. Perform a preliminary business impact analysis (BIA).
4. Define a risk profile.

The outputs of this activity are, among others, a business impact analysis report (BIAR), which is a description of the application functionality and a list of the business objectives, constrained by the requirements defined in the subactivities listed.

For example, if during this activity a business objective of creating a user community was identified, then registering customers with their personal data would be a functional requirement, and a security requirement around storing PII would be entered into the BIAR.

The input of participants with knowledge of the business processes, application requirements, and business risk posture is taken into consideration, so it is required that product owners, project managers, business owners, and even C-level executives participate in the activity.

It is safe to say that at this stage, the focus is on establishing a reason based on governance, risk, and compliance (GRC) for the remainder of the activities, which include security policies and standards, security guidelines, etc.

Define technical scope

The formal definition of the *define technical scope* stage is "defining the scope of technical assets/components for which threat enumeration will ensue."[8] High-level design documents, network and deployment diagrams, and technology needs (libraries, platforms, etc.) are used to perform these subactivities:

1. Enumerate software components.
2. Identify actors and data sources: where data is created or originates and data sinks; where it is stored away.
3. Enumerate system-level services.
4. Enumerate third-party infrastructures.
5. Assert completeness of secure technical design.

This analysis will generate lists of all assets involved in the system, their mode of deployment, and the dependencies between them, and it will permit a high-level end-to-end overview of the system.

For example, in a simple web application writing to a database hosted in a cloud provider, the analysis that we get at this stage could be as simple as the following:

- Browser: Any
- Web server: Apache 2.2
- Database: MariaDB 10.4
- Actors: User (via browser), Administrator (via browser, console)
- Data sources: User (via browser), Imported (via console)

---

8 Tony UcedaVélez, "Real World Threat Modeling Using the PASTA Methodology," *https://oreil.ly/_VY6n*, 24.

- Data sinks: Database, Log Sink (via cloud provider)
- Protocols in use: HTTP, HTTPS, and SQL over TLS
- System-level services: Fedora 30 running as an image on the cloud provider hardened using CIS Benchmarks (*https://oreil.ly/4ae7Y*) for hardening
- At this time, the system is thought to be sufficiently secured

Decompose the application

During *application decomposition*, you must identify and enumerate all the platforms and technologies in use and the services they require, down to physical security and the processes that govern these. Here are the subactivities:

1. Enumerate all application use cases.
2. Construct data flow diagrams for identified components.[9]
3. Perform security functional analysis and use trust boundaries in the system.

In this stage, PASTA considers where abuse cases may turn into many different attacks. Notice that the DFD we previously discussed also plays a central part in this stage, mapping the relationships among different components via the data flows between them and how they cross trust boundaries.

These DFDs tie together the items listed in the previous stage, "Define technical scope" on page 60, into a cohesive representation of the system. Actors, technology components, and all of the elements in the system start expressing a security posture that can be tested with abuse cases. By placing trust boundaries for the first time in the process, the data flows start expressing how they may be vulnerable to abuse, or how certain abuse cases do not apply to the system.

In addition to data flows, the decomposition reaches down to the smallest details of the system, in a way that many times gets confused with "define technical scope." For example, a system may be expected to run on a certain brand of Intel-based server. That may lead to the unexpected presence of many subsystems that may not have been evaluated fully in the technical scope phase. For example, a baseboard management controller (BMC) may go ignored in the technical scope phase but on application decomposition, it will show up (for example, when listing all subsystems of the motherboard) and will have to be evaluated accordingly.

---

9 Recall we referred to elements in our description of DFDs in Chapter 1; these elements can include system components.

Perform threat analysis

In the words of its creators, "PASTA diverges from other application threat models, as it attempts to focus on the most viable threats both inherent to the technology footprint of the environment as well as the industry segment and the data managed by the application environment."[10] The *threat analysis* stage of PASTA supports this assertion by giving you the background necessary to identify those viable threats. It does this by using all available sources of knowledge to build attack trees and threat libraries that are relevant to the system being modeled:

1. Analyze the overall threat scenario.
2. Gather threat intelligence from internal sources.
3. Gather threat intelligence from external sources.
4. Update the threat libraries.
5. Map the threat agents to assets mapping.
6. Assign probabilities to identified threats.

The value of this stage comes from identifying those threats that are actually applicable and relevant to the system in question, preferring quality of threat identification over quantity of results.

Detect vulnerabilities

In the *vulnerability detection* stage, you focus on identifying areas of the application that are open to risks or vulnerable to attacks. From the information gathered in previous stages you should be able to find tangible and relevant threats by mapping that information into the attack trees or libraries built earlier. One of the main objectives here is to limit (or remove) the amount of false threat findings identified against the system:

1. Review and correlate existing vulnerability data.
2. Identify weak design patterns in the architecture.
3. Map threats to vulnerabilities.
4. Provide context risk analysis based on threats and vulnerabilities.
5. Conduct targeted vulnerability testing.

Lastly, you should review the architecture of the system security, looking for those issues such as missing or sparse logging, data unprotected at rest or in transit, and

---

10 *Risk Centric Threat Modeling: Process for Attack Simulation and Threat Analysis*, Tony UcedaVélez, Marco M. Morana, Chapter 7.

---

failures in authentication and authorization. Review trust boundaries to verify that access control is properly placed and that levels of information classification are not breached.

Enumerate attacks

In the *attack enumeration* stage, you analyze the vulnerabilities that you identified previously, according to their probability of turning into attacks. To do this, you use a probability calculation that involves the probability of a threat (remember that in PASTA, a threat is anything that can unfavorably impact an asset) and weakness (which is a tangible fact or event that realizes a threat) coexisting and generating an impact, mitigated by the countermeasures in place.

The following are the steps for performing attack enumeration analysis:

1. Update the attack library and vectors and the control framework by using the latest entries in threat intelligence sources—like the United States Computer Emergency Readiness Team, known as US CERT (*https://www.us-cert.gov*), and CVE (*https://cve.mitre.org/*)—in order to keep up with latest identified vectors.
2. Identify the attack surface of your system and enumerate the attack vectors matching the previous analysis.
3. Analyze identified attack scenarios in the previous steps by correlating them with the threat library, and validate which attack scenarios are viable by cross-checking paths in the attack trees that match the attack scenarios.
4. Assess the probability and impact of each viable attack scenario.
5. Derive a set of cases to test existing countermeasures.

The use of previously built attack trees and libraries is central here, especially in identifying how those might overcome the assets and controls in place to generate a possible impact. At the end of the day, you want to finish this stage with a measurement and understanding of the probability of an attack for each vulnerability identified.

Perform risk and impact analysis

At the *risk and impact analysis* stage, you mitigate the threats that you have identified as those most probable to result in attacks. You do this by applying countermeasures that are effective and relevant to your system. But what does *effective and relevant* mean in this context? That decision is reached by a calculation that includes the following:

1. Determine the risk of each threat being realized.

2. Identify the countermeasures.

3. Calculate the residual risks: do the countermeasures do a good enough job in reducing the risk of the threats?

4. Recommend a strategy to manage residual risks.

You should not determine the risk by yourself. For example, you may want to include risk assessment and governance professionals, depending on the possible impact of the threats. You and your team will review artifacts generated in the previous stages (attack trees and libraries, attack probabilities, etc.) to come up with a proper risk profile for each threat and calculate the immediacy of countermeasures and the residual risk after the countermeasures are applied. Once you know these risks, you can calculate the overall risk profile of the application, and you and your team can suggest strategic direction to manage that risk.

If we consult the RACI (responsible/accountable/consulted/informed) diagram for PASTA,[11] we can see the complexity inherent to the process—at least in terms of the people/roles involved and the information flow among them.

As an example, let's look at stage 3, "Decompose the application" on page 61, with its three activities:

- Enumerate all application use cases (login, account update, delete users, etc.).
  - Responsible: Threat modeler (a specific role defined by PASTA)
  - Accountable: Development, threat modeler
  - Consulted (two-way): Architect, SysAdmin
  - Informed (one-way): Management, project manager, business analyst, quality assurance, security operations, vulnerability assessment, penetration tester, risk assessor, compliance officer
- Construct data flow diagram of identified components.
  - Responsible: Threat modeler
  - Accountable: Architecture, threat modeler
  - Consulted (two-way): Development, SysAdmin
  - Informed (one-way): Management, project manager, business analyst, quality assurance, security operations, vulnerability assessment, penetration tester, risk assessor, compliance officer

---

11 UcedaVélez, Morana, *Risk Centric Threat Modeling*, Chapter 6, Figure 6.8.

- Perform security functional analysis and use trust boundaries.
  - — Responsible: None
  - — Accountable: Development, SysAdmin, threat modeler
  - — Consulted (two-way): Architect
  - — Informed (one-way): Management, project manager, business analyst, quality assurance, security operations, vulnerability assessment, penetration tester, risk assessor, compliance officer

Of course, these information flows also occur in other methodologies. This description provides an overview, covering the whole set of roles responsible for a project's development. Nevertheless, when the process is strictly followed, we can see how these interactions might result in a somewhat tangled web over time.

Even from this brief and incomplete view of PASTA, we can already reach some conclusions by using our parameters to classify it as a methodology (see Table 3-4).

Table 3-4. PASTA as a methodology

Parameter	Score	Explanation
Accessible	1	PASTA requires the continued involvement of many roles, and a sizeable time investment to be completed properly. Teams may have difficulty budgeting this time.
Scalable	3	Much of the framework can and should be reused across instances of PASTA in the same organization.
Educational	1	PASTA relies on a "threat modeler" role that is responsible or accountable for most of the activities. In this sense, any educational benefits the team receives come via its interaction with the final threat model, its findings and recommendations, and, as such, it is of limited value.
Useful	4	A well-executed and documented PASTA threat model offers views from many angles, including the most viable and probable attacks and attack vectors as well as useful mitigation and risk acceptance.
Agile	1	PASTA is not a lightweight process, and performs better when all the design and implementation details of the system are known beforehand. Imagine how much work needs to be redone if components get refactored or a new technology is introduced.
Representative	2	This one is a bit problematic. If the whole design, architecture, and implementation are well-known beforehand, and changes are limited and incorporated well in the process, then PASTA could offer some of the most representative threat models out there. On the other hand, if the development process is anything but a completely efficient waterfall, the changes will result in a system model that may not reflect the complete, final state of development. Since nowadays this situation is rare, we chose to move forward with the Agile assumption.
Unconstrained	2	The PASTA coauthors take a deep look at CAPEC (*https://capec.mitre.org*) as a source for attack trees and threat libraries, and suggest heavy reliance on CVE and CWE libraries to identify vulnerabilities and weaknesses, respectively. There is little consideration of system-specific threats, and the calculus of risk relies a lot on previously identified vulnerabilities. In this sense, the process feels constrained and limited.

Threat Assessment and Remediation Analysis

The *Threat Assessment and Remediation Analysis* (*https://oreil.ly/EWtgz*), was developed at MITRE by Jackson Wynn et al. in 2011. He describes it as an "assessment approach [that] can be described as conjoined trade studies, where the first trade identifies and ranks attack vectors based on assessed risk, and the second identifies and selects countermeasures based on assessed utility and cost."[12] It has been used in many assessments by the US Army, Navy, and Air Force since its adoption.

One of the many things that makes TARA stand out is its aim to protect against mid-to-high state-sponsored adversaries, in order to maintain what it calls "mission assurance" of systems under attack. This approach assumes that the attacker has enough knowledge and resources to bypass perimeter controls like firewalls and intrusion detection, and so the methodology focuses on what to do after the adversary has crossed the moat. How does the system survive and continue to function when the attacker is already inside?

TARA is focused on the acquisition phase of a traditional system development life cycle. As a government-sponsored activity, it assumes that development happens elsewhere, with assessment performed by the body aiming to absorb the system.

During the acquisition program, architecture analysis is performed to build a representative model of the system. This model provides the foundation for a list of plausible attack vectors against the system (with their associated mitigations), which are then ranked based on their risk level, producing a vulnerability matrix. This process is called a Cyber Threat Susceptibility Assessment. By the end of the CTSA phase, it should be possible to create a table mapping TTPs and their potential impact against each identified component. Each row of the table would contain the following:

- The target TTP name
- A source of reference for the TTP (such as the attack pattern being considered, as an entry from the Common Attack Pattern Enumeration and Classification, or CAPEC[13])
- And for each component in the system, two entries:
  - Plausible?: Is the TTP plausible when considering the component in question? (Yes, No, or Unknown.)
  - Rationale?: What is the rationale or reasoning behind the answer to the question of plausibility?

---

12 J. Wynn, "Threat Assessment and Remediation Analysis (TARA)," *https://oreil.ly/1rrwN*.

13 Common Attack Patterns Enumeration and Classification, *https://capec.mitre.org*.

For example, consider a system component—a local area network (LAN) Network Switch. The TTP "target programs with elevated privileges," which is sourced from CAPEC-69 (*https://oreil.ly/Wsi17*), may indicate that plausibility exists (which will be marked in the table as "Yes"), and a rationale or reasoning states that "the switch runs a flavor of Unix as its operating system, which supports the use of scripts and programs that may elevate their own privileges." Clearly the LAN switch is at risk.

By associating mitigations to each identified vulnerability, the analysis generates a list of countermeasures, which are then ranked according to their effectiveness and cost to implement. The result of this ranking is a mitigation mapping table, which is then fed back to the acquisition program by using a "solution effectiveness table." This table shows the extent to which each mitigation adds protection to the system, and prioritizes those that add the most value and effectiveness. This analysis is referred to as the Cyber Risk Remediation Analysis (CRRA) step of the process.

Paraphrasing the paper's author, TARA is similar to other threat modeling methodologies, but its uniqueness derives from basing itself on a catalog of mitigation mapping data and the way it is used in selecting countermeasures so that the overall risk is reduced to an acceptable level of risk tolerance.[14]

 A word about *threat catalogs*, also known as *threat libraries* (*https://oreil.ly/uz2Ci*): In our experience, threat modeling methodologies based exclusively on threat libraries, especially if these are the result of a statistical analysis of past issues encountered in the systems being analyzed, will intrinsically create a mindset in the analysis team of "threat modeling via rearview analysis." Considering that technologies are constantly changing and new attack vectors are regularly being introduced, it is myopic to use *only* a past history of identified threats as a guide to the future. Without a doubt, such a collection has immense value as an educational device, in order to illustrate past issues to the development team, set a reference point of "unforgivable" security concerns, and guide the choice of security training to be made available to the team. But as a conceptual exercise, it is valuable for you to analyze threats as they may appear, and not only as they once did. On the other hand, you could interpret threat libraries as a different approach to an attack tree, in which case they are used as starting points to derive further attack vectors and methodologies to which the system may be subjected. In the threat modeling realm, the real value is in how the catalog is used rather than in its existence or lack thereof.

---

14 Wynn, "Threat Assessment and Remediation Analysis."

The key features of TARA are as follows:[15]

1. You can perform TARA assessments on deployed systems or on systems still in their acquisition life cycle.

2. Use of stored catalogs of TTPs and countermeasures (CMs) promote consistency from one TARA assessment to the next.

3. TTP and CM catalog data is derived from open source and classified sources, and can be selectively partitioned/filtered based upon the scope of the TARA assessment.

4. TARA is not a one-size-fits-all approach; the level of rigor applied in the assessments can be adjusted up or down as necessary.

5. The TARA toolset provides default scoring tools to quantitatively assess TTP risk and CM cost-effectiveness. These tools can be tailored or omitted entirely based on the assessment scope and/or the needs of the program.

Since we are using TARA as an example of a threat library–based approach, it is helpful to look at how the TTP and CM catalogs are constructed and kept current and how TTPs are scored to create a ranking model.

The mission assurance engineering (MAE) catalog of TTPs and CMs is based on threat intelligence available in open sources like MITRE ATT&CK (*https:// attack.mitre.org/*), CAPEC (*https://capec.mitre.org*), CWE (*https://cwe.mitre.org/*), CVE (*https://cve.mitre.org/*), the National Vulnerability Database, or NVD (*https:// oreil.ly/oCpaU*), and others,[16] as well as specialized and classified sources that would include electronic warfare (using attacks in the electromagnetic spectrum to disrupt system operations), state-level cyberwarfare vectors, and supply-chain attacks less familiar to the civilian public (see Table 3-5).

---

15 Wynn, "Threat Assessment and Remediation Analysis."

16 For example, NIST 800-30 contains a very extensive list in Appendix E: *https://oreil.ly/vBGue*.

Table 3-5. Default TTP risk scoring model (source: https://oreil.ly/TRNFr)

Factor Range	1	2	3	4	5
Proximity: What proximity would an adversary need in order to apply this TTP?	No physical or network access required	Protocol access through DMZ and firewall	User account to target system (no admin access)	Admin access to target system	Physical access to target system
Locality: How localized are the effects posed by this TTP?	Isolated single unit	Single unit and supporting network	External networks potentially impacted	All units in theater or region	All units globally and associated structures
Recovery time: How long would it take to recover from this TTP after the attack was detected?	<10 hours	20 hours	30 hours	40 hours	>50 hours
Restoration cost: What is the estimated cost to restore or replace the affected cyber asset?	<$10K	$25k	$50k	$75k	>$100k
Impact: How serious an impact is loss of data confidentiality resulting from successful application of this TTP?	No impact from TTP	Minimal impact	Limited impact requiring some remediation	Remediation activities detailed in continuity of operations (*https://oreil.ly/jxltf*) (COOP) plan	COOP remediation activities routinely exercised
Impact: How serious an impact is loss of data integrity resulting from successful application of this TTP?	No impact from TTP	Minimal impact	Limited impact requiring some remediation	Remediation activities detailed in COOP	COOP remediation activities routinely exercised
Impact: How serious an impact is loss of system availability resulting from successful application of this TTP?	No impact from TTP	Minimal impact	Limited impact requiring some remediation	Remediation activities detailed in COOP	COOP remediation activities routinely exercised
Prior use: Is there evidence of this TTP in the MITRE threat DB?	No evidence of TTP use in MITRE DB	Evidence of TTP use possible	Confirmed evidence of TTP use in MITRE DB	Frequent use of TTP reported in MITRE DB	Widespread use of TTP reported in MITRE DB
Required skills: What level of skill or specific knowledge is required by the adversary to apply this TPP?	No specific skills required	Generic technical skills	Some knowledge of targeted system	Detailed knowledge of targeted system	Knowledge of both mission and targeted system
Required resources: Would resources be required or consumed in order to apply this TTP?	No resources required	Minimal resources required	Some resources required	Significant resources required	Resources required and consumed

Factor Range	1	2	3	4	5
Stealth: How detectable is this TTP when it is applied?	Not detectable	Detection possible with specialized monitoring	Detection likely with specialized monitoring	Detection likely with routine monitoring	TTP obvious without monitoring
Attribution: Would residual evidence left behind by this TTP lead to attribution?	No residual evidence	Some residual evidence, attribution unlikely	Attribution possible from characteristics of the TTP	Same or similar TTPs previously attributed	Signature attack TTP used by adversary

This scoring model used by TARA is based on 12 separate measurements. Apart from the more common ones (impact, how difficult it is to realize the attack, likelihood, etc.), it is worth paying attention to more unique ones, like restoration costs and stealth, which refer to the initial assumption that the attacker was successful in breaching the external defenses and is now inside the system.

Likewise, it is interesting to note how impact is divided in the confidentiality, integrity, and availability (CIA) triad, but unlike CVSS (which measures impact as None, Low, Medium, High, and Critical), TARA is interested in the amount of remediation needed to overcome the impact (see Table 3-6).

Table 3-6. TARA scoring model

Parameter	Score	Explanation
Accessible	5	TARA depends on a threat modeling individual or team taking a system over the whole process. As such, it presupposes the existence of these resources, and by definition should be fully accessible to them.
Scalable	5	By definition, the process can be reused as is in all model tasks across the assessing organization. If there are resources to execute the assessment, the process should be fully available to them.
Educational	2	TARA relies on a modeling individual or team that is responsible or accountable for most of the activities. As with PASTA, the development team receives a list of to-dos in the form of recommended countermeasures, and as such it is of limited value as a knowledge-expanding device. But the catalog itself serves to educate what is possible as attacks, and can be used to train the team.
Useful	2	A well-executed and documented TARA threat model will offer views from many angles, including the most viable and probable attacks and attack vectors as well as useful mitigation and risk acceptance in the "solutions effectiveness table." On the other hand, being part of an acquisitions model, TARA operates on fully formed systems and is less suited to influence design choices during development time.
Agile	1	TARA is not a lightweight process, and performs better when all the design and implementation details of the system are known beforehand. Imagine how much work needs to be redone if components get refactored or a new technology is introduced.
Representative	5	For the same reasons as PASTA, TARA looks at fully formed systems in its analysis of the attack surface.

Parameter	Score	Explanation
Unconstrained	2	TARA builds on the TTPs and CMs catalog for its analysis. This imposes a predefined view of the threats the system may be subject to, somewhat limiting the flexibility of the analysis. On the other hand, the catalog is supposed to be a living entity constantly updated, but its sources move slowly and additions come from past-observed events. For a TTP catalog example, see this ENISA page (*https://oreil.ly/uC6KTENISA*).

Trike

Developed in 2005 by Paul Saitta, Brenda Larcom, and Michael Eddington, Trike v1 stands out from other threat modeling methodologies by trying to generate threats semiautomatically, without an explicit need for brainstorming. This directly targets the inexperienced developer, who is not asked to "think like a hacker" because it relies uncharacteristically on the use of a tool.[17]

Trike positions itself as a "framework for security auditing from a risk management perspective" (*https://oreil.ly/YagrU*). Version 2, which remains a work in progress for documentation, *appears* to have ceased development of the methodology and associated tool(s) as of 2012. This is an important detail—Trike version 2 brings forward interesting and useful concepts, yet it should be treated as experimental and unproven in the field. So we focus here on Trike version 1.

The methodology tries to be well-defined regarding what to analyze and when to stop the analysis (trying to stay out of rabbit holes). While it tries to put a lot of analysis power in the hands of the developer, it approaches security as a separate technical domain, and a subject matter expert is required to take the analysis "to the next level."

By formalizing system design, Trike allows the use of both tools (a desktop version and an Excel-based one) to (semi-)automatically identify threats *and* most important, provide a guarantee that all threats covered by the analysis have indeed been evaluated. Another unique characteristic of Trike is its point of view, which focuses on the defender instead of the attacker.

Requirements model

The first activity, as in many of the other methodologies we have discussed, is to understand the purpose of the system being threat modeled and how it achieves those goals, by examining the interactions of actors and the environment with the system assets. This is the *requirements model* phase. Build a table that includes the assets, the actors, and the actions possible.

---

17 The name Trike has no specific meaning—the authors say in the FAQ, "If anyone asks, invent a story—it is probably what we'd do."

In Trike, actions follow the CRUD (create, read, update, delete) model of atomic access, and these (and their chaining) are the only possible actions. Each system action is represented by a tuple of <actor, asset, rules>, with the rules acting as limits on which actors or roles may affect the action. Actions are added to the list if they are part of the normal functioning state of the system—that is, if an action is not a fully expected part of the system (i.e., is not documented), it does not count for the purpose of this analysis. In other words, only valid use cases for the system go in this list, while no misuse or abuse cases are added. The resulting set of actions serves to completely describe, in a formal way, the system under evaluation.

This translates into analyzing every asset and actor pair in sequence, and evaluating each CRUD action. Once these are understood, rules are enunciated by using Boolean logic declarative sentences, as in "actor must be in Admin role *and* asset must be in Suspended state."

We examined Trike by running the Trike1.1.2a tool (*https://oreil.ly/kM3od*) on a Squeak virtual machine running on Ubuntu. Your mileage may vary. Unfortunately, the Squeak-based tool doesn't seem to have been kept up-to-date with the methodology, since the authors appear to prefer that practitioners to use the spreadsheet-based tool.

The tool comes with a sample threat model of a blog system, which sufficiently exemplifies its use.

 We encourage you to check out the Trike project on SourceForge for more images and details about this methodology.

Implementation model

Once you collect actors and rules and create a formal definition of requirements, it is time to assess the implementation. This is done by excluding actions that do not belong in the action framework—these are not the actions we are looking for!—and understanding how the remaining actions interact with the rest of the system.

Trike distinguishes between supporting and intended actions. *Supporting* actions are those that move the system along from a bookkeeping and infrastructural point of view, *supporting* the workings of the system. The example given is the login operation, which takes a user from one state (not logged in) to another (logged in). We do not delve into the creation of these supporting actions here, as the process is complex and does not add much to our discussion. You may want to examine the explanation in the Trike documentation. *Intended actions* and the state machine that is created from them are considered experimental features by the Trike authors, and have undergone changes across the versions of the methodology.

Next, the system is represented, as is the case for many threat modeling methodologies, using DFD. This follows the same symbology and approach as when describing STRIDE, including the partitioning of the system into more detailed separated DFDs providing more in-depth information in particular areas. The important point here is that for Trike, the "definition of done" of DFD representation is "until there are no longer any processes which cross trust boundaries."

The diagram is again annotated, building a complete representation of the system, and looking to capture the technology stack used by the elements—OS, types of data stores, etc. As needed, you can complete the DFD with a network deployment diagram.

Gather all this data and compile a list of all possible use flows for the system. These map actions into the implementation, showing how assets in the system are impacted by actor actions affecting changes into the application state.

Gathering data and compiling use flows is achieved by tracing the paths of both intended and supporting actions into the DFD; every time an external actor is in the path, the use flow is segmented. Since the changes to the system state correspond to states in a state machine (which might be more clearly represented with a sequence diagram, as seen in Chapter 1), there might be pre- and post-conditions that are also part of the flow. As an example, submitting a blog entry to a mythical blogging platform has two stages. The first stage is writing the post and approving its entry into the system, so that flow adds a "post submitted" state to the system. This then becomes a precondition to the "post allowed" state.

Again, use flows are (based on the information available from the Trike project page on SourceForge) considered experimental in the Trike methodology. In fact, the Trike authors identified them as prone to be cumbersome and a possible way to introduce errors in the model.

The threat model

Having the requirements and the implementation models, the next step is to generate threats. In Trike, threats are events (not technology or implementation specific) and express a deterministic set derived from the actor-asset-action matrix and the associated rules. All threats are either denial of service or elevation of privilege, another unique feature of Trike. A *denial of service* happens when an actor cannot execute an action, and an *elevation of privilege* happens when an actor either performs an action they are not intended to in a particular asset, or when an actor performs an action even though rules disallow it, or when an actor co-opts the system to perform an action.

How do you generate a list of threats? Create one denial-of-service threat for each intended action; then invert the set of intended actions and remove the set of disallowed actions, which creates a set of elevation-of-privilege threats. These sets comprehend the full set of threats against the system.

Using the implementation model and the derived set of threats, you can decide which of those threats can be successfully translated into an attack. You can do this by using attack trees, by identifying threats at the root of each tree.

Even though automation is a central tenet of Trike, the generation of attack trees and graphs is not fully automated, and human intervention in the form of subject matter experts is required at this step.

The risk model

In- and out-of-scope risks are central to Trike. When evaluating risk, you must consider the exact part of the system and the risks it is under before you can decide whether a risk applies to the system. Assets are given a monetary value, based on their business value to the enterprise, which is decided by the business, not the threat modeling leader. Next, you must rank the set of intended actions by assigning a value of 1 to 5 to the undesirability of any given action being prevented (the value of a denial-of-service threat), with 5 meaning it is most undesirable to have this action prevented. Then rank all actors with a trust level between 1 and 5, with 1 being a highly trusted actor and 5 being an anonymous one.

Trike defines *exposure* as the value of an asset times the action-specific risk, and this index ranks threats in order of seriousness of their impact to the organization.

The probability that a weakness will be exploited is also part of the calculus of Trike. It is a function of reproducibility (how easy it is to reproduce an attack), the exploitability (how easy it is to perform the attack), and the actor trust value. This value currently is purely informational.

For each threat, the exposure value multiplied by the largest applicable probability risk gives you a threat risk value, which relates business impact to technical execution of the threat.

The authors of Trike realize that this is a coarse and naive approach to risk modeling, but maintain that it is enough to produce an expressive set of capabilities. With the generation of threats and their associated values, you can derive which mitigations to those threats you should apply, in which order, and the extent to which the threats will be removed or at least diminished (see Table 3-7). You can see an interesting overview of Trike in a presentation by one of its authors, Brenda Larcom (*https://oreil.ly/S44fV*), at Mozilla.

Table 3-7. The scoring model

Parameter	Score	Explanation
Accessible	1	Trike proposes a sound approach to threat modeling, and some of its basic ideas are sound. Unfortunately, the execution of the methodology is poorly documented, and discussion of it seems to have stopped. Available tools offer partial implementation or convoluted workflows.
Scalable	5	By definition, the process can be reused as is in all model tasks across the assessing organization. If there are resources to execute the assessment, the process should be fully available to them.
Educational	3	By cataloging all possible threats into two categories (elevation of privilege and denial of service), Trike encourages discussion as rules are created and actors and assets are examined. This dialogue and deep dive should generate additional security education to the team (guided by the security lead).
Useful	2	Too many dangling points remain in the methodology, which makes for an interesting intellectual exercise but offers limited practical value.
Agile	2	Trike focuses on all being known about the system at the time of modeling. As such, it is less suited to systems whose development (or at least design) isn't complete and whose capabilities and characteristics can be fully examined at the time of modeling. The Trike authors claim the methodology "adapts easily to piecemeal expansion, and as such fits just as easily into spiral development or XP/Agile models," but we respectfully disagree. Even if the information flow does support revising the model, the operational cost of applying the differences between the previous and new models is too high.
Representative	5	For the same reasons as TARA—Trike looks at fully formed systems in its analysis of the attack surface.
Unconstrained	2	Trike builds on attack trees and graphs for attack generation, and highly supports the notion that attack trees are "one of the more useful time-saving features of the Trike methodology." While that is true, it also acts as a constraint on the threats being evaluated. Dynamic generation of threats is seen as an operational concern, and not one linked to the methodology itself.

Specialized Methodologies

In addition to the methodologies we've presented, several are more focused on specific aspects of product security than straightforward development and protection. Straying into the domain of threat modeling, some of these focus on looking for privacy-related issues rather than strictly security-related ones. We mention some here for completeness and for comparison—to show how you can apply the same basic ideas from this chapter in different manners in order to identify threats to other categories of sensitive assets, classified data, and other forms of "crown jewels."

LINDDUN

As a privacy variation, *LINDDUN* (linkability, identifiability, nonrepudiation, detectability, disclosure of information, unawareness, and noncompliance) is a systematic approach to privacy threat modeling. The LINDDUN site (*https://linddun.org/*) provides extensive tutorial and guidance material, and is a valuable resource. The methodology was developed at the DistriNet Research Group at KU Leuven, a university in Belgium, by Dr. Kim Wuyts, Professor Riccardo Scandariato, Professor Wouter Joosen, Dr. Mina Deng, and Professor Bart Preneel.

Unlike a traditional security-focused threat model, which is primarily concerned with the CIA triad, LINDDUN assesses threats against unlinkability, anonymity, pseudonymity, plausible deniability, undetectability and unobservability, content awareness, and policy and consent compliance—all with a focus on the data subject's privacy. This thus not only involves the point of view of an (external) attacker, but also an organizational perspective as certain system behavior could violate the privacy of data subjects. Without extending too much (a full discussion of each property can be seen in the LINDDUN paper[18]), the properties are as follows:

Unlinkability
Two or more actions, elements, identities, or other pieces of information cannot be linked together—that is, a relationship between them cannot be safely established based on available information.

Anonymity
The actor's identity cannot be established.

Pseudonymity
An actor can use a separate identifier than the one that (directly) identifies the actor (i.e., the pseudonym does not directly lead to the natural person).

Plausible deniability
An actor can deny having performed an action, and other actors are not able to confirm or deny that affirmation.

Undetectability and unobservability
An attacker cannot sufficiently distinguish whether the item of interest (action, data, etc.) exists. Unobservability means that an item of interest (IOI) is undetectable and that the subjects involved in the IOI are anonymous against the other involved subjects.

Content awareness
Users should be aware of the information they are making available to service providers by using the more dynamic elements of web interaction (forms, cookies, etc.), or by inviting into their systems content not available at installation time (like ad networks downloading executables after installation). The property of content awareness maintains that "only the minimum necessary information should be sought and used to allow for the performance of the function to which it relates."

---

18 Mina Deng et al., "A Privacy Threat Analysis Framework: Supporting the Elicitation and Fulfillment of Privacy Requirements," June 2010, *https://oreil.ly/S44fV*.

Policy and consent compliance

> The system is aware of the privacy policy offered and the data it stores and processes, and actively informs the owner of the data about compliance with legislation and policy, before accessing that data

Many of the steps in Figure 3-4 will look familiar—they operate the same as the phases of STRIDE, so focus on where LINDDUN differs from the security-focused methodology.

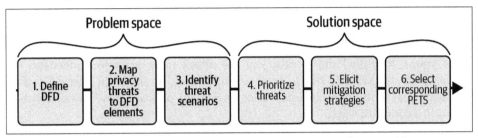

Figure 3-4. The steps of LINDDUN (Figure 6.12 in Kim Wuyts, "Privacy Threats in Software Architectures" (Ph.D. thesis, KU Leuven, 2015), 135.)

The LINDDUN authors created a distinct mapping of privacy-oriented threats into the DFD elements, as shown in Figure 3-5.

	L	I	N	D	D	U	N
Entity	✗	✗				✗	
Data store	✗	✗	✗	✗	✗		✗
Data flow	✗	✗	✗	✗	✗		✗
Process	✗	✗	✗	✗	✗		✗

Figure 3-5. Mapping of DFD elements to LINDDUN threats

You can see the full definitions of the threat categories in "LINDDUN: A Privacy Threat Analysis Framework" (*https://www.linddun.org/*):

- L: Linkability threats against unlinkability
- I: Identifiability threats against anonymity and pseudonymity
- N: Nonrepudiation threats against plausible deniability
- D: Detectability threats against undetectability and unobservability
- D: Disclosure of information threats against confidentiality
- U: Unawareness threats against content awareness

- N: Noncompliance threats against policy and consent compliance

Consider this mapping when examining use cases the system personifies. For example, a user writing a blog entry would result in the user of the entry form as an "external entity" and the blog system as a "process storing the entry in a data store via two data flows (user to blog system, blog system to data store)." In a process parallel to STRIDE per Element, the intersections between each DFD element and a privacy threat that contain an "X" mean that the related element is susceptible to that threat.

An extensive discussion of how each threat affects each element is outside the scope of this book, but is addressed in the LINDDUN paper.

Once you've identified the threats, you use attack trees again to understand the approach an attacker may take to reach a specific goal. As shown in Figure 3-6, if an attacker's goal is to force noncompliance of consent policies, they may direct their efforts in a couple of ways.

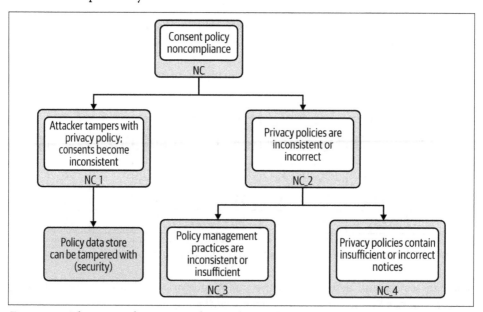

Figure 3-6. Threat tree for noncompliance threats (source: based on https://oreil.ly/afYUJ)

The direct route is to tamper with the data store that houses the policies by leveraging a security concern; if they are successful, they can create a situation that makes compliance difficult or impossible (by altering key aspects of the policies themselves or changing the way consent is obtained or managed). Indirectly, they can influence the organization into making mistakes or subvert internal practices to force a noncompliance situation. In addition to this attacker-centric perspective, compliance violation can also occur from the organizational perspective, by, for instance, not respecting data protection principles such as minimization and purpose limitation and thereby processing more personal information than would be strictly required.

The LINDDUN site contains a catalog of privacy threat trees including a generic explanation of the tree and detailed discussion of its leaf nodes. Each threat tree includes guidance for the consumer of the trees on how to interpret the information for each leaf.[19] Each guidance block usually ends with a standard disclaimer indicating that the tree describes potential areas for concern at a high level, and that users should seek legal advice to ensure compliance.

LINDDUN does not suggest a risk classification technique or taxonomy, instead relying on existing methodologies like the ones we mentioned in the Introduction. You need to construct a misuse case (MUC) that translates the information gathered in the previous steps and translates it into a usable story that you can compare to other stories so you can rank them. From the LINDDUN paper, we show an example of noncompliance that will be familiar to any user of social media:

Title
    MUC 10: Policy and consent noncompliance

Summary
    The social network provider doesn't process the user's personal data in compliance with user consent; e.g., disclose the database to third parties for secondary use.

Assets, stakeholders, and threats
    PII of the user

    1. The user: revealed identity and personal information

    2. The system/company: negative impact on reputation

Primary misactor
    Insider

Basic flow
    1. The misactor gains access to social network database.

    2. The misactor discloses the data to a third party.

Trigger
    A malicious actor; can always happen.

---

19 See *https://oreil.ly/afYUJ* for an example of guidance provided for each leaf node.

Preconditions
1. The misactor can tamper with privacy policies and makes consents inconsistent. *or*

2. The policies are not managed correctly (not updated according to user's request).

Prevention capture points
1. The design system is in compliance with legal guidelines for privacy and data protection and keeps internal policies consistent with policies communicated to the user.

2. Legal enforcement: users can sue the social network provider whenever their personal data is processed without consent.

3. Employee contracts: employees who share information with third parties will be penalized (fired, pay fine, etc.).

Prevention guarantee
Legal enforcement will lower the threat of an insider leaking information, but it will still be possible to breach user's privacy.

Note that the preconditions come directly from the threat tree. Once you describe a misuse case, you can extract requirements from it in the form of prevention capture points and prevention guarantees. LINDDUN steers threat mitigation toward the use of privacy-enhancing technology (PET) solutions, rather than purely legal or contractual devices. The LINDDUN paper does a great job of listing PET solutions and mapping them to the privacy properties that they address. We do not reproduce that mapping here, and you should be sure to read the paper to become familiar with the method, should you decide to use it. Given LINDDUN's similarity with STRIDE per Element, reapplying our measurement parameters would not be logical, as they would be equal to STRIDE's parameters. On the other hand, LINDDUN is a great illustration of how you can apply the processes of threat modeling to domains other than security (i.e., C, I, and A), and generate similarly valuable results.

Madness? This Is SPARTA!

Security and Privacy Architecture Through Risk-Driven Threat Assessment, or *SPARTA*, is a framework and tool to facilitate continuous threat elicitation that we "discovered" during research for this book. Originating at KU Leuven (University) in Belgium, this framework was created by Laurens Sion, Koen Yskout, Dimitri Van Landuyt, and Wouter Joosen. (As you can see from SPARTA and LINDDUN, great research is being done at this university in the threat modeling space!)

The premise of SPARTA is that while traditional methodologies like STRIDE are successful in identifying threats, they lead to considerable effort because the threat modeling activity happens separately from the development effort.[20] This creates artifacts that may end up scattered and must be kept organized, which also require more effort. This creates a barrier to reviewing the resulting threat model when changes are made to the developing system or to the underlying security characteristics. In the view of the SPARTA authors, these changes may have far-ranging effects that justify reviewing the complete set of results in the threat model.

Presented as a tool, SPARTA provides a GUI (based on the popular Eclipse framework) for DFD creation with the usual drag-and-drop workflow.[21] SPARTA enriches the DFD with metadata that provides enhancements in the following areas:

Semantics
> Adding a representation of security solutions and their effects to a DFD promotes verification of that data and of the consequences it forces on the system you're representing.

Traceability
> The relationship between a security mechanism and its consequences on the system should be mappable.

Separation of concerns
> A threat library and a catalog of possible security solutions and mitigations should evolve independently from each other.

Dynamic and continuous threat assessment
> Much like the continuous threat modeling methodology (which we describe in Chapter 5), SPARTA believes that threat elicitation should happen whenever it is necessary rather than at specific times in the development cycle; thus, as possible, automatically.

Without going deeply into each area (rich and interesting academic discussion is provided in complementary papers by the SPARTA authors), it is relevant to say that the model for the additional DFD security metadata adds instances of `SecuritySolution` to enable capturing security solutions as part of the DFD. Each `SecuritySolution` contains `Roles`, which list the DFD elements that are involved in that solution; a `Role` can implement `CounterMeasures` that mitigate `ThreatTypes`, and can specify which `Roles` that countermeasure applies to (see Figure 3-7).

---

20 "SPARTA: Security and Privacy Architecture through Risk-driven Threat Assessment," SPARTA, *https://oreil.ly/1JaiI*.

21 As of October 2020, in closed access mode: contact the SPARTA authors for access.

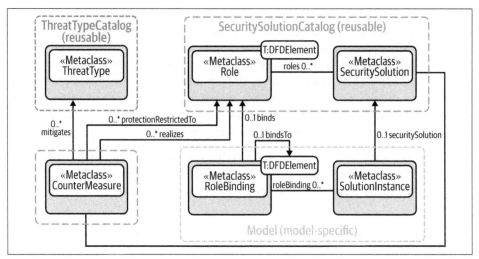

Figure 3-7. SPARTA UML representation of the security meta-model (from https://oreil.ly/nNSm0)

Once the DFD reflects the system being represented and adequate instantiations are provided in the security meta-model, the tool iterates over all `ThreatTypes` in the threat library (part of the tool, expandable by the user). This allows it to identify those DFD elements that may be susceptible to the `ThreatType` by verifying that they do not execute a corresponding `CounterMeasure`.

At this step, we see one of the unique characteristics of the SPARTA threat identification method: it doesn't matter whether the `ThreatType` in a particular element is mitigated by a specific `SecuritySolution`, as long as one exists and is defined that will mitigate that particular threat. For example, if the threat is "data in transit over a public network is not encrypted," SPARTA will recognize the threat as mitigated if the data flow is declared to be running over TLS, or if the whole system is declared to be using a VPN for all its data flows. To us, that means that the architect is at liberty to play "what if" with systemic or focused mitigations and understand how those choices impact the security posture of the whole system.

Risk analysis in SPARTA uses FAIR, which is mentioned in the Introduction, and adds Monte Carlo simulations for *each* risk component from FAIR:

- Countermeasure strength
- Threat capability
- Contact frequency
- Probability of action
- Vulnerability
- Threat event frequency
- Loss event frequency
- Loss magnitude and risk

To perform the risk analysis, add to the DFD (a) the security instances of the solution, which are specified according to the meta-model and (b) the estimates for each `ThreatType` of each one of the FAIR factors; these are added by security experts and system and risk stakeholders. The additions take into account attack profiles and values already in the security solution (for example, the capabilities of a possible attacker, and countermeasures, respectively). Once you've identified all threats in the DFD, you perform a risk estimation for each one, generating a probability that an attack defeats a countermeasure.

The statistical considerations are beyond the scope of this book—for those so inclined, we heartily recommend the SPARTA authors' academic papers. Take into consideration defense in depth: if multiple countermeasures to a given threat exist, the final probability is the probability of defeating all of the countermeasures.

SPARTA also utilizes distinct personas to represent attackers with varying capabilities—for example, the risk evaluation when the attacker is an entry-level variety (a script kiddie) will be different from the evaluation of an attacker as a nation-state.

These are fully customizable, so a team could, for example, choose an "unskilled external website user" or a "nation-state-level actor" (for an example, see Figure 3-8).

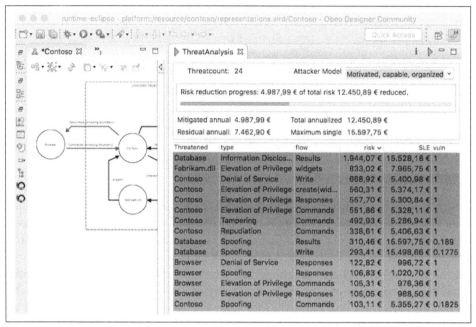

Figure 3-8. SPARTA example DFD and list of associated threats (source: https:// oreil.ly/VC3oh)

The goal is to continuously consider the probability, and the threats you identify, when changes to the DFD, security meta-model, threat libraries, countermeasures, etc., happen. This adds a real-time component to SPARTA via an instantaneous impact analysis that we found intriguing. The user can sort the risk list in different ways to help plan for optimal mitigation.

SPARTA continues to evolve as we write these lines, and we look forward to these developments and hope to soon see a complete tool available to the community.

INCLUDES NO DIRT

INCLUDES NO DIRT (*https://oreil.ly/0TepP*) has recently been made available publicly. This methodology focuses on bridging the gaps between security, privacy, and compliance, and then applying that construct to the world of clinical environments. It combines the best of both STRIDE and LINDDUN, with a focus on healthcare. It could have been called "SuperSTRIDE" since INCLUDES NO DIRT is an acronym that contains the LINDDUN and STRIDE acronyms, and then adds "C" and "O," as shown in the following:

I: Identifiability
Avoid anonymity, support traceability of actions (domain: privacy).

N: Nonrepudiation
Avoid plausible deniability (domain: privacy).

C: Clinical error
Ensure correct application of clinical standards (domain: compliance).

L: Linkability
Relate information throughout the system (domain: privacy).

U: Unlicensed activity
Ensure users have proper credentials or licensure (domain: compliance).

D: Denial of service
Maintain availability (domain: security).

E: Elevation of privilege
Ensure correct authorization for actions (domain: security).

S: Spoofing
Avoid impersonation (domain: security).

N: Noncompliant to policy or obligation
Enforce policy or contractual obligation (domain: compliance).

O: Overuse
Enforce usage restrictions (domain: compliance).

D: Data error
Maintain data integrity from mistakes or component failures (domain: security).

I: Information disclosure
Maintain confidentiality of data (domain: security).

R: Repudiation
Reinforce association of user to action (domain: security).

T: Tampering
Maintain data integrity from misuse or abuse (domain: security).

This threat modeling methodology generally follows the approach of STRIDE, but it also helps to guide the nonsecurity practitioner through an extensive questionnaire and "choose-your-own-adventure" (*https://www.cyoa.com*) style process flow. However, in a sense, it is inflexible in practice because of the rigid nature of how it is constructed. The documentation suggests the approach "must be accessible by non-security/non-privacy practitioners," at which it mostly succeeds because they have baked a ton of knowledge into the process itself. Unfortunately, in order to tailor the methodology to an area other than the clinical healthcare setting on which it focuses, extensive security and/or privacy experience is required.

Shall We Play a Game?

Throughout this book, we have gone back to the problem of teaching developers and architects what they need to know about security to be effective in their threat modeling activities. Many solutions out there aim to provide faster and more comprehensive return on investment for this need—some of them taking the form of games and game-like helping material that builds on the creativity, curiosity and competitiveness inherent to most people in the information field. We chose to address these in this chapter because of their documented efficacy in some situations and their pairing with established threat modeling technologies, while at the same time being in the forefront of threat modeling as a discipline. We do not claim this to be an exhaustive list, but these are the ones that we have encountered (and in some cases used, either in a teaching environment or "in production"). If you explore on your own, you'll surely be able to find variants of these and others.

Adam Shostack, himself a pioneer in the gamification of threat modeling by authoring the Elevation of Privilege game, maintains a running list of these gamified helpers on his personal blog site (*https://oreil.ly/CkLhg*)—you should visit it regularly if this approach is of interest.

We won't discuss whether the game is exciting, deep, or even playable. We consider that as educational tools, they are all valid, and their efficacy will vary widely depending on how they are used. We see gamification as a powerful tool that encourages threat modeling and are intrigued by new developments in the area.

Game: Elevation of Privilege

Author: Adam Shostack

Threat methodologies implemented: STRIDE

Main proposition: The suits in this card deck follow the STRIDE methodology: spoofing, tampering, repudiation, information disclosure, denial of service, and elevation of privilege. Each card proposes a threat; for example, the Ten of Spoofing proposes, "An attacker can choose to use weaker or no authentication." If the player of that card can apply that threat to the system, then that gets documented as a finding; otherwise the game proceeds according to low/high value card rules (see Figure 3-9).

Obtain from: *https://oreil.ly/NRwcZ*

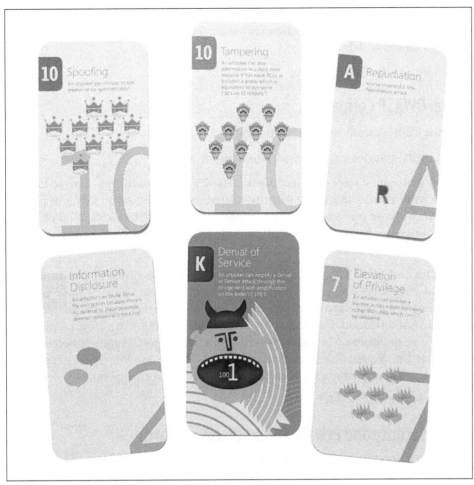

Figure 3-9. Elevation of Privilege sample cards[22]

Game: Elevation of Privilege and Privacy

Author: Mark Vinkovits

Threat methodologies implemented: STRIDE

Main proposition: As part of the threat modeling practice at LogMeIn, a team identified the need of formalizing the brainstorming activity around threat modeling and privacy-related discussions and decided to add a Privacy suit to the original Elevation of Privilege game. The suit would have cards that were actionable and presented a

---

22 These are pictures of Izar's personal collection of security games.

high privacy risk. For example, the Ten of Privacy reads, "Your system does not implement erasure or anonymization for personal data once the legal ground for processing has been withdrawn."

Obtain from: *https://oreil.ly/rorks*

Game: OWASP Cornucopia

Authors: Colin Watson and Dario De Filippis

Threat methodologies implemented: None specifically

Main proposition: Rather than identify threats, OWASP Cornucopia aims to identify *security requirements* and create security-related user stories. As an OWASP project, it does focus more on web-based development: it is a further modification of Elevation of Privilege, but in its current published form, OWASP Cornucopia values threats that are relevant to ecommerce websites.

The suites in OWASP Cornucopia are derived from the OWASP Secure Coding Practices cheatsheet and the OWASP Application Security Verification Standard. The game has six suits: Data Validation and Encoding, Authentication, Session Management, Authorization, Cryptography, and a catch-all suit, Cornucopia. For example, the Ten of Session Management reads, "Marce can forge requests because per-session or per-request for more critical actions, strong random tokens (i.e., anti-CSRF tokens) or similar are not being used for actions that change state."

Obtain from: *https://oreil.ly/_iUlM*

Game: Security and Privacy Threat Discovery Cards

Authors: Tamara Denning, Batya Friedman, and Tadayoshi Kohno

Threat methodologies implemented: None specifically

Main proposition: This card deck, created by a team of researchers at the Computer Science department at the University of Washington, proposes four non-numbered suits (dimensions): Human Impact, Adversary's Motivations, Adversary's Resources, and Adversary's Methods. Some activities are suggested to make use of the cards: sorting them by threat importance to the system being analyzed, or combining cards ("which Adversary's Method best serves this specific Adversary's Motivation?"), or creating new cards exploring the dimensions, perhaps motivated by current events in the news.

Less of a game and more of a directed educational activity, discussion and analysis of the dimensions and of the cards in them supports understanding and exploration of security issues. For example, a random card in the Adversary's Resource dimension reads, "Unusual Resources—What kinds of unexpected or uncommon resources might the adversary have access to? How might unusual resources enable or amplify attacks on your system?" Incidentally, while this deck does not promote it, it is used in the Hybrid Threat Modeling Methodology (*https://oreil.ly/JTBzU*), developed by Nancy Mead and Forrest Shull at the Software Engineering Institute of Carnegie Mellon University, where the cards are used to support brainstorming sessions to identify threats relevant to the system being threat modeled (see Figure 3-10).

Obtain from: *https://oreil.ly/w6GWI*

Figure 3-10. Security and Privacy Threat Discovery Cards[23]

---

23 These are pictures of Izar's personal collection of security games.

Game: LINDDUN GO

Authors: The LINDDUN Team

Threat modeling methodologies implemented: LINDDUN

Main proposition: LINDDUN GO provides more lightweight support for the elicitation phase by means of a simplified method and a set of privacy threat type cards (inspired by the Elevation of Privilege cards). LINDDUN GO is therefore a good start for those new to the field as well as for more experienced threat modelers who are looking for a less heavy approach. For beginners, this serves as a great educational tool to get started, not requiring privacy expertise (see Figure 3-11).

Obtain from: *https://www.linddun.org/go*

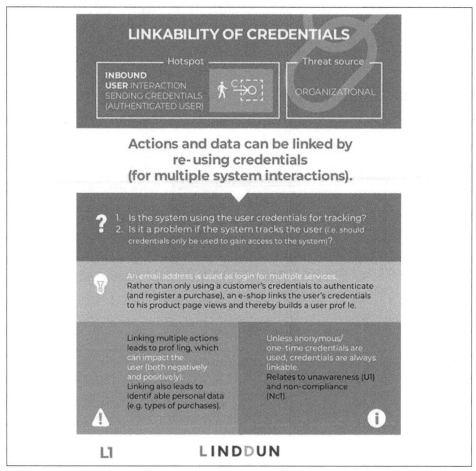

Figure 3-11. LINDDUN GO sample card: Linkability of credentials (https://www.lind dun.org/go)

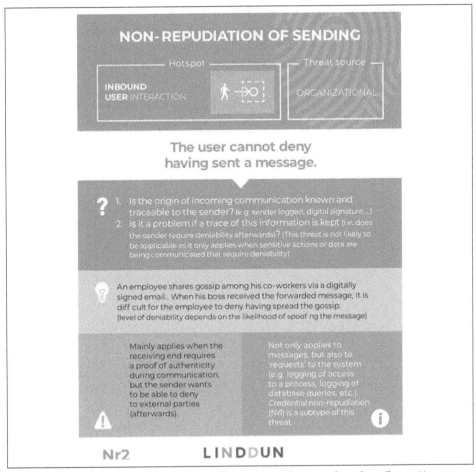

Figure 3-12. LINDDUN GO sample card: Non-repudiation of sending (https://www.linddun.org/go)

Summary

In this chapter, you learned of the wide variety of threat analysis approaches that are well established and practical, since the birth of STRIDE until today. Through this overview, you should have a good understanding of which technique tends to be used in particular environments, development styles, organizational structures, or specific challenges, or expectations from the threat modeling process. You also learned how to play with your design in order to generate threats for your threat models.

We would like to ask something of you: if after trying to find a methodology for your environment you still don't have one that seems to fit, try some of the most popular ones; then leverage your newfound experience to design your own approach to identifying threats from your models. Then come back to the threat modeling community (on Reddit's *r/ThreatModeling*, or on OWASP's Slack workspace on *#threat-modeling*, or in "Birds-of-a-Feather" gatherings at popular security conferences that explore threat modeling as a topic!) and show us what you came up with. We look forward to learning from your experience.

In the next chapter, we show ways to perform threat modeling through the use of automation—both to describe models and to "automagically" identify security and privacy threats.

## CHAPTER 4

Automated Threat Modeling

There didn't seem to be any computer-driven process that couldn't be improved upon by humans crawling around on the actual structure and writing on it with grease pencils.

—Neal Stephenson, *Atmosphæra Incognita*

In Chapter 1 you got an in-depth look into the mechanics of building different types of system models "by hand," by drawing on a whiteboard or using an application like Microsoft's Visio or draw.io. You also saw the information you need to gather when constructing those models. In Chapter 3, you got an overview of threat modeling approaches that consume the system models you create, allowing you to identify areas of security concern within your system under evaluation. You learned of methods that find high-level *threats*, with a consideration for the adversaries who have the capability and intent to carry out an attack. You also saw methodologies that look deeper in the threat "stack" to analyze the underlying causes that lead to threats (and adversarial targets)—weaknesses and vulnerabilities, which alone or in combination result in disaster for your system's functionality and data (as well as your reputation and brand).

These techniques and methodologies are an effective approach to both system and threat modeling, *if you have the time and energy*, and can convince your organization that this approach is important. However, in this age of continuous everything, and everything as code, a lot of pressure is placed on development teams to deliver more in less time. Therefore, security practices that were accepted as necessary evils because they consumed more than a few minutes of developer time are being abandoned as too costly (perceived or otherwise). That leaves people who focus on security in a difficult position. Do you try to influence your organization to bite the bullet and be more rigorous in applying security engineering practices, or do you try to get as much done as possible with your shrinking resources, knowing that the quality of your results (and, by extension, the security of the end product) may suffer? How do you maintain high security standards and the attention to detail that is necessary to create a well-engineered system?

One way you can facilitate good security engineering is to limit the need to build system and threat models by hand and turn to automation to help reduce the burden on you, to meet the needs of the business *and* the security team. While the human element is arguably an important part of a threat modeling activity, construction and analysis of system models is something a computer can accomplish with ease; you, of course, must supply the input.

Automation not only helps you to design the model, but also can assist with answering questions. For example, if you're not sure whether data flow A between endpoints X and Y leaves your critical data exposed to the mythical Eve,[1] you can use a program to figure that out.

In this chapter, we explore an evolution in the making. When it comes to creating the state of the art in threat modeling techniques, performing threat analysis and defect elicitation, you can use automation techniques dubbed threat modeling with code and threat modeling from code.[2]

You may be wondering—how will threat modeling automation make your life easier, and not one more tool/process/responsibility to care about in the long run? We wondered the same, too.

Why Automate Threat Modeling?

Let's face it—threat modeling the traditional way is hard, for many reasons:

- It takes rare and highly specialized talent—to do threat modeling well, you need to tease out the weaknesses in a system. This requires training (such as reading this or other primers on threat modeling) and a healthy dose of pessimism and critical thinking when it comes to what is and what could be (and how things could go wrong).

- There is a lot to know, and that will require a breadth and depth of knowledge and experiences. As your system grows in complexity, or changes are introduced (such as the digital transformation many companies are going through these days), the changes in technologies brings an accelerating number of weaknesses:

---

1 Randall Munroe, "Alice and Bob," *xkcd* webcomic, *https://xkcd.com/177*.

2 Some people also use the encompassing phrase *threat modeling as code* to align to the DevOps jargon. Much like DevOps (and its jargon!) a couple of years ago, the whole vocabulary is in transition—many people mean many different things by it, but we feel that slowly a convention is coalescing.

new weaknesses and threats are identified, and new attack vectors created; the security staff must be constantly learning.

- There are myriad options to choose from.[3] This includes tools and methodologies to perform threat modeling and analysis, as modeled representations, and how to record, mitigate, or manage findings.

- Convincing stakeholders that threat modeling is important can be difficult, in part because of the following:

  — Everyone is busy (as mentioned previously).

  — Not everyone in the development team understands the system as specified and/or as designed. What is designed is not necessarily what was in the specification, and what is implemented may not match either. Finding the right individuals who can correctly describe the current state of the system under analysis can be challenging.

  — Not all architects and coders have a complete understanding of what they are working on; except in small, highly functioning teams, not all team members will have cross-knowledge of one another's areas. We call this the Three Blind Men and the Elephant (*https://oreil.ly/9EJxo*) development methodology.

  — Some team members (hopefully, only a small number) have less-than-perfect intentions, meaning they may be defensive or provide intentionally misleading statements).

- While you may be able to read the code, that does not show you the whole picture. If you have code to read, you may have missed your chance to avoid potentially serious mistakes introduced by the design that coding cannot mitigate. And sometimes it can be hard to derive the overlaying design from code only.

- Creating a system model requires time and effort. And since nothing is ever static, maintaining a system model takes time. A system's design will change as the system requirements are modified in response to implementation, and you need to keep the system model in sync with any changes.

These are some of the reasons that some long-time members of the security community have expressed concerns on the practical use of threat modeling as a defensive activity during the development life cycle.[4] And to be honest, these reasons *are* challenging.

But fear not! The security community is a hardy bunch who are never shy to take on a challenge to address a real-world problem, especially those problems that cause you

---

3 At last check, we counted more than 20 methodologies and variations.

4 "DtSR Episode 362—Real Security Is Hard," Down the Security Rabbit Hole Podcast, *https://oreil.ly/iECWZ*.

pain, anguish, and sleepless nights. And automation can help address these concerns (see Figure 4-1).

Figure 4-1. "Very small shell script" (source: https://oreil.ly/W0Lqo)

The difficult part of using automation is the complexity of systems and the relative inability for a program to do something the human brain can do better: pattern recognition.[5] The difficulty is expressing the system in a way a computer can understand without *actually creating the system*. As a result, two related approaches are available:

Threat modeling from code
> Creating computer code in a programming language or in a newly defined domain-specific language (DSL) that results, when executed, in analysis of threats being performed on a model that represents the input data provided

Threat modeling with code (aka threat modeling in code)
> Using a computer program to interpret and process information provided to it to identify threats or vulnerabilities

Both approaches can be effective as long as you resolve the GIGO problem. The results you get must bear a direct relationship to the quality of your input (the description of the system and its attributes) for the automation. Both methods also require the algorithms and rules used in the analysis to be "correct," such that a given set of inputs generates valid and justifiable outputs. Either implementation can eliminate the need for specialized talent to interpret a system model and understand information about elements, interconnections, and data to identify the indicators of a potential security concern. Of course, this does require that the framework or language supports this analysis and is programmed to do it correctly.

---

5 Ophir Tanz, "Can Artificial Intelligence Identify Pictures Better than Humans?" *Entrepreneur*, April 2017, *https://oreil.ly/Fe9w5.*

We will talk first about the construction of a system model in a machine-readable format, and then present the theories for each type of automated threat modeling and provide commercial and open source projects that implement them. Later in the chapter (and in the next chapter), we leverage these concepts to deliver information on further evolutionary threat modeling techniques that strive to work within the rapidly accelerating world of DevOps and CI/CD.

Fundamentally, threat modeling relies on input in the form of information that contains or encodes data sufficient for you to analyze; this information enables you to identify threats. When using code rather than human intelligence to perform threat modeling, you describe the system to be evaluated (e.g., the entities, flows, or sequences of events that make up a system, along with the metadata necessary to support analysis and documentation of findings), and the application renders and analyzes the system representation to produce results, and optionally render the representation as diagrams.

Threat Modeling from Code

Threat modeling from code processes information about a system stored in machine-readable form to generate output information related to weaknesses, vulnerabilities, and threats. It does this based on a database or set of rules of things it should be looking for, and needs to be resilient to unexpected input (since these types of applications take input data to *interpret*). In other words, threat modeling from code is an interpreted approach to create a system model from which to generate threats.

Threat modeling from code may also be referred to as *threat modeling in code*, such as in the case of Threatspec (described in "Threatspec" on page 98).

The phrase "threat modeling from code" is an evolution of thought, combining two concepts of how a system captures, maintains, and processes information to identify threats. The idea of threat modeling in code came from conversations Izar had with Fraser Scott (the creator of Threatspec, described later) around the notion that code modules can store system representation and threat information alongside code or other documentation and can be maintained throughout the life cycle. Tooling that processes the information can be executed to output meaningful data. In threat modeling from code—came about from another conversation between Izar and the creator of ThreatPlaybook, Abhay Bhargav—threat information can be encoded but needs to be "wrangled" and correlated by *something* to be meaningful. Collectively, these paradigms form the basis for this evolving area of threat modeling as code, whereby interpretation and manipulation of data from various sources are the key operations.

How It Works

In threat modeling from code, you use a program (code) to analyze information created in a machine-readable format that describes a system model, its components, and data about those components. The program interprets the input system model and data, and uses a taxonomy of threats and weaknesses, and detection criteria, to (a) identify potential findings and (b) produce results that can be interpreted by a human. Usually, the output will be a text document or PDF-type report.

Threatspec

Threatspec is an open source project geared toward both development teams and security practitioners. It provides a convenient way to document threat information alongside code, allowing you to generate documentation or a report that enables informed risk decisions. Threatspec is authored and maintained by Fraser Scott at *https://threatspec.org*.

 Threatspec is called out here in this class of tool because of what it does versus what it does not do:

- It does require code to exist.
- It does make documentation of threat information easier.
- It does not perform analysis or threat detection on its own.

Some of the benefits of using Threatspec include the following:

- Brings security to coders by using code annotations (with which they are probably familiar)
- Allows the organization to define a common lexicon of threats and other structures for development teams to use
- Facilitates the security discussion of threat modeling and analysis
- Automatically generates detailed and useful documentation, including diagrams and code snippets

On the other hand, while Threatspec is an excellent tool for giving coders a way to annotate their code with threat information and thus bring security closer into the development process, it has a couple of downsides to keep in mind.

First, the tool first *requires* code to exist, or to be created together with annotations, which may mean that the design is already solidified. In this case, the development team is mainly creating security documentation, which is highly valuable but different from threat modeling. Effectively, for these types of projects, threat modeling "shifts right," which is in the wrong direction.

But the Threatspec documentation does make it clear that the most productive use of the tool is in environments that have bought into the everything-as-code mentality, such as DevOps. For those environments, the chicken-and-egg of design versus code development is not a concern. Threatspec has also recently added the capability to document threats and annotations without having written code, by putting this information into plain-text files that can be parsed. This may help mitigate this potential concern for teams that have more structure to their development life cycle or follow more stringent systems engineering practices.

Second, the development team requires expert knowledge. The team needs guidance from an expert, of what a threat is and how to describe it. This means you cannot address the problem of scalability directly. This approach lends itself, as described by the tool's documentation, to discussions or guided exercises between the development team and security personnel. But in doing so, scalability is further challenged, by adding back the bottleneck of the security expert. Extensive training of development teams may overcome this hurdle, or having security embedded within the development group may help facilitate conversations closer to where and when code is being developed.

In the future, Threatspec may be especially suited for taking the output of static code analysis tools and generating annotations describing threats from the nature of the code (rather than just what the coders are able or willing to document themselves). Because Threatspec has direct access to source code, it may, as an enhancement, perform verification activities and provide feedback directly into the source code when it discovers threats, risks, or weaknesses. Finally, extending threats into functional safety and privacy domains can produce a comprehensive view of the security, privacy, and safety posture of a system, which is especially important when dealing with compliance officers or regulators (e.g., for PCI-DSS compliance, GDPR, or other regulatory environments) or for guiding root cause or hazard analysis as follow-up activities.

You can obtain Threatspec from GitHub at *https://oreil.ly/NGTI8*. It requires Python 3 and Graphviz (*https://www.graphviz.org*) to run and generate reports. The creator/maintainer of Threatspec is active in the security community, especially the OWASP Threat Modeling working group and in the Threatspec Slack, and encourages contributions and feedback on the tool.

ThreatPlaybook

ThreatPlaybook is an open source project brought to you by the folks at we45, led by Abhay Bhargav. It is marketed as a "DevSecOps framework [for] collaborative Threat Modeling to Application Security Test Automation." It is geared toward development teams to provide a convenient way to document threat information and to drive automation of security vulnerability detection and validation. ThreatPlaybook has a stable release (V1) and a beta release (V3); there is no V2 release.[6]

ThreatPlaybook's specialty is to facilitate the use of threat modeling information:

- It makes documentation of threat information easier.
- It connects with other security tools for orchestration and validation of vulnerabilities, such as through security test automation.
- It does not perform analysis or threat detection on its own.

ThreatPlaybook uses GraphQL (*https://graphql.org*) in MongoDB, and YAML-based descriptions of use cases and threats with descriptive constructs, to support test orchestration for vulnerability verification. It also offers a full API, a capable client application, and a decent report generator. For test automation integrations, it has two options: the original Robot Framework Libraries[7] and in V3 its own Test Orchestration Framework functionality. The documentation suggests that ThreatPlaybook has good integration (via Robot Framework) with OWASP Zed Attack Proxy (*https://oreil.ly/-MRM1*), Burp Suite from PortSwigger (*https://oreil.ly/59620*), and npm-audit (*https://oreil.ly/ZvpkT*).

You can obtain ThreatPlaybook from GitHub at *https://oreil.ly/Z2DZd* or via Python's pip utility. A companion website (*https://oreil.ly/KVrxC*) has good, although somewhat sparse, documentation, and videos explaining how to install, configure, and use ThreatPlaybook.

Threat Modeling with Code

Unlike Threatspec and ThreatPlaybook described previously, which are examples of using code to facilitate the threat modeling activity in the system development life cycle, threat modeling with code takes an architecture or system description that is encoded in a form such as one of the description languages described previously, and

---

6 See the ThreatPlaybook documentation for more details, at *https://oreil.ly/lhSPc*.

7 See the Robot Framework, an open source framework for testing, at *https://oreil.ly/GWGKP*.

performs analysis for automated threat identification and reporting. Utilities following the "with code" paradigm are tools that can read system model information and generate meaningful results that encapsulate the knowledge and expertise of security professionals, and enable security pros to scale across a larger development community.

How It Works

A user writes a program in a programming language to construct a representation of a system and its components, and information about those components. This program describes information about the system in code and provides constraints to performing the analysis. The resulting process uses a set of APIs (functions) to perform threat analysis on the modeled system state and properties. When the "source code" is compiled and executed (or interpreted, depending on the specifics of the language in use), the resulting program produces security threat findings based on the characteristics and constraints of the modeled system.

The concept of creating models without drawing on a whiteboard has been around since at least 1976, when A. Wayne Wymore, then a professor at the University of Arizona, published *Systems Engineering Methodology for Interdisciplinary Teams* (Wiley). This book, and others that followed, set the groundwork for the technical domain known as model-based systems engineering (*https://oreil.ly/oPYSL*) (MBSE). Lessons the industry learned from MBSE influenced the system-modeling constructs referenced in Chapter 1, and the languages of describing systems for computational analysis that we will briefly discuss.[8]

Architecture description languages (ADLs) describe representations of systems. Related to ADLs are system design languages, or SDLs (*https://oreil.ly/BbyQZ*). Within the set of ADLs, two related languages provide the ability to build and analyze system models that look for security threats:[9]

- Architecture Analysis & Design Language, or AADL (*https://oreil.ly/lZdg0*)
- The Acme (*https://oreil.ly/rVV2G*) description language for component-based system modeling

Systems engineering uses AADL, which is larger and more expressive, when creating system models of embedded and real-time systems. This is true especially in the fields of avionics and automotive systems, which require functional safety—the property of preserving health and life of human occupants when it comes to system behavior.

---

8 A. Wymore's autobiography is available on this University of Arizona site (*https://oreil.ly/mPG3s*).

9 A survey of ADLs is available from "Architecture Description Languages" by Stefan Bjornander, *https://oreil.ly/AKo-w*.

ACME is less expressive and therefore more applicable for systems that are less complex or smaller in size (defined by number of components and interactions). ACME is also a freely available language specification, while AADL requires a paid license (*https://oreil.ly/zotv4*), although some training material is available for free so you can become familiar with the language.[10]

These languages introduce simple concepts that system and software engineers still use today. You may notice similarities to the concepts we described in Chapter 1:

Components
Represent functional units such as processes or data stores

Connectors
Establish relationships and communication pipelines among components

Systems
Represent specific configurations of components and connectors

Ports
Points of interaction between components and connectors

Roles
Provide useful insights into the function of elements within the system

Properties, or annotations
Provide information regarding each construct that can be used for analysis or documentation

 In both ACME and AADL (*https://oreil.ly/yKn-I*), ports exist as connection points between objects and flows. Our discussion of modeling techniques uses this concept, both through drawings and manual analysis techniques, and through automated methodologies using objects with properties. We recommend this as an enhancement on the traditional DFD (as described in Chapter 1) to improve readability of the system model. This concept also supports the inclusion of architectural constraints or capabilities into the system model, where holding protocols or protection schemes on the data flows alone is not easy to process for complex systems with multiple data flows that are harder to analyze. Using ports helps with this analysis and to render your diagram.

---

10 "AADL Resource Pages," Open AADL, *http://www.openaadl.org*.

Minimalist architecture description language for threat modeling

What information is necessary to describe and analyze a system model? Let's refresh your memory of what you learned in Chapter 1 about building a representative drawing "by hand." You need information on the following:

- The entities that exist in the system

- How these entities interact—which elements connect to one another via data flows

- Characteristics of the elements and data flows

These are the core requirements for describing a system model so that automation can identify patterns that represent potential weaknesses and threats. More specifically, the language or constructs that describe the system must allow you to specify basic entity relationships and describe the core units of elements (and collections of elements), ports, and data flows.

Additionally, you should include *metadata* in the properties of the objects—the who, what, and why—of the systems and its elements. There are multiple reasons that this is necessary when you build a representation of the system, as metadata does the following:

- Metadata provides background information that helps to identify gaps in security controls and processes, as well as to generate a report or document that the development team will use. This metadata includes items such as the name of the object within the system model, application or process name, who or which team is responsible for its implementation and/or maintenance, and the object's general purpose within the system.

- Assigns each object a short identifier for easier reference in the future and to facilitate documentation and the rendering of diagrams.

- Allows you to provide specific information such as the value (financial value, or the importance of the data for users of the system, for instance) of the data managed and/or stored by the system under consideration. You should also provide the value that the system's functionality provides, how much the system supports risk identification and prioritization, and other information needed for documentation. This information is not strictly *necessary* to *identify* security concerns, but it should be considered necessary when you perform risk assessment, prioritization, and reporting.

Elements and collections

Objects connect to other objects within a system, and have properties pertinent for threat analysis; these objects are referred to as elements. Elements can represent a process, an object, or an individual (actor). Elements also represent data within a system. Data is associated with elements or data flows (for details, see "Data and data flows" on page 109).

Collections are a special form of element. Collections form an abstract relationship grouping of elements (and by extension their data flows or any arbitrary orphaned elements and/or ports) to establish commonality or a reference point for analysis. They allow you to create a representation of a group of items, where the value or purpose of the group is important to you in some way. Grouping may inform analysis independent of the members of the group—if certain elements operate or exist as part of a group, that may offer clues about their shared functionality that each element by itself would not indicate. Recommended collections include the following:

System

> This allows you to indicate that a set of elements comprises members of a larger compound element. For the purposes of drawing, and for analysis at varying degrees of granularity, a system can be represented both as a collection or as an element. As we discussed in Chapter 1, when drawing system models, a process exists for starting with an element and decomposing it into its representative parts. Recall when creating the context, or initial layer, showing the major components of the system, a single shape was used to represent a collection of subcomponent parts; when drawn at a higher level of specificity (i.e., zoomed in), the representative parts become individualized. When creating a system model in a description language, the representative parts need to be specified individually and, for convenience, grouped together (usually by assigning a shared label or indicator of their relationships to one another).

Execution context

> It is critically important to be able to account for the context in which a process executes, or the scope of a unit of data, during analysis. Use an execution context collection to associate things like processes with other things such as virtual or physical CPUs, compute nodes, operating systems, etc., in the scope in which it operates. Understanding this helps you identify cross-context concerns and other opportunities for abuse.

Trust boundary

> A collection of elements may be purely abstract and/or arbitrary, not requiring physical or virtual adjacency, to have meaning to you. At the time of defining the objects in the system model, not all system components may be known. So it can be helpful to be able to associate a set of elements as a collection that shares a

trust relationship, or for which trust changes between them and other elements not in the collection.

Information associated with nodes—another name for elements—is encoded as properties or characteristics of the object, and provides critical information for analysis and documentation. To support correct system model checking and threat analysis, elements need to have basic properties.[11] A representative sample is shown here:

```
Element:
    contains        ❶
    exposes         ❷
    calls           ❸
    is_type:        ❹
        - cloud.saas
        - cloud.iaas
        - cloud.paas
        - mobile.ios
        - mobile.android
        - software
        - firmware.embedded
        - firmware.kernel_mod
        - firmware.driver
        - firmware
        - hardware
        - operating_system
        - operating_system.windows.10
        - operating_system.linux
        - operating_system.linux.fedora.23
        - operating_system.rtos
    is_containerized        ❺
    deploys_to:
        - windows
        - linux
        - mac_os_x
        - aws_ec2
    provides
        - protection            ❻
        - protection.signed
        - protection.encrypted
        - protection.signed.cross       ❼
        - protection.obfuscated
    packaged_as:            ❽
        - source
        - binary
        - binary.msi
        - archive
```

---

11 There are many possible ways to represent objects within a system; this shows an idealized or representative set of properties based on our research. The list has been modified for placement in this text, and the original can be found at *https://oreil.ly/Vdiws*.

```
source_language:                    ❾
   - c
   - cpp
   - python
uses.technology:                    ❿
   - cryptography
   - cryptography.aes128
   - identity
   - identity.oauth
   - secure_boot
   - attestation
requires:                           ⓫
   - assurance
   - assurance.privacy
   - assurance.safety
   - assurance.thread_safety
   - assurance.fail_safe
   - privileges.root
   - privileges.guest              ⓬
metadata:                           ⓭
   - name
   - label
   - namespace
   - created_by
   - ref.source.source             ⓮
   - ref.source.acquisition        ⓯
   - source_type.internal          ⓰
   - source_type.open_source
   - source_type.commercial
   - source_type.commercial.vendor
   - description                   ⓱
```

❶ List (array or dictionary) of elements connected to this element (for a system of systems, for example), which may include data

❷ List of port nodes

❸ One element to another, establishing a data flow

❹ Elements have a type (generic or specific)

❺ Boolean characteristics might be True or False, or (set) or (unset)

❻ Generic protection scheme

❼ Use of Microsoft Authenticode cross-signature support

❽ What form is the element in use?

⑨ If the system is or contains software, what language(s) is in use?

⑩ Specific technology or capabilities that are used by the component

⑪ What does the component need, or assume, to exist?

⑫ Set only values that apply. Be careful of conflicting attributes

⑬ General information for reporting, reference, and other documentation

⑭ Reference to where source code or documentation resides

⑮ Reference to where this component came from (project site, perhaps)

⑯ This component was internally source

⑰ Arbitrary user-defined information

Elements should support particular relationships to other entities or objects:

- Elements can contain other elements.
- An element may *expose* a port (ports are described in the next section).
  — Ports are associated with data.
- Elements can *connect* to other elements by way of a port, establishing a data flow.
- An element can make a *call* to another element (such as when an executable makes a call into a shared library).
- An element can read or write data. (Data objects are described in "Data and data flows" on page 109.)

Ports

Ports provide an entry or connection point where interactions between nodes occur. Ports are exposed by nodes (especially nodes representing processes) and are associated with a protocol. Ports also identify requirements on their security, such as any expectation of security in subsequent communications that pass through the port. Methods offered by the port protect exposed communication channels; some of these methods come from the node exposing the port (such as a node opening a port for traffic protected by TLS) or from the port itself (e.g., for a physically secure interface).

For consumption and readability by a computer program,[12] it is imperative to identify and segregate communication flows per protocol. Since different protocols may offer varied configuration options that can impact the overall security of the design, try to avoid overloading communication flows. For example, an HTTPS server that allows RESTful interactions as well as WebSockets through the same service and the same port should use two communication flows. Likewise, a process that supports both HTTP and HTTPS through the same interface should be described in the model with distinct communication channels. This will facilitate analyzing the system.

Properties related to ports may include the following:

```
Port:
  requires:              ❶
    - security           ❷
    - security.firewall  ❸
  provides:              ❹
    - confidentiality
    - integrity
    - qos
    - qos.delivery_receipt
  protocol:              ❺
    - I2C
    - DTLS
    - ipv6
    - btle               ❻
    - NFS                ❼
  data:                  ❽
    - incoming           ❾
    - outbound           ❿
    - service_name       ⓫
    - port               ⓬
  metadata:              ⓭
    - name
    - label
    - description        ⓮
```

❶ What does this port require or expect?

❷ When set, this means some form of security mechanism is expected to be in place to protect the port

❸ This port must have a firewall in place to protect it (as a specific security protection example)

❹ What capabilities does the port offer?

---

12 As in any good code, simplicity is best to make the program flow intelligibly to the "next maintainer."

⑤ What protocol does the port use?[13]

⑥ Bluetooth Low Energy

⑦ Network File System

⑧ What data is associated with this port?

⑨ Data being communicated *to* this port (data nodes, list)

⑩ Data being communicated *from* this port (data nodes, list)

⑪ Describe the service that is exposed, especially if this object represents a well-known service[14]

⑫ Numeric port number, if known (not ephemeral)

⑬ General information for reporting, reference, and other documentation

⑭ Arbitrary user-defined information

Data and data flows

Data flows (see Chapter 1 for examples of data flows) are sometimes referred to as *edges* because they become connecting lines in a diagram.[15] Data flows are the paths upon which data objects travel between elements (and through ports).

You may be wondering why it is important or useful to separate data from data flows. The answer is that a communication channel usually is just a path or pipe upon which arbitrary information can travel, similar to a highway. The data channel itself usually has no context regarding the sensitivity of the data that flows through it. Nor does it have any sense of business value, criticality, or other factors that may impact its use or protection requirements. By using data nodes and associating them with data flows, you can create an abstraction that represents a system that passes different types of data across data flows.

It may be obvious, but you should assign the most restrictive classification of the data going through the data flow as the data classification for the data flow itself, as this

---

13 For readers unfamiliar with I2C, see Scott Campbell's "Basics of the I2C Communication Protocol" (*https://oreil.ly/2YkQX*) Circuit Basics page.

14 See "Service Name and Transport Protocol Port Number Registry," IANA, *https://oreil.ly/1XktB*.

15 For a discussion on edges and graphs, see "Graph Theory" by Victor Adamchik, *https://oreil.ly/t0bYp*.

will drive the requirements on the data flow to protect the data that passes within it. This allows the system representation to be templated to support variant analysis, which means testing various combinations of data associated with the data flows to predict when a security issue may arise.

These are some suggested properties for data:

```
Data:
  encoding:
    - json
    - protobuf
    - ascii
    - utf8
    - utf16
    - base64
    - yaml
    - xml
  provides:
    - protection.signed
    - protection.signed.xmldsig
    - protection.encrypted
  requires:
    - security
    - availability
    - privacy
    - integrity
  is_type:                              ❶
    - personal
    - personal.identifiable        ❷
    - personal.health              ❸
    - protected
    - protected.credit_info        ❹
    - voice
    - video
    - security
  metadata:                           ❺
    - name
    - label
    - description                      ❻
```

❶ Type of data this object represents

❷ Personally identifiable information (PII)

❸ Protected health information (PHI)

❹ PCI-DSS protected data

❺ General information for reporting, reference, and other documentation

⑥ Arbitrary user-defined information

Services that expose the port define the capabilities and properties of the data flow (the data flow inherits properties represented by the port). Data flows may still benefit from having metadata, allowing them to differentiate each flow when, for example, generating a diagram or report.

Other model description languages

To round out your knowledge, let's discuss a couple of other languages, some of which fit into the SDL category. We encourage you to investigate them if you are interested.

The Common Information Model, or CIM (*https://oreil.ly/TpaVq*), is a Distributed Management Task Force (DMTF) standard for representing, at a granular level of detail, a computing system and its properties. You can use CIM, and variants like SBLIM (*https://oreil.ly/OuEvz*) for Linux systems, to understand and document the configuration of a system for tasks such as policy orchestration and configuration management. For a guide on the type of data to use when annotating system models, review the list of available properties the CIM offers for systems the specification describes.

Unified Modeling Language, or UML (*https://www.uml.org*) is an Object Management Group, or OMG (*https://oreil.ly/28YEs*), standard with a heavy lean toward describing software-centric systems. You may already be familiar with UML, as it is commonly taught as part of a computer science curriculum. The sequence diagram (which we discussed in Chapter 1) is a part of the UML specification. Recently, research has been presented at the academic level that uses UML more for the description of software systems when looking to identify threats than for the analysis to identify those threats.[16]

Systems Modeling Language (*http://www.omgsysml.org*) (SysML) is also an OMG standard. This variant of UML is designed to be more directly applicable for systems engineering (rather than purely software) than UML. SysML adds two diagram types to UML, and slightly modifies a couple of the other diagram types to remove software-specific constructs, but overall reduces the diagrams available from 13 to 9.[17] In theory, this makes SysML "lighter"-weight and more functional for general systems engineering use. Companies and organizations that rely on highly structured systems engineering processes, and of course academia, have published case studies

---

16 Michael N. Johnstone, "Threat Modelling with Stride and UML," Australian Information Security Management Conference, November 2010, *https://oreil.ly/QVU8c*.

17 "What is the Relationship Between SysML and UML?" SysML Forum, accessed October 2020, *https://oreil.ly/xL7l2*.

on how to apply SysML for modeling systems for threats, although at the time of writing there is limited availability of case studies showing the automation of analysis for threats.[18,19]

The types of system models, or abstractions, available, and the data that can be associated with them, in both UML and SysML, are key for application in the area of threat modeling, and specifically threat modeling via code. Both provide a means to specify objects and interactions, and parameters about those objects and interactions. Both also use XML as their data interchange format. XML is designed to be processed by computer applications, which makes this ideal for creating system models that you can analyze for threats.

Analysis of graphs and metadata

Let's consider for a moment the simple example shown in Figure 4-2.

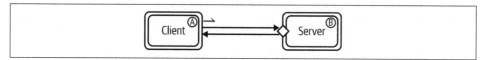

Figure 4-2. Simple client/server system model

These annotations accompany the system diagram in Figure 4-2:

- The client is written in C and calls out to the server on port 8080 to authenticate the user of the client.

- The server checks an internal database, and if the information sent by the client matches what is expected, the server returns an authorization token to the client.

Put your security hat on (refer to the Introduction if you need to brush up on authentication and other applicable flaws) and identify the security concerns in this simple system model.[20] Now, think about *how* you came to the conclusion you did. You (probably) looked at the system model, saw the information provided as annotations, and determined potential threats. You performed pattern analysis against a database of threat information stored in your memory. This is what security advisors for development teams do regularly, and is one of the challenges of scalability—not enough "memory" and "compute power" to go around.

---

18 Aleksandr Kerzhner et al., "Analyzing Cyber Security Threats on Cyber-Physical Systems Using Model-Based Systems Engineering," *https://oreil.ly/0ToAu*.

19 Robert Oates et al., "Security-Aware Model-Based Systems Engineering with SysML," *https://oreil.ly/lri3g*.

20 Hint: Using this system model carries at least five potential threats such as spoofing and credential theft.

This pattern analysis and extrapolation is easy for a human brain to do. Our brains, given the right knowledge, can easily see patterns and make extrapolations. We even have a subconscious that allows us to have "gut feelings" about our analysis. We make connections to and between things that seem random and ambiguous. We don't even process all of the steps that our brains take when working; our thoughts "just happen." Computers, unlike our brains, do things quickly, but they need to be aware of every step and process that's needed. Computers can't infer or assume. So, what we take for granted, computers need to be programmed to do.

So, how would a computer program analyze this scenario?

First, you need to develop a framework for analysis. This framework must be able to accept input (from the model) and perform pattern analysis, draw inferences, make connections, and occasionally guess, to produce an outcome that humans can interpret as meaningful. Ready with that AI yet?

Actually, it is not that much of a challenge, and has not been for quite some time. The basic approach is simple:

1. Create a format for describing a system representation with information, using something like an ADL.

2. Create a program to interpret the system model information.

3. Extend the program to perform analysis based on a set of rules that govern the patterns of information present in the system model.

So let's look at that simple example again, in Figure 4-3.

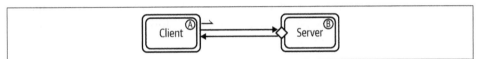

Figure 4-3. Simple client/server system model revisited

Now, let's use our idealized description language from earlier in the chapter to describe the information in the system model. To reference each object distinctly in the system model, we use a placeholder identifier for each object, and connect properties to that identifier:

```
# Describe 'Node1' (the client)
Node1.name: client
Node1.is_type: software
Node1.source_language: c
Node1.packaged_type: binary

# Describe 'Node2' (the server)
Node2.name: server
Node2.is_type: software
```

```
# Describe 'Node3' (an exposed port)
Node3.is_type: port
Node3.port: 8080
Node3.protocol: http

# Establish the relationships
Node2.exposes.port: Node3
Node1.connects_to: Node3

# Describe the data that will be passed on the channel
Data1.is_type: credential
Data1.requires: [confidentiality, integrity, privacy]
Data1.metadata.description: "Data contains a credential to be checked by
the server"

Data2.is_type: credential
Data2.requires: [confidentiality, integrity]
Data2.metadata.description: "Data contains a session token that gives/
  authorization to perform actions"

Node3.data.incoming = Data1
Node3.data.outbound = Data2
```

Now, obviously, in the preceding example (which we completely made up and created only for the purpose of explanation), you may notice one or two things of concern. Your human brain is able to make inferences about the meaning of the properties and what the system might look like. In Chapter 3, you learned how to determine some of the vulnerabilities that may exist in a sample system.

But how will the computer program do this same task? It needs to be programmed to do so—it needs a set of rules, and structures to piece information together to achieve the results necessary for analysis.

Constructing rules means looking at available sources of threats and identifying the "indicators" that reveal a threat is possible. The CWE Architectural Concepts list (*https://oreil.ly/pKzO4*) or CAPEC Mechanisms of Attack (*https://oreil.ly/oulfi*) are repositories that are excellent resources to consider.

 You may have noticed that we refer to the CWE and CAPEC databases multiple times throughout the book. We are particularly fond of using these as central resources because they are open, public, and filled with consumable and applicable information that has been contributed by experts across the security community.

For our demonstration, let's take a look at two possible sources of a rule:

- CWE-319: Cleartext Transmission of Sensitive Information (*https://oreil.ly/6psXE*)
- CAPEC-157: Sniffing Attacks (*https://oreil.ly/xg2A1*)

CWE-319 tells us the weakness occurs when "the software transmits sensitive or security-critical data in cleartext in a communication channel that can be sniffed by unauthorized actors." From this simple description, you should be able to identify the indicators that need to be present for a potential threat to exist in a system:

- A process: This performs an action.
- "Transmits": The software unit communicates with another component.
- "Sensitive or security-critical data": Data of value to an attacker.
- Without encryption: On the channel or protecting the data packets directly (one of these conditions needs to exist).
- Impact: Confidentiality.

CAPEC-157 describes an attack against sensitive information as "in this attack pattern, the adversary intercepts information transmitted between two third parties. The adversary must be able to observe, read, and/or hear the communication traffic, but not necessarily block the communication or change its content. Any transmission medium can theoretically be sniffed if the adversary can examine the contents between the sender and recipient." From this description, we get details of how an attacker may perform this attack:

- Traffic between two parties (endpoints) is intercepted.
- The attack is passive; no modification or denial of service is expected.
- The attacker (actor) requires access to the communication channel.

So with these two descriptions, we might consider the following unified rules (in text):

- The source endpoint communicates to the destination endpoint.
- The data flow between endpoints contains sensitive data.
- The data flow is not protected for confidentiality.

The impact of having these conditions present in a system would enable a malicious actor to obtain sensitive data through sniffing.

The code to identify this pattern and to indicate the condition of threat existence might look like (in pseudocode, minus all the safety checks) the following:

```
def evaluate(node n, "Threat from CWE-319"):
    if n.is_type is "software":
        for i in range(0, len(n.exposes)):
            return (n.exposes[i].p.data.incoming[0].requires.security)
            and
            (n.exposes[i].p.provides.confidentiality)
```

This is an extremely simplified example of what a tool or automation could accomplish. More efficient algorithms for performing this pattern matching certainly exist, but hopefully this example gives you an idea of how threat modeling uses code to perform automatic threat detection.

While threat modeling with code is a pretty neat trick, threat modeling from code makes the technology potentially more accessible. In this paradigm, instead of using code to assist in managing threat information, or using a program to analyze a textual description of a model "with code" to match constructs to rules to determine threats, an actual program is written that, when executed, performs the threat modeling analysis and rendering "automagically."

For this to be possible, a program author needs to create program logic and APIs to describe elements, data flows, etc. and the rules by which they will be analyzed. Developers then use the APIs to create executable programs. Execution (with or without precompilation, dependent on the language choice for the APIs) of the program code results in these basic steps:

1. Translate the directives that describe objects to build a representation of the system (such as a graph, or just an array of properties, or in an other representation internal to the program).

2. Load a set of rules.

3. Walk the graph of objects performing pattern matching against the set of rules to identify findings.

4. Generate results based on templates for drawing the graph as a diagram that is (hopefully) visually acceptable to a human and for outputting details of findings.

Writing code to autogenerate threat information provides a few benefits:

- As a coder, you are already used to writing code, so this offers an opportunity for you to have something actionable on your terms.

- Threat modeling as code neatly aligns with the everything as code or DevOps philosophies.

- You can check in code and keep it under revision control in tools you, as a developer, are already used to, which should help with adoption as well as management of the information.

- If the APIs and libraries that are built to contain the knowledge and expertise of security professionals support the capability to dynamically load rules for analysis, the same program can service multiple domains. A program can re-analyze a system previously described in code as new research or threat intelligence reveals new threats so they are always up-to-date, without changing the model or having to redo any work.

This method has a few detractions to consider as well, however:

- Developers such as yourself already write code every day to deliver value to your business or customers. Writing additional code to document your architecture may seem like an additional burden.

- With so many programming languages available today, the likelihood of finding a code bundle that uses (or supports integration with) a language your development team uses may be a challenge.

- The focus is still on developers who, as the keepers of code, need the skills to understand concepts like object-oriented programming and functions (and calling conventions, etc.).

These challenges are not insurmountable; however, the threat modeling from code space is still immature. The best example we can offer for a code module and API for performing threat modeling from code is pytm.

 Disclaimer: we are really, really, *really* biased toward pytm, as creators/leaders of the open source project. We want to be fair in this book to all the great innovations in the field of threat modeling automation. But we do honestly feel pytm has addressed a gap in methods that have been made available to security practitioners and development teams trying to make threat modeling actionable and effective for them.

pytm

One of the main reasons we wrote this book was the sincere desire for individuals involved with development to have immediately accessible information that helps them further develop their security capabilities in the secure software development life cycle. This is why we talk about training, the challenge of "thinking like a hacker," attack trees and threat libraries, rules engines, and diagrams.

As experienced security practitioners, we have heard many arguments from development teams against the use of threat modeling tooling: "It is too heavy!", "It is not platform-agnostic; I work in X, and the tool only works in Y!", "I don't have the time to learn one more application, and this one requires me to learn a whole new syntax!"

Apart from the presence of a lot of exclamation points, a common pattern in these declarations is that the coder is asked to step outside their immediate comfort zone and add one more skill to their toolbox or interrupt a familiar workflow and add an extraneous process. So, we thought to ourselves, what if we were to instead try to approximate the threat modeling process to one already familiar to the coder?

Much as can be seen in continuous threat modeling (which we describe in depth in Chapter 5), reliance on tools and processes already known to the development team helps create commonality and trust in the process. You are already comfortable with these and use them every day.

Then we looked at automation. Which areas of threat modeling offered the most challenges to the development team? The usual suspects stepped forward: identifying threats, diagramming and annotating, and keeping the threat model (and by extension, the system model) current with minimum effort. We bantered about description languages, but they fell into the category of "one more thing for the team to learn," and their application felt heavy in the development process, while the teams were trying to make it lighter. How could we help the development team meet its (efficiency/reliability) goal and still achieve our security education goal?

Then it struck us: why not describe a system as a collection of objects in an object-oriented way, using a commonly known, easy, accessible, existing programming language, and generate diagrams and threats from that description? Add Python, and there you have it: a Pythonic library for threat modeling.

Available at *https://oreil.ly/nuPja* (and at *https://oreil.ly/wH-Nl* as an OWASP Incubator project), in its first year of life, pytm has captured the interest of many in the threat modeling community. Internal adoption at our own companies and others, talks and workshops by Jonathan Marcil at popular security conferences like OWASP Global AppSec DC (*https://oreil.ly/yrf1q*) and discussions at the Open Security Summit (*https://oreil.ly/SGrB0*) and even use by Trail of Bits (*https://oreil.ly/iWv7O*) in its Kubernetes threat model indicate that we are moving in the right direction!

 pytm is an open source library that has profited immensely from the discussions, work, and additions of individuals including Nick Ozmore and Rohit Shambhuni, co-creators of the tool; and Pooja Avhad and Jan Was, responsible for many central patches and improvements. We look forward to the community's active involvement in making it better. Consider this a call to action!

Here is a sample system description using pytm:

```python
#!/usr/bin/env python3    ❶


from pytm.pytm import TM, Server, Datastore, Dataflow, Boundary, Actor, Lambda    ❷


tm = TM("my test tm")    ❸
tm.description = "This is a sample threat model of a very simple system - a /
web-based comment system. The user enters comments and these are added to a /
database and displayed back to the user. The thought is that it is, though /
simple, a complete enough example to express meaningful threats."

User_Web = Boundary("User/Web")    ❹
Web_DB = Boundary("Web/DB")

user = Actor("User")    ❺
user.inBoundary = User_Web    ❻

web = Server("Web Server")
web.OS = "CloudOS"
web.isHardened = True    ❼

db = Datastore("SQL Database (*)")
db.OS = "CentOS"
db.isHardened = False
db.inBoundary = Web_DB
db.isSql = True
db.inScope = False

my_lambda = Lambda("cleanDBevery6hours")
my_lambda.hasAccessControl = True
my_lambda.inBoundary = Web_DB

my_lambda_to_db = Dataflow(my_lambda, db, "(&lambda;)Periodically cleans DB")    ❽
my_lambda_to_db.protocol = "SQL"
my_lambda_to_db.dstPort = 3306

user_to_web = Dataflow(user, web, "User enters comments (*)")
user_to_web.protocol = "HTTP"
user_to_web.dstPort = 80
user_to_web.data = 'Comments in HTML or Markdown'
user_to_web.order = 1    ❾

web_to_user = Dataflow(web, user, "Comments saved (*)")
web_to_user.protocol = "HTTP"
web_to_user.data = 'Ack of saving or error message, in JSON'
web_to_user.order = 2

web_to_db = Dataflow(web, db, "Insert query with comments")
web_to_db.protocol = "MySQL"
```

```
web_to_db.dstPort = 3306
web_to_db.data = 'MySQL insert statement, all literals'
web_to_db.order = 3

db_to_web = Dataflow(db, web, "Comments contents")
db_to_web.protocol = "MySQL"
db_to_web.data = 'Results of insert op'
db_to_web.order = 4

tm.process()    ❿
```

❶ pytm is a Python 3 library. No Python 2 version is available.

❷ In pytm, everything revolves around elements. Specific elements are `Process`, `Server`, `Datastore`, `Lambda`, (Trust) `Boundary`, and `Actor`. The `TM` object contains all metadata about the threat model as well as the processing power. Import only what your threat model will use, or extend `Element` into your own specific ones (and then share them with us!)

❸ We instantiate a `TM` object that will contain all of our model description.

❹ Here we instantiate a trust boundary that we will use to separate distinct areas of trust of the model.

❺ We also instantiate a generic actor to represent the user of the system.

❻ And we immediately put it in the correct side of a trust boundary.

❼ Each specific element has attributes that will influence the threats that may be generated. All of them have common default values, and we need to change only those that are unique to the system.

❽ The `Dataflow` element links two previously defined elements, and carries details about the information flowing, the protocol used, and the communication ports in use.

❾ Apart from the usual DFD, pytm also knows how to generate sequence diagrams. By adding an `.order` attribute to `Dataflow`, it is possible to organize them in a way that will make sense once expressed in that format.

❿ After declaring all our elements and their attributes, one call to `TM.process()` executes the operations required in the command line.

Besides the line-by-line analysis, what we can learn from this piece of code is that each threat model is a separate individual script. This way, a large project can keep the pytm scripts small and colocated with the code that they represent, so that they can be more easily kept updated and version controlled. When a specific part of the system changes, only that specific threat model needs editing and change. This focuses effort on the description of the change, and avoids the mistakes made possible by editing one large piece of code.

By virtue of the process() call, every single pytm script has the same set of command-line switches and arguments:

```
tm.py [-h] [--debug] [--dfd] [--report REPORT] [--exclude EXCLUDE] [--seq] /
[--lis] [--describe DESCRIBE]

optional arguments:
  -h, --help              show this help message and exit
  --debug                 print debug messages
  --dfd                   output DFD (default)
  --report REPORT         output report using the named template file /
(sample template file is under docs/template.md)
  --exclude EXCLUDE       specify threat IDs to be ignored
  --seq                   output sequential diagram
  --list                  list all available threats
  --describe DESCRIBE  describe the properties available for a given element
```

Of note are --dfd and --seq: these generate the diagrams in PNG format. The DFD is generated by pytm writing in Dot, a format consumed by Graphviz (*https://www.graphviz.org*) and the sequence diagram by PlantUML (*http://plantuml.com*). also has multiplatform support. The intermediate formats are textual, so you can make modifications, and the layout is governed by the respective tools and not by pytm. Working this way, every tool can focus on what it does best.[21]

See Figures 4-4 and 4-5.

---

21 Graphviz has packages for all major operating systems.

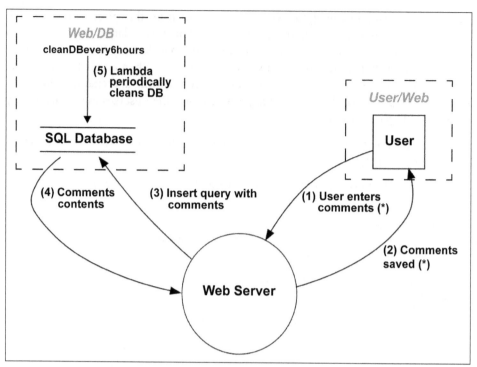

Figure 4-4. DFD representation of the sample code

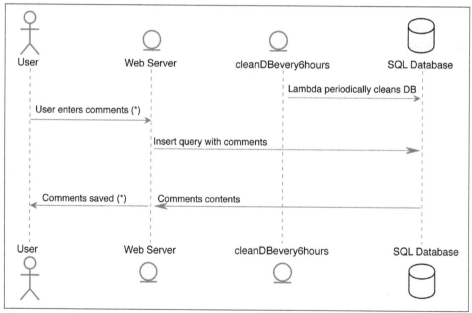

Figure 4-5. The same code, now represented as a sequence diagram

Being able to diagram at the speed of code has proven to be a useful property of pytm. We have seen code being jotted down during initial design meetings to describe the system in play. pytm allows team members to leave a threat modeling session with a functional representation of their idea that has the same value as a drawing on a whiteboard but can be shared, edited, and collaborated upon immediately. This approach avoids all the pitfalls of whiteboards ("Has anyone seen the markers? No, the black markers!", "Can you move the camera a bit? The glare is hiding half of the view," "Sarah is responsible for turning the drawing into a Visio file. Wait, who's Sarah?", and the dreaded "Do Not Erase" signs).

But while all of that is valuable, a threat modeling tool is quite lacking if it doesn't, well, reveal threats. pytm does have that capability, albeit with a caveat: at this stage in its development, we are more concerned with identifying initial capabilities than being exhaustive in the threats identified. The project started with a subset of threats that roughly parallels the capabilities of the Microsoft Threat Modeling Tool described in this chapter, and added some lambda-related threats. Currently, pytm recognizes more than 100 detectable threats, based on a subset of CAPEC. You can see some of the threats pytm is able to identify here (and all threats can be listed by using the --list switch):

```
INP01 - Buffer Overflow via Environment Variables
INP02 - Overflow Buffers
INP03 - Server Side Include (SSI) Injection
CR01 - Session Sidejacking
INP04 - HTTP Request Splitting
CR02 - Cross Site Tracing
INP05 - Command Line Execution through SQL Injection
INP06 - SQL Injection through SOAP Parameter Tampering
SC01 - JSON Hijacking (aka JavaScript Hijacking)
LB01 - API Manipulation
AA01 - Authentication Abuse/ByPass
DS01 - Excavation
DE01 - Interception
DE02 - Double Encoding
API01 - Exploit Test APIs
AC01 - Privilege Abuse
INP07 - Buffer Manipulation
AC02 - Shared Data Manipulation
DO01 - Flooding
HA01 - Path Traversal
AC03 - Subverting Environment Variable Values
DO02 - Excessive Allocation
DS02 - Try All Common Switches
INP08 - Format String Injection
INP09 - LDAP Injection
INP10 - Parameter Injection
INP11 - Relative Path Traversal
INP12 - Client-side Injection-induced Buffer Overflow
AC04 - XML Schema Poisoning
```

```
DO03 - XML Ping of the Death
AC05 - Content Spoofing
INP13 - Command Delimiters
INP14 - Input Data Manipulation
DE03 - Sniffing Attacks
CR03 - Dictionary-based Password Attack
API02 - Exploit Script-Based APIs
HA02 - White Box Reverse Engineering
DS03 - Footprinting
AC06 - Using Malicious Files
HA03 - Web Application Fingerprinting
SC02 - XSS Targeting Non-Script Elements
AC07 - Exploiting Incorrectly Configured Access Control Security Levels
INP15 - IMAP/SMTP Command Injection
HA04 - Reverse Engineering
SC03 - Embedding Scripts within Scripts
INP16 - PHP Remote File Inclusion
AA02 - Principal Spoof
CR04 - Session Credential Falsification through Forging
DO04 - XML Entity Expansion
DS04 - XSS Targeting Error Pages
SC04 - XSS Using Alternate Syntax
CR05 - Encryption Brute Forcing
AC08 - Manipulate Registry Information
DS05 - Lifting Sensitive Data Embedded in Cache
```

As mentioned earlier, the format pytm uses to define threats is undergoing a revision
to accommodate a better rule engine and provide more information. Currently, pytm
defines a threat as a JSON structure with the following format:

```
{
    "SID":"INP01",
    "target": ["Lambda","Process"],
    "description": "Buffer Overflow via Environment Variables",
    "details": "This attack pattern involves causing a buffer overflow through/
manipulation of environment variables. Once the attacker finds that they can/
modify an environment variable, they may try to overflow associated buffers./
This attack leverages implicit trust often placed in environment variables.",
    "Likelihood Of Attack": "High",
    "severity": "High",
    "condition": "target.usesEnvironmentVariables is True and target.sanitizesInp
ut is False and target.checksInputBounds is False",
    "prerequisites": "The application uses environment variables.An environment/
variable exposed to the user is vulnerable to a buffer overflow.The vulnerable/
environment variable uses untrusted data.Tainted data used in the environment/
variables is not properly validated. For instance boundary checking is not /
done before copying the input data to a buffer.",
    "mitigations": "Do not expose environment variables to the user.Do not use /
untrusted data in your environment variables. Use a language or compiler that /
performs automatic bounds checking. There are tools such as Sharefuzz [R.10.3]/
which is an environment variable fuzzer for Unix that support loading a shared/
library. You can use Sharefuzz to determine if you are exposing an environment/
```

```
        variable  vulnerable to buffer overflow.",
          "example": "Attack Example: Buffer Overflow in $HOME A buffer overflow in
          sccw allows local users to gain root access via the $HOME
          environmental variable. Attack Example: Buffer Overflow in TERM A
          buffer overflow in the rlogin program involves its consumption of
          the TERM environment variable.",
          "references": "https://capec.mitre.org/data/definitions/10.html, CVE-1999-090
        6, CVE-1999-0046, http://cwe.mitre.org/data/definitions/120.html, http://cwe.mit
        re.org/data/definitions/119.html, http://cwe.mitre.org/data/definitions/680.html
          "
      },
```

The target field describes either a single or a tuple of possible elements that the threat acts upon. The condition field is a Boolean expression that evaluates to True (the threat exists) or False (the threat does not exist) based on the values of the attributes of the target element.

> Interestingly enough, the use of Python's eval() function to evaluate the Boolean expression in a condition introduces a possible vulnerability to the system: if pytm is installed system-wide, for example, but the threat file's permissions are too permissive and any user can write new threats, an attacker could write and add their own Python code as a threat condition, which would happily be executed with the privileges of the user running the script. We aim to fix that in the near future, but until then, be warned!

To complete the initial set of capabilities, we added a template-based reporting capability.[22] While simple and succinct, the templating mechanism is enough to provide a usable report. It enables the creation of reports in any text-based format, including HTML, Markdown, RTF, and simple text. We have opted for Markdown:

```
# Threat Model Sample
***

## System Description
{tm.description}

## Dataflow Diagram
![Level 0 DFD](dfd.png)

## Dataflows
Name|From|To |Data|Protocol|Port
----|----|---|----|--------|----
{dataflows:repeat:{{item.name}}|{{item.source.name}}|{{item.sink.name}}/
|{{item.data}}|{{item.protocol}}|{{item.dstPort}}
}
```

---

22 See "The World's Simplest Python Template Engine" by Eric Brehault, *https://oreil.ly/BEFIn*.

```
## Potential Threats
{findings:repeat:* {{item.description}} on element "{{item.target}}"
}
```

This template, applied to the preceding script, would generate the report you can see in Appendix A.

We truly expect to continue growing and developing more capabilities in the near future, hopefully bringing down the entry barrier to threat modeling by development teams while providing useful results.

Threagile

A new (as of July 2020) entry in the threat-modeling-as-code space, Threagile (*https://threagile.io*) by Christian Schneider is a promising system. It is currently in stealth mode but will soon be made available, open source!

Much like pytm, Threagile falls under the category of threat modeling with code, but uses a YAML file to describe the system it will evaluate. A development team is able to use the tools that team members already know, in their native IDE, and that can be maintained together with the code of the system it represents, version controlled, shared, and collaborated on. The tool is written in Go.

Since at the time of this writing the tool is still under development, we advise you to visit the Threagile's author's website (*https://oreil.ly/A96sg*) to see examples of the reports and diagrams generated.

The main elements of the YAML file describing the target system are its data assets, technical assets, communication links, and trust boundaries. For example, a data asset definition looks like this:

```
Customer Addresses:
        id: customer-addresses
        description: Customer Addresses
        usage: business
        origin: Customer
            owner: Example Company
            quantity: many
            confidentiality: confidential
        integrity: mission-critical
        availability: mission-critical
        justification_cia_rating: these have PII of customers and the system /
    needs these addresses for sending invoices
```

At this time, the data asset definition is the main difference in approach between Threagile and pytm, since the definitions of technical assets (in pytm, elements like Server, Process, etc.), trust boundaries, and communication links (pytm data flows) follow more or less the same breadth of information about each specific element in the system.

Differences are more marked in that Threagile considers different types of trust boundaries, like Network On Prem, Network Cloud Provider, and Network Cloud Security Group (among many others) explicitly, while pytm does not differentiate. Each type mandates different semantics that play a role in the evaluation of threats.

Threagile has a plug-in system to support rules that analyze the graph of the system described by the YAML input. At the time of this writing, it supports around 35 rules, but more are being added. A random pick of sample rules shows the following:

- cross-site-request-forgery
- code-backdooring
- ldap-injection
- unguarded-access-from-internet
- service-registry-poisoning
- unnecessary-data-transfer

Unlike pytm, which works as a command-line program, Threagile also provides a REST API that stores (encrypted) models, and allows you to edit and run them. The Threagile system will maintain the input YAML in a repository, together with the code the YAML describes, and the system can be told to perform processing either via the CLI or the API. Output of Threagile consists of the following:

- A risk report PDF
- A risk tracking Excel spreadsheet
- A risk summary with risk detail as JSON
- A DFD automatically laid out (with coloring expressing the classification of assets, data, and communication links)
- A data asset risk diagram

This last diagram is of particular interest, as it expresses, for each data asset, where it is processed and where it is stored, with color expressing risk state per data asset and technical asset. To the best of our knowledge, this is the only tool offering that view right now.

The format of the generated PDF report is extremely detailed, containing all the information necessary to flow risk up to management or for developers to be able to mitigate it. The STRIDE classification of identified threats is present, as is an impact analysis of risks per category.

We look forward to seeing more of this tool and getting involved with its development, and heartily suggest you take a look at it after it is opened to the public.

An Overview of Other Threat Modeling Tools

We tried to represent these tools as impartially as we could, but overcoming confirmation bias can be difficult. Any errors, omissions, or misrepresentations are solely our responsibility. No vendor or project participated in this review, and we do not suggest one tool over another. The information presented here is simply for educational purposes and to help you start your own research.

IriusRisk

Methodologies implemented: Questionnaire-based, threat library

Main proposition: The free/community edition of IriusRisk (see Figure 4-6) provides the same functionality as the Enterprise version, with a limitation on the kinds of reports it can produce and the elements offered in its menu for inclusion in the system. The free edition also does not contain an API, but it is enough to show the capabilities of the tool. Figure 4-6 shows an example of the analysis results performed by IriusRisk on the model of a simple browser/server system. Its threat library appears to be based on CAPEC at least, with mentions of CWE; Web Application Security Consortium, or WASC (*http://www.webappsec.org*); OWASP Top Ten; and the OWASP Application Security Verification Standard (ASVS) and OWASP Mobile Application Security Verification Standard (MASVS).

Freshness: Constantly updated

Obtain from: *https://oreil.ly/TzjrQ*

ANALYSIS	
● Alert	Use of a random value in an e-mail or SMS to recover a password should be a last resort and is known weak.
● Info	Sensitive data is received by the component
● Info	Password reset functionality.
● Info	Sensitive data is processed by the component
● Info	Authentication required
● Advice	**Google Environment, Mobile Client, PCI DSS, EU GDPR, AWS, Microsoft Azure related questions and risk patterns are not available in the Community Edition** If you'd like to see a demo of the unrestricted edition of IriusRisk please contact us
● Security Policy	The security standard: PCI-DSS-v3.2 will be applied

Figure 4-6. IriusRisk real-time analysis results

A typical finding on an IriusRisk report would contain the component where it was identified, the kind of flaw ("Access sensitive data"), a short explanation of the threat ("Sensitive data is compromised through attacks against SSL/TLS") and a graphic/color representation of the risk and progress of countermeasures.

Drilling into a given threat shows a unique ID (containing CAPEC or other index information), a division of impact into confidentiality, integrity, and availability, a longer description and a list of references, associated weaknesses, and countermeasures that will inform the reader on how to address the identified issue.

SD Elements

Methodologies implemented: Questionnaire-based, threat library

Main proposition: At the time of writing in version 5, SD Elements aims to be a full-cycle security management solution for your enterprise. One of the capabilities it offers is questionnaire-based threat modeling. Given a predefined security and compliance policy, the application tries to verify the compliance of the system in development to that policy by suggesting countermeasures.

Freshness: Frequently updated commercial offering

Obtain from: *https://oreil.ly/On7q2*

ThreatModeler

Methodologies implemented: Process flow diagrams; Visual, Agile, Simple Threat (VAST); threat library

Main proposition: ThreatModeler is one of the first commercially available threat modeling diagramming and analysis tools. ThreatModeler uses process flow diagrams (which we briefly mention in Chapter 1) and implements the VAST modeling approach to threat modeling.

Freshness: Commercial offering

Obtain from: *https://threatmodeler.com*

OWASP Threat Dragon

Methodologies implemented: Rule-based threat library, STRIDE

Main proposition: Threat Dragon is a project recently out of incubator status at OWASP. It is an online and desktop (Windows, Linux, and Mac) threat modeling application that provides a diagramming solution (drag and drop), and a rule-based analysis of the elements defined, suggesting threats and mitigations. This cross-platform, free tool is usable and expandable (see Figure 4-7).

Freshness: In active development, led by Mike Goodwin and Jon Gadsden

Obtain from: *https://oreil.ly/-n5uF*

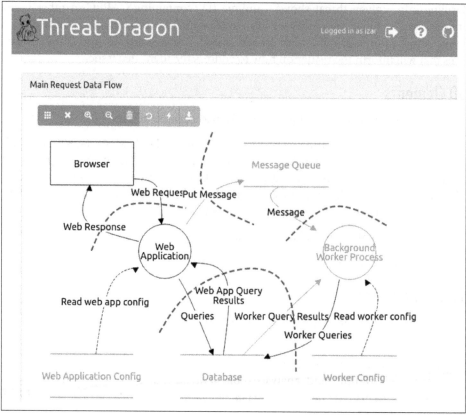

Figure 4-7. A sample system, available as a demonstration

Notice in Figure 4-7, that the DFD conforms to the simple symbology presented throughout the book; each element has a property sheet that provides details and context about it. The element is shown in the context of the full system, and basic information about whether it is in scope for the threat model, and what it contains, and how it is stored or processed, is available.

Users also can create their own threats, adding a level of customization that enables an organization or team to stress those threats that are particular to their environment or to the functioning of their system. There is a direct correlation with STRIDE threat elicitation and a simple High/Medium/Low criticality ranking without direct correlation to a CVSS score.

Threat Dragon offers a comprehensive reporting capability that keeps the system diagram in focus, and provides a list of all findings (with their mitigations, if available) sorted by elements, or the reason if a given element is part of the diagram but marked out of scope for the threat model.

Microsoft Threat Modeling Tool

Methodologies implemented: Draw and annotate, STRIDE

Main proposition: Another major contribution of Adam Shostack and the SDL Team at Microsoft, the Microsoft Threat Modeling Tool is one of the earliest appearances in the threat modeling tool space. Initially based on a Visio library (and thus requiring a license for that program), that dependency has been dropped, and now the tool is a standalone installation. Once installed, it offers options to add a new model or template, or load existing ones. The template defaults to an Azure-oriented one, with a generic SDL template for systems that are not Azure-specific. Microsoft also supports a library of templates (*https://oreil.ly/ygSun*), which, although not extensive at the moment, is surely a welcome contribution to the landscape. The tool uses an approximation of the DFD symbology we used in Chapter 1, and offers tools that let you annotate each element with attributes, both predefined and user-defined. Based on prepopulated rules (that live in an XML file and can, in theory, be user-edited), the tool generates a threat model report containing the diagram, the identified threats (classified based on STRIDE), and some mitigation advice. Although the elements and their attributes are heavily Windows oriented, the tool does have value for non-Windows users (see Figure 4-8).

Freshness: Seems to be updated every couple of years.

Obtain from: *https://oreil.ly/YL-gI*

Much as in other tools, each element can be edited to provide its properties. The main difference here is that some element properties are very Windows-related; for example, the OS Process element contains properties like Running As, with Administrator as a possible value, or Code Type: Managed. When the program generates threats, it will ignore options that won't be applicable to the targeted environment.

Reporting in this tool is closely tied to STRIDE, with each finding having a STRIDE category, in addition to a description, a justification, a state of mitigation, and a priority.

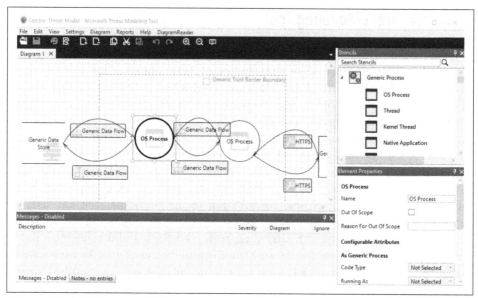

Figure 4-8. DFD for sample demo system provided with the tool

CAIRIS

Methodologies implemented: Asset-driven and threat-driven security design

Main proposition: Created and developed by Shamal Faily, CAIRIS, which stands for Computer Aided Integration of Requirements and Information Security, is a platform to create representations of secure systems focusing on risk analysis that is based on requirements and usability. Once you define an environment (i.e., a container in which the system exists—an encapsulation of assets, tasks, personas and attackers, goals, vulnerabilities, and threats), you can define the contents of the environment. Personas define users, and tasks describe how personas interact with the system. Personas also have roles, which can be stakeholder, attacker, data controller, data processor, and data subject. Personas interact with assets, which have properties including Security and Privacy (like CIA), Accountability, Anonymity, and Unobservability, valued as None, Low, Medium, and High. Tasks model the work that one or more personas perform on the system in environment-specific vignettes. CAIRIS is able to generate UML DFDs with the usual symbology, as well as textual representations of a system. The system is complex, and our description will never do it justice, but during the course of our research, CAIRIS intrigued us enough to warrant further exploration. A book that expands on the tool and the ways it should be used, and that provides a complete course on security by design is *Designing Usable and Secure Software with IRIS and CAIRIS*, by Shamal Faily (Springer).

Freshness: Under active development

Obtain from: *https://oreil.ly/BfW2l*

Mozilla SeaSponge

Methodologies implemented: Visually driven, no threat elicitation

Main proposition: Mozilla SeaSponge is a web-based tool that works on any relatively modern browser and provides a clean, good-looking UI, which also promotes an intuitive experience. At this time, it does not offer a rule engine or a reporting capability, and development appears to have ended in 2015 (see Figure 4-9).

Freshness: Development seems to have stagnated.

Obtain from: *https://oreil.ly/IOlh8*

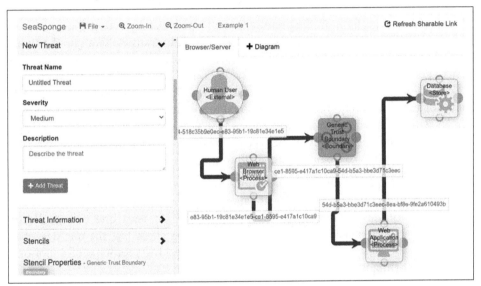

Figure 4-9. Mozilla SeaSponge user interface

Tutamen Threat Model Automator

Methodologies implemented: Visually driven, STRIDE, and threat libraries

Main proposition: Tutamen Threat Model Automator is a commercial software-as-a-service (SaaS) offering (as of October 2019, in free beta) with an interesting approach: upload a diagram of your system in draw.io or Visio formats, or an Excel spreadsheet, and receive your threat model. You must annotate your data with security-related metadata, zones of trust, and permissions you want to assign to elements. The generated report will identify the elements, the data flows, and the threats, and will propose mitigations.

Freshness: Frequently updated commercial offering

Obtain from: *http://www.tutamantic.com*

Threat Modeling with ML and AI

This is the age of "AI solves everything."[23] However, the state of the security industry is such that we're not ready to make that leap (yet) for threat modeling.

Some research has been has been done in using machine learning (ML) and AI in threat modeling. This is natural, given that today's AI is an advancement of the expert systems of the (recent) past. These systems were based on rules processed by inference engines trying to satisfy a set of requirements to bring the system being modeled into a satisfactory state. Or the systems would point out any discrepancies that deemed the solution impossible. Sounds familiar, no?

Machine learning is built on the premise that after you classify enough data, patterns emerge that allow you to classify any new data. Trying to translate that into the threat modeling domain can be tricky. For example, in the field of network security, it is easy to generate vast amounts of data carrying both "good" and "bad" traffic to train a classification algorithm. However, in threat modeling, a sufficient corpus of data may not exist, meaning you would be unable to train an algorithm to recognize threats with fidelity. That immediately takes you back to the approach where a threat is an expression of an unwanted state caused by the configuration of the system, in a specific constellation of elements and attributes.

Machine learning approaches to threat modeling are primarily still an academic exercise, with little in the way of published papers or proofs of concept that would allow us to demonstrate a functioning AI/ML system.[24,25] At least one patent already addresses a generic machine learning threat modeling chain like the one described previously, but as of today, we are not aware of a working prototype of a tool or a dataset supporting it.

Even as they are called upon and leveraged to improve security in other systems, ML systems have a need to be modeled for threats. Here are some examples of research done in this area:

---

23 Corey Caplette, "Beyond the Hype: The Value of Machine Learning and AI (Artificial Intelligence) for Business (Part 1)," Towards Data Science, May 2018, *https://oreil.ly/324W3*.

24 Mina Hao, "Machine Learning Algorithms Power Security Threat Reasoning and Analysis," NSFOCUS, May 2019, *https://oreil.ly/pzIQ9*.

25 M. Choras and R. Kozik, ScienceDirect, "Machine Learning Techniques for Threat Modeling and Detection," October 6, 2017, *https://oreil.ly/PQfUt*.

- The NCC Group has provided results of its research into this area and has developed threat models for ML systems that highlight how they can be attacked or abused by unscrupulous adversaries.[26] The researchers at NCC Group used one of the oldest non-ML tools available for threat modeling—Microsoft's Threat Modeling Tool, 2018 Edition—in their research.
- Researchers at the Institute of Computer Engineering, Vienna University of Technology, published their threat model for ML algorithm training and inference mechanisms, along with a good discussion on vulnerabilities, adversary goals, and countermeasures to mitigate the threats identified.[27]
- Berryville Institute of Machine Learning, cofounded by famed security scientist Gary McGraw, PhD, published an architectural risk analysis of ML systems that reveals interesting areas of concern in the field of security when applied to ML systems (some of which may themselves be applied to detecting security issues in other systems).[28]

MITRE's CWE is beginning to include security weaknesses for machine learning systems, with the addition of CWE-1039, "Automated Recognition Mechanism with Inadequate Detection or Handling of Adversarial Input Perturbations" (*https://oreil.ly/2wT_M*).

Summary

In this chapter, we took a longer look at some of the existing challenges of threat modeling and how you can overcome them. You learned about architecture description languages and how they provided the foundation for the automation of threat modeling. You learned about the various options for automating threat modeling, from simply generating better threat documentation to performing full modeling and analysis by writing code.

We discussed tools that use techniques from threat modeling with code and threat modeling from code (collectively referred to in the industry as threat modeling as code) while implementing threat modeling methodologies from Chapter 3. Some of these tools also implement other features, such as security test orchestration. We

---

26 "Building Safer Machine Learning Systems—A Threat Model," NCC Group, August 2018, *https://oreil.ly/BRgb9*.

27 Faiq Khalid et al., "Security for Machine Learning-Based Systems: Attacks and Challenges During Training and Inference," Cornell University, November 2018, *https://oreil.ly/2Qgx7*.

28 Gary McGraw et al., "An Architectural Risk Analysis of Machine Learning Systems," BIML, *https://oreil.ly/_RYwy*.

showed you our threat-modeling-from-code tool, pytm, and we finished by briefly discussing the challenge of applying machine learning algorithms to threat modeling.

In the next chapter, you will get a glimpse into the near-future of threat modeling with exciting new techniques and technologies.

## CHAPTER 5

Continuous Threat Modeling

"Who are you?" said the Caterpillar.

This was not an encouraging opening for a conversation.

Alice replied, rather shyly, "I—I hardly know, Sir, just at present—at least I know who I was when I got up this morning, but I think I must have been changed several times since then."

"What do you mean by that?" said the Caterpillar, sternly. "Explain yourself!"

"I can't explain myself, I'm afraid, Sir," said Alice, "because I am not myself, you see."

   —Lewis Carroll, *Alice in Wonderland*

This chapter introduces you to the process of continuous threat modeling. We also present one implementation, and describe the results from use of this methodology in the real world.

Why Continuous Threat Modeling?

Chapter 3 covered various threat modeling methodologies and pointed out some of their advantages and shortcomings from our experience. When we discussed the parameters used to "grade" those methodologies, you may have noticed that we were leaning heavily toward, for the lack of a better label, something we all call *Agile Development*.

What we mean by this is any of the existing development technologies that stray away from the waterfall model (whereby a design is first developed, then implemented and tested, with no further modification until the next iteration of the system). We are also talking about those systems that get DevOps'ed a thousand times a day, with developers making frequent changes in their constant drive to improvement. How does threat modeling survive and thrive in these environments without slowing everyone down?

In our experience, developers live at the speed of deployment. Architects set the speed of progress. Security people run at the speed of their caution.

How can you reconcile different speeds and rhythms, and make sure that you can conduct threat modeling in a way that meets everyone's points of view, expectations, and requirements? You want to have a multispeed process, one that captures the system as it initially exists, and then continues to capture it as it evolves, revealing threats as they appear, evolve, and change. And, of course, you want this as you continue to address all of the other challenges we've discussed in the previous chapters! To achieve all of this, you need continuous threat modeling.

The Continuous Threat Modeling Methodology

Still using the grading parameters we introduced in Chapter 2, the continuous threat modeling (CTM) methodology relies on a simple set of guiding principles:

- A product team will always know its own system better than any security expert that is not part of that team.
- A team cannot be expected to stop what it is doing to engage in threat modeling (*accessible, Agile*).
- An individualized increasing-returns learning curve replaces training. The quality of the analysis of threats grows with experience (*educational, unconstrained*).
- The state of the threat model must reflect the present state of the system being modeled (*representative*).
- Today's threat model needs to be better than yesterday's (*scalable, educational*).
- The findings need to match the system (*useful*).

It is not by chance that the educational parameter gets invoked twice in the principles. The whole idea is to enable a team with little or no security knowledge and with or without access to a security expert to engage in effective threat modeling. It is also not by chance that the first principle does not connect to any of the measurement parameters we explored in Chapter 2: the whole methodology is based on the product team taking *ownership* of its own threat model, in a way that will enable team members to reap the benefits of the process and not be dependent on an external source of knowledge. We had no measurement for that in Chapter 2.

Evolutionary: Getting Better All the Time

One of our main propositions is that threat models must be *evolutionary*. This means that the threat model gets better every day. This also means that a team does not need to feel paralyzed by the need to "catch them all!" being comprehensively thorough and effectively identifying all the possible threats in the system, before proceeding with mitigation.

Knowing that your threat model will evolve over time also enables scalability by letting different teams move at different speeds and interactions through the same steps. While it is important to have a methodology that works for all your teams, they do not need to be locked in step in order for that methodology to be immediately effective. You may let each team evolve as it will, and intervene (with advice, or expert support) as needed.

The Autodesk Continuous Threat Modeling Methodology

 Before we begin this section that highlights how the Autodesk Continuous Threat Modeling (A-CTM) methodology embodies the principles of CTM and its benefits and usage, we would like to recognize and thank the people who directly contributed to the development, deployment, and day-to-day betterment of A-CTM: Reeny Sondhi and Tony Arous, who saw the value in an untried solution and decided to pursue it, the valiant AppSec Team: Hemanth Srinivasan, Esmeralda Nuraliyeva, Allison Schoenfield, Rohit Shambhuni, John Roberts, and the product teams at Autodesk who embraced and improve the methodology daily.

A-CTM is a real-world instantiation of the continuous threat modeling approach. It took the theory of CTM and applied it to a fast-changing organization, with many teams located all over the world, and experienced all the growing pains of a new methodology. Based on the results observed, corrections were made over time, and the methodology continues to evolve, as do the threat models it fosters.

The methodology is described in operational detail in the "Continuous Threat Modeling Handbook," available in the Autodesk GitHub repository (*https://oreil.ly/ MrDsa*). It may be applied at any time in the life cycle of a system, from design to deployment. The following is the Autodesk continuous threat modeling mission statement from the handbook:

The full threat modeling service that a security department typically provides for development teams can be thought of as a good set of training wheels. We see an increasing need to scale this process, and have taken the approach of transferring knowledge to development teams. The approach outlined in this Handbook provides a structure for teams to apply security principles to the threat modeling process, which enables them to translate their product knowledge into security findings, following a guided approach to questioning its security posture. The goal of this approach is to support and strengthen the development team's security capabilities across multiple iterations to the point where the quality of the threat model executed by the development team will require minimal involvement of your security team.

For the purposes of this chapter, we interchangeably use CTM, A-CTM, and Autodesk CTM to refer to the same methodology. By and large, mentions of CTM by itself refer to the base methodology and philosophy, and A-CTM to the Autodesk implementation.

To solve the dichotomy between "what do we have up to now" and "how it changes over time," CTM adopts a dual-speed approach. In this manner, you build a threat model (the *baseline threat model*) by using whatever information is available for the system at that moment, and then you and the team adopt a "Threat Model Every Story" approach (covered in detail in the following sidebar): each developer evaluates changes they make in the system from a security standpoint as they are planned, applied, or tested, and appropriate action is then taken. The baseline threat model becomes a living document that changes and evolves accordingly, and at the end (or at any given milestone) of the process reflects the present status of the system with all its changes. This idea is examined in deeper detail in the following sidebar, which first appeared as an article by Izar in the Threat Modeling Insider Newsletter (*https://oreil.ly/cJCZn*).

How Often Do Living Documents Need to Breathe?

The idea of a threat model report as a living document is not novel. It has been championed repeatedly and famously by thought leaders in threat modeling including Adam Shostack and Brook S.E. Schoenfield, and is reflected in many threat modeling methodologies, implicit or explicitly, by their last step: now do it again. Microsoft introduced the idea of security spikes to address changes in design during Agile development, and many a threat modeling tool is based on the idea of facilitating the expression of on-the-fly changes into a current threat model. The currently popular fast development and deployment philosophy expressed in DevOps sees systems deployed and redeployed a hundred (if not more) times a day, with small changes moving from inception to customer-facing in record times. This would surely tax even the most flexible threat modeling tool.

But between the "once and done, then again" and a "change at the speed of thought" situations there lies a spot that appears to be promising. Here, changes to a system's design and implementation can be reflected in the threat model in a way that allows

---

reaping the benefits of this conceptual process and yet keeps the model reflecting the system as it moves along, while offering the developer a consumable ramping up in their experience of security as a programming subdiscipline. The fact is that if we wait many scrums (or any other unit of development cycles) to address change in the threat model, important and secure-significant details will likely be lost.

On the other hand, of the hundreds of changes a day that are enabled by DevOps, only a very small number will be "security notable events" that modify the attack surface, the security posture, or the secure configuration of the system. These events are more effectively identified at the time they are, for the lack of a better word, designed —at the time the architect or developer needs to add or modify the system in a way that changes its security assertions and/or assumptions. This magic spot is the feature, fix, or story. As Schoenfield so aptly puts in *Secrets of a Cyber Security Architect* (Auerbach Publications):

> Threat modeling doesn't have to take a long time. As I've noted in this book, if an inexperienced team finds just one requirement that significantly improves a security posture, this is a win and should be celebrated as such. This implies that threat models needn't be the long, exhaustive exercise often promulgated by software security programs. Rather, get developers thinking about credible attack scenarios. Over time, they will likely get better at the analysis, identify more scenarios that apply, and thus identify more security requirements.

My interpretation of Schoenfield's experience is that we trust developers with mission-critical decisions when they are writing their code, but for some reason we decided that threat modeling is something better left to the experts—looking for the big bang of a complete solution. But if we want incremental, evolutionary answers, we must trust them, give them the tools, and more than that, give them the understanding of security fundamentals so they can do their own threat modeling or at least identify their own security notable events. By queueing these events and having that queue addressed in able time by a curator—who ultimately decides what goes into the threat model and what needs to be addressed in documentation, testing procedures, or deployment changes—the threat model keeps apace with development. At all times, the changes are reflected in the threat model, with fewer opportunities for lost details and wrong assumptions and at a granularity that addresses only potential security flaws rather than every little change in the system.

This is the basis of continuous threat modeling, or "Threat Model Every Story," a threat model methodology currently deployed at Autodesk and under consideration by a few other companies. You can view the talk, "Threat Model Every Story: Practical Continuous Threat Modeling Work for Your Team" (*https://oreil.ly/aSaXr*), from OWASP AppSec California 2019.

At first look, CTM appears to be as "heavy" as other methodologies we've seen, but in truth it tries to make things simple, and more than anything, collaborative. Threat modeling is a team sport.

Everyone in the development team is a full stakeholder in the CTM process:

- Product owners and product managers want to verify that security requirements are met appropriately.
- Architects want to validate the design.
- Developers want to both receive guidance and provide feedback on changes made to the design during implementation.
- Testers want to use it as a road map for security testing.
- DevOps uses it for architectural review and security controls on deployment.

While these are distinct roles with separate expectations from the threat modeling exercise, they provide different views of the same system that creates a comprehensive view of the system with enough detail to make appropriate security and risk decisions.

At this time in the process, you should select one or more (but not too many!) *curators*. The role of threat model curator is more of a process minder than technical, but it is important that the curator knows who is responsible for what in the team, and can clearly communicate. This person will also need dedicated time during the whole development process to perform CTM bookkeeping.

The curator will own a queue in the team's bug repository (or any other mechanism used to keep track of tasks and bugs). This queue is formed by items (for clarity, we will refer to them simply as *tickets*) that are labeled according to their status relative to the threat model:

security-tm
> These are tickets that express and track *findings* in the threat model; that is, verified issues that need to be solved.

potential-tm-update
> These are tickets that express changes in the design, implementation, deployment, documentation, or any other characteristic of the system development that is deemed of potential interest to the threat model as a whole.

The curator will use *potential-tm-update* tickets and promote them to *security-tm* by using their own judgment, or after discussion with others in the team, and if needed, consultation with a security expert if one is available. With time, patterns will evolve in the *potential-tm-update* tickets that will allow the process to flow faster.

There are two outcomes for the *potential-tm-update* consideration by the curator. The ticket may become a *security-tm* ticket, which is tracked as a finding up to its full resolution. Or the *potential-tm-update* is considered something that may be resolved in another way, for example, a change in documentation, a notification to the

DevOps team that deployment needs have changed, or a new test case for quality engineering. This is where the methodology shines in transforming potential issues into actionable tasks that improve the overall clarity of the system as it is developed.

Baselining

The first step of the CTM process includes building a baseline of the existing system or design. Your team must come together and identify and investigate any known characteristics of the system. This includes the following actions:

Define the scope
> Are you threat modeling a full system or just a small design change? Decide which elements of the system will be part of the threat model.

Identify all important assets
> The model must include all relevant parts of the system. If you are worried about too much detail, start with a top-level description of the system and repeat the process for more detailed views of smaller parts.

Draw diagram(s)
> Create diagrams of your system based on the scope. These should include, minimally, the personas who use the system (e.g., users, administrators, operators), and the way they interact with the system, browsers, desktop clients, servers, load-balancers, and firewalls, etc.

Draw data flows
> Picture the interactions between the system's pieces in terms of data flow. Annotate the interactions with details such as protocols and authentication.

Mark where the important data lives, transits, and is transformed
> This is important, as here you'll discover which assets you are trying to protect and where they appear in the system. You can create a diagram on a whiteboard, or in any of the many diagramming solutions we discussed in Chapter 1. To make it easy to keep the diagram up-to-date, you might want to use an open source toolchain using pytm (*https://github.com/izar/pytm*), which we discussed in Chapter 3.

At this stage, the "definition of done" is that team members agree that the diagram that you've just created correctly represents the system's pieces and their interactions to a level that satisfies the team's understanding of all the relationships among the elements.

It is important to note that the format of the DFD and the threat model report that contains it is critical. If all of your organization's teams follow the same format, it will become easier to locate information in distinct threat models, and for members of your security team to quickly absorb this information when working with multiple development teams. CTM highly encourages the use of the basic DFD symbology we discussed in Chapter 1.

At this point, your team learns what to present in the DFDs. As we have stated many times in this book, we have found that as a rule, threat modeling is a GIGO activity. You will get outcomes as good as the quality of the information available to you and your team. For this reason, CTM leans heavily toward having the DFD as well annotated as possible. If adding all of this detail to the high-level DFD (Level-0) gets too dense for readability, the team can break the diagram into separate, more detailed DFDs (Level-1).

The methodology also requires that your team provide additional characteristics that would allow an external observer to obtain the minimum amount of information needed to make educated observations about the security of your system. You should also suggest a standard format for the report. If the attending security expert is not always the same person, or is dealing with many products at the same time, having a standard format allows them to quickly and effectively context switch. The sample threat model in Appendix A reflects these points. Using a consistent format for the threat model is also beneficial when team members move between teams, and when there is an interest in data mining the threat models to extract useful data.

The following is a DFD checklist for CTM:

1. Provide a complete diagram of your system, including deployment.
2. Label each component in the system overview DFD (L0).
3. Label the direction of each data flow by using arrows (to/from/bidirectional).
4. Label the main actions that each arrow represents.
5. Label the protocol used for each data flow.
6. Label the trust boundaries and networks.
7. Label the main types of data and how they flow through the application (control flow) in the detailed DFD (L1).
8. Describe the personas who use the system (users, administrators, operators, etc.) and show how data flow/access differs for each person.
9. Label each part of the authentication process.
10. Label each part of the authorization process.
11. Label the order of these actions numerically.
12. Label the "crown jewels," or the most sensitive data. How is it handled? What is the most critical application functionality?

The format for findings should follow a set structure:

A unique identifier
This is how the finding will be identified throughout its life cycle.

A fully descriptive attack scenario
Many times, findings get interpreted in more than one way by different members of the team. Specifying a full attack scenario makes it easier for the team to understand whether everyone is referring to the same issue or whether more than one issue is lying under a single finding. Having enough information helps establish the impact and likelihood of the finding, as does (if necessary) breaking the finding into several smaller ones.

Severity
While not, strictly speaking, a *risk* rating system, CVSS is a viable, although sometimes imperfect, way to establish a ranking of findings. CVSS offers a simple way to quickly establish an indication of severity for an issue that can give you an apples-to-apples comparison of findings.[1] It is not the best for all use cases, but it is easy to use and descriptive enough, and it is used as a standard by enough tools, to make it a useful and representative metric. Nothing in CTM mandates the use of CVSS, and the team is free to adopt a metric that speaks to them, or is more representative of risk than severity—but it is crucial that all threat modeling efforts in an organization use the same method, so that prioritization can occur and so that discussions center around the same standards for finding "importance."

Mitigation
A proposed solution to the problem identified. Together with the *potential-tm-update* and the ticketing system, this field creates a space where the final conclusion about the finding can be recorded and consulted as necessary.

Baseline Analysis

As we've discussed, the first problem that CTM tries to address is security education. The second problem is the need for a security expert who conducts the threat model exercise to identify flaws. The question always comes back to how can the team identify those flaws independently, if team members do not have the expert knowledge themselves?

Threat modeling trainers usually open with the line "think like a hacker!" This is as useful as pushing an inexperienced cook into a kitchen and telling them to just think like a Michelin-rated chef. Better order those pizzas, or everybody will starve. Asking

---

1 CVSS is discussed in more detail in Chapter 3.

a person to do this is more than addressing a knowledge issue; it is a mindset shift that not everyone will be able or ready to undertake: stop "coding to spec" and start "coding/designing/testing to break." It requests that people change their point of view, which isn't easy to do.

With that in mind, CTM nudges the team to think in terms of security flaws, but with an approach of "have we done the right thing?" We think that leading your team in a discussion of the security aspects of its design will bring out findings, while increasing team members' security knowledge. It does that by requiring the team to go over a subject list that points out domains of security and examine a couple of *leading* questions to begin the discussion (see Table 5-1).[2]

Table 5-1. Leading questions to begin the discussion

Subject	Sample questions under that subject
Authentication and authorization	• How do users and other actors in the system, including clients and servers, authenticate each other so that there is a guarantee against impersonation? • Do all operations in the system require authorization, and are these given to only the level necessary, and no more (for example, a user accessing a database has limited access to only those tables and columns they really need access to)?
Access control	• Is access granted in a role-based fashion? Are all access decisions relevant at the time access is performed (token/permissions updated with state-changing actions; token/permissions checked before access is granted)? • Are all objects in the system subject to proper access control with the appropriate mechanisms (files, web pages, resources, operations on resources, etc.)? • Is access to sensitive data and secrets limited to only those who need it?
Trust boundaries	• Can you clearly identify where the levels of trust change in your model? • Can you map those to access control, authentication, and authorization?
Auditing	• Are security-relevant operations being logged? • Are logging best practices being followed: no PII, secrets are logged. Logging to a central location, compatible with industry standards such as SIEM, RFC 5424 and 5427, and OWASP. Is AWS CloudTrail being properly used?
Cryptography	• Are keys of a sufficient length, and algorithms in use known to be good (no collisions, no easy brute-forcing, etc.)? • Are all implementations of crypto well tested and up to their latest known secure patch, and is there no use of cryptography developed in house? • Can cryptography be easily configured/updated to adapt to changes?

---

2 Autodesk Continuous Threat Modeling Handbook, *https://oreil.ly/39UsH*.

Subject	Sample questions under that subject
Defense of secrets	• What are the tokens, keys, credentials, secrets, etc. in your system? • How are they protected? • Are any secrets distributed with the application (hardcoded)? • Are well-established and tested systems being used to store secrets? • Are any secrets (API or SSH keys, client secrets, AWS access keys, SSL private keys, chat client tokens, etc.) stored unencrypted in repositories, document shares, container images, local storage in browser, etc.? • Are secrets passed in through environmental variables as part of any build/deploy procedures? • Are secrets and sensitive data scrubbed from memory as soon as they are used, or is there a possibility that they would be logged? • Can keys be easily rotated?
Injection	• Are all inputs coming from outside the system being inspected for malformed or dangerous input? (This is especially relevant to systems accepting data files; input that gets displayed as part of web pages, binaries, or scripts, or input that gets directly incorporated into SQL queries; and systems that embed interpreters of, among others, Lua, JavaScript, and LISP).
Data encryption in transit and at rest	• Is all the important data in the system, the crown jewels, protected when it is transmitted between parts of the system and when it is being stored—both from external and internal attackers?
Data retention	• Together with the issue of data protection in transit and at rest, are we saving and retaining more data than we need? • Is data being retained for the time and in the manner required by compliance requirements?
Data minimization and privacy	• If we are saving personal data, are we protecting it according to all needed standards and compliance requirements? • Do we need to minimize and/or anonymize retained data?
Resiliency	• Does the system depend on any single point of failure that could suffer a denial-of-service attack? • If the system is distributed among many service nodes, is it possible to isolate a part of them, degrading the service but not interrupting it, in case of a localized security breach? • Does the system provide feedback controls (monitoring) to allow it to call for help as a denial of service or system probing takes place?
Denial of service	• Consider multitenancy—can one tenant generate a computation or I/O that would preclude other tenants from working? • Consider storage—can one tenant fill up all storage and stop others from working?
Configuration management	• Is the system set up to be managed by a centralized configuration management tool and/or process, with backed-up and protected configuration files?

Subject	Sample questions under that subject
Third-party libraries and components	• Are all dependencies (both direct and transitive): — Updated to mitigate all known vulnerabilities? — Obtained from trusted sources (e.g., published by a well-known company or developer that promptly addresses security issues) and verified as originating from the same trusted source? • Code-signing for libraries and installers is highly recommended—has code-signing been implemented? • Does the installer validate checksums for components downloaded from external sources? • Is there an embedded browser (embedded Chromium, Electron framework, and/or Gecko)? If so, please see the "API" entry at the end of this table.
Hardening	• Has the system design taken into consideration that the system must run in a hardened environment (closed egress ports, limited file system permissions, etc.)? • Do the installer and application processes require only the minimum privileges needed to run? Do they drop privileges whenever possible? • Are hardened images being used on cloud platforms? • Does the app load libraries only using absolute paths? • Was isolation of the service (containerization, limiting consumption of host resources, sandboxing) considered in the system's design?
Cloud services	• Have the known best practices been followed in design and use of cloud services? • Role requirements and secure policies • Use of MFA where appropriate • A plan for API key rotation • Has root access (to your cloud provider management system) been correctly hardened, managed, and configured? • Have permissions been tightened for each cloud service? • Is all back-channel (server-to-server, internal APIs) communication being routed internally via VPC peering (i.e., back-channel traffic does not go over the public internet)?
Dev/stage/prod practices	• Are the environments adequately protected? • For nonproduction testing environments (especially staging/integration), is test data sourced from production? If so, is sensitive data (e.g., personally identifiable information or customer data) scrubbed or masked before nonproduction use? • Is email functionality always tested using company-managed email accounts (i.e., not using public email providers such as *test@gmail.com*)? • Are code reviews performed per commit, by a qualified person (no direct commits to release or main branches)? • Is any security feature (login, encryption, object rights management) not covered by unit/function tests?
API	• Should you be looking into CORS if your API will be made available to browsers? • Are you using the right mode of authentication and authorization? • Are you considering impersonation? Injection?

It is important to note that this is a list of leading questions, not a checklist. The team is *not* expected to simply answer each question and move forward; instead, team members should discuss the question and responses in the context of the system they are building. The goal is to elicit thoughts on "what could possibly go wrong," while nudging developers to surface those issues that were not addressed in the past, if the system is already in place—the security debt that was created when the focal need was to get the system up and running.

This has proven to be the hardest part of introducing the methodology to teams, making them overcome the feeling that they need to answer these questions and it will be sufficient. It will not. The point here is to encourage exploration, but rather than thinking, "What could be a spoofing problem in this system?" we ask, "Regarding authentication, after you have taken into consideration these initial points here where people have traditionally had problems, what else could you consider?"

Once the team applies the subject list to its system, and if a security expert is available, the team reviews all findings identified, and if needed, the expert will point the team to further inquiry. The idea is that the expert provides more ideas, but not critique, such as, "Oh here, you forgot this." This also allows the expert to identify areas where the team needs more formal education; for example, team members did a good job on authentication and authorization, but their logging or hardening approaches need more depth.

Consider the Socratic method (*https://oreil.ly/x9_Jj*), whereby a teacher leads the students to realization by using argumentative dialogue, rather than just expanding on a given point. It is widely believed that this approach is more stimulating of critical thinking and helps single out erroneous presuppositions. By "nudging" the team in a direction and leading a dialogue around a possibility, the security expert creates an opportunity for directed learning that is more effective than just listing possibilities one by one and checking whether they stick.

If an expert is not available, the team needs to exercise introspection. For example, were there no findings because the system is good, or because the team did not dig deep enough? In any case, the curator or the team leader should use any weak knowledge areas (when the team asks, "What do they mean by 'what is the key length of your keys?'" or "What is authorization?") to provide further specialized training to the team. Once that is done, you may want to initiate a smaller discussion of that specific subject area, limiting the effort to those areas that were lacking in depth.

The results of applying the subject list as a guide to the analysis are as follows:

- Findings based on the design of the system in regard to a given subject
- Learning opportunities for subjects if the team feels unable to dig deeper
- Certainty that the basics of secure system design were evaluated over the scope of the system

When Do You Know You Did Enough?

A common question in threat modeling is when to stop. When do you know you have examined enough, thought enough, and thrown enough questioning against your system that you can consider the task done? It is quite the personal question. We have repeatedly awoke in the middle of the night with a eureka moment, as we realize we didn't ask *that* question, or didn't consider *that* vector quite the right way. We are always aware that we may be forgetting something important. You don't need to be paranoid to threat model effectively. But it helps.

In CTM, the answer to the question is made easier because the threat model is by definition evolutionary, and several opportunities remain for further inquiry. But day-to-day guidelines are needed, and after much thought and trial-and-error, you should consider a threat model complete when the following criteria are met:

- All of the relevant diagrams are in the document.
- You documented the background information and findings in the agreed format, in the development team's tracking system of choice.
- A versioned copy of the threat model is stored in a central, access-controlled location shared by the product team and the security team.

In the event a security team or security expert is not available for reviews, we suggest that you choose a security-minded team member as the security "devil's advocate" who will question the security assumptions made in the threat model, poking holes in any argument made toward finding mitigation. This way, at least, you will have assurance that you thoroughly examined any weak areas.

If a security team or expert is ready to provide assistance, they should act in an education and mentorship role, trying to *elevate* the product team's security posture rather than *question* it. You can do this by providing constructive criticism of the team's performance during the threat model, by pointing out unique and potentially product-oriented subject areas for further exploration, and by making sure that the development team examines all the crucial areas like authentication and authorization, cryptography, and data protection.

Threat Model Every Story

So, hopefully, the baseline and the initial analysis solve the problem of figuring out the state of the system and what you must fix right now. But how do you solve the issue of the system progressing and the threat model falling behind? How do you prevent the need to perform the same extensive baselining exercise at the end of another development cycle?

No matter how you look at it, only one element is responsible for getting bugs into the system, and that's the coder. Ultimately, the coder is the one who makes decisions about which parameters to use, which order of operations a given flow will take, where things go, and who can do what in the system. This means that if you want to solve at least some of these issues, they have to be addressed at the developer level.

So how do you apply the solution framework of the subject list at the developer level in a way that both respects the scope of a developer's work and takes into consideration that now only one mind is focusing on many aspects of the same issue, and not the whole team trading information on already established facts? In other words, how can CTM reduce the subject list into actionable items that any overtaxed developer could immediately use? CTM's response is the Secure Developer Checklist.

The use of checklists is not novel. As physicians and nurses started using checklists, hospitals saw significant drops in surgery errors and infections.[3] Pilots have been using them since before the first wheels-up landing. You can find checklists in so many aspects of daily life that today most people barely recognize them as the mnemonic devices they are.

Most of these checklists specify conditions to configure in order to achieve a target state. For example, let's take a look at the "Before Starting Engine" checklist of a Cessna 152 aircraft:[4]

The "Before Starting Engine" checklist is as follows:

1. Preflight inspection complete

2. Seats adjusted and locked in position

3. Seat belts and shoulder harnesses fastened

4. Fuel shutoff valve on

5. Radios and electrical equipment off

6. Brakes test and hold

Phrases like "fuel shutoff valve on" describe a target state ("valve on") that the pilot must set, which is independent of the previous state. The important point here is that no matter in which state the aircraft was left in the past, before starting the engine, the pilot must turn the shutoff valve on. Otherwise, the pilot does not continue to the next step in the checklist. This is also a basic example—imagine the pre-engine start list of something incredibly complex, such as the space shuttle? It is huge![5]

---

3 Atul Gawande, *The Checklist Manifesto: How to Get Things Right* (New York: Picador, 2010).

4 "Cessna 152 Checklist," FirstFlight Learning Systems Inc., *https://oreil.ly/ATr_k*.

5 "STS-135 Flight Data Files," Johnson Space Center, NASA, *https://oreil.ly/tczMp*.

The fact is, when things can go catastrophically wrong, a checklist with all the right states in the right order is invaluable. On the other hand, in an activity like systems development, the number of possible states is enormous, and creating a checklist for every environment is impossible. CTM just can't give developers a step-by-step list that will cover all situations. It needs a different mechanism.

For that reason, the Secure Developer Checklist adopted a different approach, which is known as the If-This-Then-That format. In this mode, the checklist doesn't contain step-by-step instructions, but rather call-out and response ones. The idea is that the developer will be able to easily recognize the "if this" side and follow up with the "then that" action that is appropriate.

The Secure Developer Checklist is also purposely short and concise. It doesn't aim to be a handbook or a guide to each one of the "then that" clauses, but a memory refresher that points the developer in the right direction to more information.

The ultimate objective of the checklist is somewhat counterintuitive. Ultimately, it must be dropped. Unused. Left alone.

Going back to the earlier training rant, one of the most egregious mistakes in security training is that it doesn't try to create a muscle memory mechanism in trainees. There is an underlying assumption that by giving them massive amounts of information and multiple-choice questions, they will be able to remember it and correctly apply it in when needed. That simply doesn't happen. Developers learn their craft by developing a toolbox of algorithms, code snippets, and system configurations that they understand and know when and how to apply. In every facet of their work, they begin at the novice level, collect experience as journeymen, and eventually, after enough application of the basics, become experts. But for some reason, security is expected to be the exception to the rule, and they need to come out of their Object Oriented Language of the Day 401, "Inner Workings of Object Introspection for Security," one-hour seminar with a complete understanding of how and when to use the techniques presented.

So, we hope that you use the checklist over and over, until you develop that muscle memory that leads you (and your team!) to not need the checklist anymore. At that time, you can stop using the checklist altogether, or it can be substituted for a checklist more suited to a given stack or technology, but still following the same format.

The following is an excerpt of the Autodesk Secure Developer Checklist; refer to the most current version (*https://oreil.ly/BYTus*) (see Table 5-2).

Table 5-2. Excerpt from the Autodesk Secure Developer Checklist

If you did *this*...	...then do *that*
...added functionality that changes sensitive properties or objects in the system	• Protect with authentication. You must make sure that all new functionality is protected with authentication. Validate that an individual, entity, or server is who it claims to be by using strong authentication mechanisms like SAML, or OAuth. • Protect with authorization. Authorization enforces the permissions/authority a person has on an entity or operation. • You must make sure that you exercise least privilege access-control policies on all new functionality. You may design for coarse-grained authorization, but keep the design flexible for fine-grained authorization. • Make sure secrets are not in clear text. A secret is only as good as its protection. When using passwords or cryptographic keys, it is important to keep them protected at all times. Try to minimize the amount of time they are available in memory by scrubbing variables right after use. Do not use hardcoded secrets under any circumstances. • Exercise least privilege. When deciding the level of privilege needed by a process or service, keep in mind that it should be only as much as that process or service needs. For example, if you are only querying a database, the credentials should not be the ones of a user who can write to the database. A process that does not need elevated (root or Administrator) privileges should not be running as root or Administrator. • Account for all vectors for client bypass. Any logic used on the client side of the application is an easy target for attack. Ensure that client-side controls cannot be bypassed by skipping steps of the application, submitting incorrect values, etc.
...created a new process or actor	• Exercise least privilege. When deciding the level of privilege needed by a process or service, keep in mind that it should be only as much as that process or service needs. For example, if you are only querying a database, the credentials you are using should not be owned by a user who can write to the database. A process that does not need elevated (root or Administrator) privileges should not be running as root or Administrator. • Make sure credentials are securely stored. Store user credentials as a salted and hashed value in a database. Ensure that a strong hash algorithm and sufficiently random salt is used. • Exercise appropriate hardening. Harden your system or component (commercial, open source, or inherited from another team) by regularly patching, installing updates, minimizing attack surface, and practicing the principle of least privilege. Minimize the attack surface by reducing the number of entry points into the system. Turn off features, services, and access that is not strictly necessary. Practice the principle of least privilege by providing the lowest amount of access and permissions necessary for a role's function. Audit each of these controls to ensure compliance.

If you did *this*...	...then do *that*
...used cryptography	• Make sure you used a toolkit approved by the organization. When including outside content (libraries, toolkits, widgets, etc.), it is important to verify that these have been vetted for security issues. • Make sure you don't write your own crypto. Writing your own crypto can introduce new flaws, and a custom algorithm may not have the necessary strength to protect against attack. Ensure that you are using an industry standard cryptographic algorithm in the correct way, for the correct purpose. See the OWASP Cryptographic Storage checklist (*https://oreil.ly/Tk6Rh*) for further details. • Make sure you have the right algorithm and key size. Use an up-to-date industry standard cryptographic algorithm and key size correctly. See OWASP Cryptographic Storage checklist for details. • Make sure any secrets are correctly stored. A secret is only as good as how it is protected. When using passwords or cryptographic keys, it is important to keep them protected at all times. Try to minimize the amount of time they are available in memory by scrubbing variables right after use. Do not use hardcoded secrets under any circumstances. Follow industry best practices for key and secret management. • Verify there are no hardwired keys or secrets that cannot be user-defined. Do not hardcode any keys. Keep keys out of code, repos, team, and personal notes, and other plain-text storage. Ensure that keys are properly stored in a password manager or as a salted and hashed value in a database.

...added an embedded component	• Exercise appropriate hardening. Every embedded component must be hardened. As part of your hardening effort, you must:
	
	  1. Minimize the attack surface. Reduce the number of entry points into the system. Turn off features, services, and access that is not specifically necessary.
	  2. When choosing a third-party component (commercial, open source, or inherited from another team), become aware of its security requirements, configuration, and implications. Contact your security team if you need help hardening a component.
	
	• Consider a component threat model. When you use a third-party component, you also inherit the risks/vulnerabilities associated with it, making it necessary to perform a threat model on third-party components you want to use. Identify all the data flows to and from the third-party component in your application and use the Autodesk Threat Modeling Handbook to generate threats.
	• Some examples of things to look for when threat modeling a third-party component:
	
	  1. Make sure that the third-party component is not given more privileges than needed in the application.
	  2. Make sure that you don't have unnecessary features (like debugging services) enabled in the third-party component.
	  3. Make sure you followed any existing security and hardening guidance for the component.
	  4. Make sure you chose restrictive defaults for the component's configuration.
	  5. Document the role of the component in the security of your complete system.
	
	• Once the threats are identified for the third-party component, make sure to address them accordingly, based on the risk/severity of those threats. Don't ship your product if it has unaddressed critical or high vulnerabilities in your third-party components.
	• Add to the component inventory. Add the new embedded component to the inventory to monitor it for updates and patches. This inventory must be kept up-to-date as a living document that can be accessed quickly and easily during a security event.

... received uncontrolled input from an untrusted source	• Verify and limit the size of input. Verify the size of input (bounds checking), as failure to do so may cause memory issues such as buffer overflows and injection attacks, etc. Failure to verify and limit input size results in data being written past allocated space and overwriting contents of the stack/heap. Implement input validation close to use (not just on the GUI!) to prevent malformed/unexpected input.
	• Assume all input is malicious and protect accordingly. Treat all input as malicious. At a minimum, validate input and sanitize output before performing actions with it. This improves the overall security posture of your application. Use a known-good approach (*https://oreil.ly/IDNRy*) as opposed to a known-bad approach (*https://oreil.ly/e_RIA*) when validating input.
	• Always perform input validation server-side, even if the input is validated client-side, because client-side input validation can be easily bypassed.
	• Consider encoding the input before it's output. When user input is appended to the response and is displayed on the web page, context-sensitive encoding of the output assists in the prevention of cross-site scripting (XSS). The type and the context in which the encoding is done is just as important as having encoding, as it is possible for XSS to manifest despite encoding, if it is done incorrectly. Read more about context-sensitive encoding in this brilliant OWASP article (*https://oreil.ly/hfW-f*).
	• Consider storing input in encoded form: for example, URL-encoded nonalphanumeric characters. When user input is appended to the response and is displayed on the web page, context-sensitive encoding of the output assists in the prevention of XSS. The type and the context in which the encoding is done is just as important as having encoding, as it is possible for XSS to occur despite encoding, if it is done incorrectly. Read more about context-sensitive encoding in this brilliant OWASP Article (*https://oreil.ly/hfW-f*).
	• Consider where and how input will be used down the processing chain. If potentially malicious input originating or passing through your application is being sent to downstream applications, and if the downstream applications implicitly trust data received from your application, this could lead to their compromise. To prevent this, make sure that you treat all input as malicious. Validate the input accordingly and encode it before data is output to downstream applications.
	• Ensure that input is not used as is when it comes from an untrusted source. Validate input before performing actions with it. This improves the overall security posture of your application. Use a known-good approach (*https://oreil.ly/EHT1H*) as opposed to a known-bad approach (*https://oreil.ly/6aFPx*) when validating input.
	• Verify that any interpreters using the data know they'll be using tainted data. Some languages, like Perl and Ruby, are able to do *taint checking*. If the contents of a variable can be modified by an external actor, it is marked as tainted and will not participate in security-sensitive operations without an error. This functionality is also present in some SQL interpreters, and if you happen to be developing your own parser/interpreter, we advise you to implement this functionality.
	• Notify QA with your parsing specification to create fuzz tests. Fuzz tests throw random data of various sizes—over, under, and just right—to test the ways that parsers and other functions accepting user input behave under edge conditions. If you created a function that accepts and "understands" user input, make sure to communicate with your QA team so it can develop the corresponding tests necessary to validate your parsing.

If you did *this*...	...then do *that*

...added web (or web-like, REST) functionality

- Protect with authorization. Authorization enforces what permissions/authority a person has on an entity or operation.
- You must make sure that you exercise least-privilege access-control policies on every new functionality. You may design for coarse-grained authorization, but keep the design flexible for fine-grained authorization.
- Protect with authentication. You must make sure that every new functionality is protected with authentication. Validate that an individual, entity, or server is who it claims to be by using strong authentication mechanisms like SAML or OAuth.
- Validate use of tokens, headers, and cookies, as uncontrolled input from an untrusted source. Never trust input that comes from the request headers, as this data can be manipulated by an attacker on the client side. Treat this data as you would treat any other potentially malicious data, and apply the steps as described under "received uncontrolled input from an untrusted source" item.
- Make correct use of TLS, checking certificates appropriately. Don't use outdated versions of TLS. Don't use broken or obsolete ciphers for your TLS connection. Make sure you are using encryption keys of sufficient size. Make sure that the certificate itself is valid and that the common name on the certificate matches the domain presenting the certificate. Make sure the certificate presented is not part of the certificate revocation list (CRL). This is not an exhaustive list of things to look for in TLS and certificates. Read this brief article (*https://oreil.ly/GvalS*) to get more information on how to get TLS right.
- Use POST instead of GET to protect arguments to calls from exposure. Using POST to send sensitive data in the body of the request is safer than sending the data as arguments in the URL of a GET request. Even if you are using TLS, the URL itself will not be encrypted and might get stored in logs, browsers, etc., thus revealing the sensitive information.
- Ensure the session can't be fixated. A *fixated* session is one that is manipulated in a way that changes an identifier in order to escape the valid scope of a user and enter another. For example, if a given URL accepts any session IDs, taken from query strings with no security validation, then an attacker can send an email to a user with that URL and append their own crafted `session_id`: *http://badurl/? session_id=foo*. If the target is fooled into clicking into the URL and entering their (valid and preexisting) credentials, the attacker can use the preset session ID *foo* to hijack the user's session. For that reason, provide defense-in-depth: use TLS to protect the whole session from interception, change the session ID after initial login, provide different IDs for each request, invalidate past sessions after logout, avoid exposing the session ID on the URL, and accept only session IDs generated by the server.
- Ensure secure storage and accessibility of secrets. A secret is only as good as its protection. When using passwords or cryptographic keys, it is important to keep them protected at all times. Try to minimize the time they are available in memory by scrubbing variables right after use. Do not use hardcoded secrets under any circumstances. Follow industry best practices for key and secret management.
- Ensure high-quality randomness of identifiers. Use a sufficiently random value for all identifiers to ensure that they are not easily predicted by an attacker. Use a cryptographically secure pseudo-random number generator to produce a value with at least 256 bits of entropy for the identifier.

If you did *this*...	...then do *that*

...transmitted data over the network

- Ensure that data cannot be sniffed in transit. To protect data in transit, you must encrypt sensitive data prior to moving and/or use encrypted connections like HTTPS/SSL/TLS to protect the data from being sniffed in transit.
- Ensure that data cannot be tampered in transit. Depending on your use case, you may use hashing, MACs/HMACs, or digital signatures to make sure that data integrity is maintained. Read this article (*https://oreil.ly/ce0LA*) for more information.
- Ensure that data cannot be replayed. You may use a timestamp or a nonce to compute a MAC/HMAC of the data before transmitting it.
- Ensure that the session cannot be hijacked. Make sure that the session ID has sufficient length and is cryptographically random. Make sure that the session ID itself is transmitted over TLS. Wherever possible, set the Secure and HTTPOnly flags on the session cookie. Also make sure that you are not vulnerable to session fixation. Read this OWASP article (*https://oreil.ly/6Nejw*) for more information.
- Make sure you are not depending on the client to protect, authenticate, or authorize. A client runs in an environment that is fully under control of the user, and so also in control of the attacker. If your security controls rely on the client, they can be bypassed and expose sensitive data and functionality. For example, it is not enough to verify a credential or security property on the browser using JavaScript, given that an attacker would be able to modify it by multiple mechanisms; for example, by using a proxy. The client should not be responsible for security decisions, but pass the relevant data to the server and use that as their security decision. A proper solution offers client-side validation for feedback purposes but server-side application of security controls.

...created a computationally or storage-bound process

- Make sure you will not provoke a denial of service to other users/actors if the process goes haywire for any reason. Implement the following best practices to avoid a DoS Service situation:
  — Use a fault-tolerant design that enables a system/application to continue its intended operation in case of failure.
  — Prevent single point of failure. Avoid/limit CPU consuming operations.
  — Keep queues short.
  — Correctly manage memory, buffers, and input.
  — Implement threading, concurrency, and asynchronicity so as to avoid operations that block while waiting for completion of large tasks to proceed.
  — Implement rate-limiting (controlling traffic to and from a server or component).

...created an install or patching capability

- Make sure your installer is signed: An installer by definition contains binaries to be installed in the target host and scripts that are responsible for that installation: creating directories and files with their permissions, making changes to the registry, etc. Many times these installers run with elevated privileges. Therefore, take extra care when validating to the user that the installer they are about to execute is indeed the one that contains only trusted software.
- Make sure your keys can be rotated. Encryption keys must be rotated periodically, so that if a key is compromised, only a small amount of data is leaked. Support the ability to perform key rotation:
  — Periodically, because of compliance requirements like SOC2 or the PCI-DSS, keys must be rotated once per year.
  — Based on an event, when access provided by a key needs to be revoked.

If you did *this…*	…then do *that*

...created a CLI or execute, a system command as part of a process

- Assume all input is malicious. At a minimum, validate input and sanitize output before performing actions with it. This improves the overall security posture of your application. Use a known-good approach (*https://oreil.ly/ucz3u*) as opposed to a known-bad approach (*https://oreil.ly/LDX5i*) when validating input. Always perform input validation on the server side even if you are doing it on the client side because client-side input can be easily bypassed.

- Make sure you cannot inject extraneous commands as arguments. When building queries and commands that will be eval()uated or exec()uted by any kind of interpreter, parser, etc., you *must* make sure that you are applying the correct validation, escaping and quoting to the input to avoid injection issues. On the interpreter side, make sure you are using the safest version of the available calls, and that (if such exists) you are letting the interpreter know that the incoming data is tainted.

- Make sure you are not providing an elevation-of-privilege vector to an attacker (least privilege). When deciding the amount of privilege needed by a process or service, keep in mind that it should be only as much as that process or service needs. For example, if you are only querying a database, your credentials should not be those of a user who can write to the database. A process that does not need elevated (root or Administrator) privileges should not be running as root or Administrator.

- Make sure you are limiting the reach of the command to those operations and areas of the filesystem you intend to (input validation and least privilege). If, for example, you are accepting an input to a file-related operation, make sure you are verifying, close to execution (not on the GUI!) that the full path you are trying to access is, indeed, in the area where you intend the user to be. Make sure strings that modify the scope of the path, like ".." and leading "/" are accounted for. Consider links when accessing a file or directory. Always use the canonical format of a path (and not relative paths) to perform a command.

- Make sure the language mechanism you are using to execute commands does not have unsafe side effects: A popular example is the yaml.load() function in the PyYAML library. It allows an attacker to supply Python code inside a YAML file, which then gets executed. Even though it is the right function for the needed use, instead use yaml.safe_load(). This difference is noted in the documentation, but many do not pay attention to it. This is why you need to be aware of side effects of any function that reads, parses, and executes code inside your code. Examples are exec(), eval(), any kind of load(), pickle(), serialization and deserialization functions, etc. See this resource for an in-depth analysis of this popular issue, but in a Ruby environment (*https://oreil.ly/bK8Fw*).

- Prefer using a well-established command execution library instead of creating a new one. Chances are that if you try to roll your own command execution library, you may end up forgetting a specific and obscure way of character quoting, black- and white- listing, or another way to manipulate input to bypass filters. Give preference to an established, tried, and tested library that takes that responsibility off your hands. At the same time, of course, make sure to choose a good library and keep an eye open for any caveats, updates, and bug fixes for it.

If you did *this*...	...then do *that*
...added a capability that can destroy, alter or invalidate customer data and/or system resources	• Consider adding two-factor authentication as a barrier before executing the procedure. Two-factor authentication is an out-of-band method of providing an additional layer of protection against an attacker performing unauthorized actions. Two-factor authentication must be out-of-band and a different method of authentication than the primary authentication method (something you know, are, or have). For example, if you log in with a password (something you know) by using a browser, a method of two-factor authentication could be using a hard token (something you have that is out of band, as in, not online or on your computer) to get a random value. • Make sure you cannot inject extraneous commands as arguments. When building queries and commands that will be `eval()`uated or `exec()`uted by any kind of interpreter, parser, etc. you MUST make sure that you are applying the correct validation, escaping and quoting to the input in order to avoid injection issues. On the interpreter side, make sure you are using the safest version of the available calls, and that (if such exists) you are letting the interpreter know that the incoming data is tainted. • Verify the operation is being logged with a timestamp and the identity of the requester. To track malicious actions of an attacker, it is important to log both the identity of the person making changes and the time of the change. In this way, if an attacker takes over an account, malicious actions can be pinpointed by verifying activity with the owner of the account.
...added a log entry	• Make sure you are not logging sensitive information (passwords, IPs, cookies, etc.). It is tempting to log as much information as possible in the case something goes wrong. But, in many cases this approach may fall short of compliance targets like GDPR, and in some cases, this may expose sensitive information like clear-text forms of passwords, sensitive cookie contents, etc. Make sure that you are not collecting more data from your users than what is strictly necessary. Ensure that your logging is not saving more than what is needed or for longer than necessary, especially when dealing with personal and/or sensitive data. • Strive to provide nonrepudiation capabilities to the logged messages. A security event is not a matter of if, but when. To be ready for that event, we want to provide timely and detailed information to anyone investigating issues. To do that, we need to assure them that whatever message they see in the logs is not only correct but also appears in the log, only as a result of the operation on which it is reporting. Verify that the logs cannot be modified by an unauthorized user (configuration), that they are received in order, and that their source is clearly established. If possible, implement signed log entries.

Several aspects of this checklist apart from the If-This-Then-That format need to be clarified. First, you will notice the concise use of guidance language. There are references to the more complex issues, but not a lot. This is so that you can get enough to start looking into the issue, but not too much to be overwhelmed.

Second, the list is as concise as it can be (but, hopefully, not more than that!). It fits on a two-sided page with a reasonable-sized font when you print it off GitHub. The idea is that a developer will print the list and have it laying around (even though it contains URLs...) and consult it without having to interrupt their workflow.

Third, the repetition of actions for items is intentional. Remember that repeated use helps the developer create muscle memory, so it is advantageous to have each "this" totally encapsulated, which avoids internal referrals and jumping up and down the text. The developer has to be able to say "here's what I did" and see the totality of "here's what I need to do now" even at the price of a few trees.

Fourth, and finally, the overuse of the language "make sure" is intentional. How do you "make sure" of something? By becoming acquainted with it in detail. If you are not able to "make sure," then you have doubts, and those need answering—either by contacting a security expert or by embarking into research, or even by consulting a colleague that may offer insight. The use of "make sure" is there as an incentive to further research and communication: you're not sure until you make sure.

Once a developer picks up a story to implement, they should evaluate it with the Secure Developer Checklist in mind. If the story has a security value—that is, it alters the threat model in any way or has security implications outside the immediate vicinity of the implementation (for example, it creates an output that another system will consume and therefore a security contract needs to be worked out)—then the story receives a *potential-tm-update* label, which the threat model curator will consider, with the outcomes we described previously. If the security value is contained, the developer implements the story securely, adding enough information to its ticket to permit documentation. The documentation in the threat model focuses on "this story brought up these threats, and here is how the team mitigated them." This ensures that the threat is not reevaluated next time the full threat model is visited, and that there is enough information if it does to establish the effectiveness of the mitigation.

Over time, we have seen that developers start implementing their stories before they look at the checklist. However, as they become familiar with the list, they refer to it before implementing. This lets them take into account what they can do differently to either eliminate or more fully mitigate any issues identified.[6]

To put this in numerical terms, when a developer first begins to implement stories without looking at the checklist, they need additional time, which includes identification of issues and corresponding remediation. Let's call that T1. Once the developer gets comfortable using the checklist before they begin development, they still need time that includes analysis and remediation. Let's call that T2. Because the developer uses the checklist *before* development, T2 < T1, simply because repeatedly using the checklist has enabled the developer to quickly see and identify issues, as well as to code securely. Over time, T2 will shrink even further, giving you and your organization a bigger delta, allowing them to prove the efficacy of continuous threat modeling. But, alas, the reality is that an ever-changing environment always has a learning curve, and developers are continually pulled in different directions. T2 will shrink, but possibly bounce back as technology changes and developers need to adapt.

---

6 Similar results have been reported by Brook S.E. Schoenfield when documenting his work at McAfee, opening the threat models as a general knowledge tool available in the Agile stand-up room—so from his experience and ours, we learn the importance of making findings available to developers.

Findings from the Field

Currently A-CTM has been in use at Autodesk for about two years (as of late 2020), and it is starting to be used outside Autodesk. The feedback, especially from the application security community, has mostly been positive; any criticism has been overwhelmingly constructive, and it directly improved the methodology along the way.

In January 2020, Allison Schoenfield and Izar presented some initial results of the use of A-CTM.[7] Schoenfield is continuously collecting information to measure and enhance the methodology, but now you can examine some initial findings:

- Development teams seem to embrace CTM to varying levels of enthusiasm, mostly based on their corporate culture. Teams that have a more independent, research-oriented culture seem to embrace a do-it-yourself effort, while teams with a more regimented background sometimes feel a lack of guidance or are overwhelmed by what's perceived as a lack of guidance offered by the methodology. For those teams, the presence and intervention of a security expert from the central AppSec team is many times invaluable and hard to replace.

- The AppSec team has less involvement in the day-to-day execution and review cycle of threat modeling, which reduces the burden on a small team to serve many product teams. The yearly (or upon-major-features) review times had to be adjusted accordingly. Given that Autodesk currently maintains more than 400 products, once all teams adopt A-CTM, there will be an ongoing need for reviews. This queue has to be managed and kept running smoothly, which does impose a certain workload on the team. The AppSec Team had to create review guidelines and agree on them with the product teams. The AppSec team also tabulated previous findings, looking for patterns pointing to areas and issues to focus on, in case those did not appear in the subject list.

- The use of a standard for the resulting report of threat models further reduced the workload on the App Sec team, since it enabled security engineers and architects to move reviews among one another with minimal investment in finding the details needed to understand the system being reviewed; security engineers and architects have a facilitated dialogue because everything is always in the same place.

- Most product teams expressed satisfaction at the evolutionary character of the system. Since they can have a continuous discussion over threats and findings when they are identified at "the right time" in the system, they feel able to

---

7 Allison Schoenfield and Izar Tarandach, "Scaling Up Is Hard To Do—The Threat Modeling Cover," You-Tube, February 2020, *https://oreil.ly/xobBx*.

respond to issues at an efficient pace and time, reducing the amount of security issues that land and then remain on the backlog.

- Because of the evolutionary nature of the approach, missed flaws generate less blame, and a more supportive educational approach instead ("Take the win or learn!").

Overall, we feel that CTM is achieving the results it set out to. The methodology is by no means perfect, but we look forward to your participation to make it better. We want your input!

Summary

In this chapter, you saw how to promote threat modeling from a single-point-in-time activity to a continuous one. It can be meshed into the fabric of development, in a way that many organizations can adopt, from those using waterfall methodologies to those more oriented to the Agile ones, and to teams that have a more independent culture or a more regimented, solidified one. We showed you how to overcome the initial speed bump of creating a "how things look like right now" threat model by creating a two-speed process, and then how to iterate over new additions to the system (at whichever speed they happen!) in order to maintain the threat model fresh and up-to-date with development.

Hopefully, you'll be able to use this methodology in your own environment. Fork the Autodesk repository and add your own modifications—and don't forget to share it with the threat modeling community!

## CHAPTER 6

Own Your Role as a Threat Modeling Champion

You can't make people listen to you. You can't make them execute. That might be a tempo-rary solution for a simple task. But to implement real change, to drive people to accomplish something truly complex or difficult or dangerous—you can't make people do those things. You have to lead them.

—Jocko Willink

In this chapter, we provide answers to common questions, and approach angles and details that didn't fit in the previous chapters. We use a Q&A style to address some of the questions we get on a daily basis. These questions come to us from all sides: the development teams we work with, our immediate management or theirs; peers both experienced and novice; and sometimes, ourselves. We hope they will give you some more thinking points to address what it means to be a threat modeler, a security prac-titioner, and a leader for change.

How Do I Get Leadership On-Board with Threat Modeling?

Q: Our team's leadership is not fully on-board with the value of threat modeling. They don't see the benefit of having this capability or making the investment neces-sary to build it out. Are there things that I (as the security champion or expert) can do to help facilitate this conversation and gain their buy-in?

A: Remind them of what happens if they don't. Leadership may not appreciate the impact that threat modeling can have on the security and/or quality of your system.

You can try to use two main arguments that do not depend on "the experts said we should" (which is an argument more in favor of spending additional money on con-sultants than on gaining value). Try telling your leadership the following:

- The development team members will be more knowledgeable about the nooks and crannies of the system if they do the analysis. This will shorten the time it takes for them to modify it when the need arises, and will foster the rise of a culture of security.

- The exercise itself is an educational tool to sharpen the development team's approach to what a secure system is. Even if no flaws are discovered during the exercise, they'll have a heightened sense of secure development going forward.

If you can, use existing data about your own product to shore up your position:

- Does your system have defects that are the result of design flaws?
- Were these flaws identified too late to address them?
- Did they cause impact to the customer or to the business?
- How much, in time or material, did it cost to fix them?

If you maintain a risk register or simply have a defect list, capture this cost and value information to use to build your case for deploying this capability. If you are able to demonstrate value in reducing problematic issues in the system, and show it can be done in a way that minimizes the cost to address them (i.e., by employing the capability early enough to outright avoid the problems in the first place), then leadership is likely to back your proposal.

In addition, use cross-industry sources like SAFECode (*https://www.safecode.org*) or the Building Security In Maturity Model (BSIMM) (*https://www.bsimm.com*), for example. While these may fall under the category of "the experts say we should," SAFECode is a consortium, and BSIMM is a collection of survey results from companies existing in distinct verticals, with both pointing to supporting data that shows threat modeling as a practice is central to an effective product security program. In this way, the "who said so" becomes the observed experience of well-regarded companies, and less an exercise of appeal to authority.

At the end of the day, point out that the overall result will lead to measurably more secure products by creating a framework to identify and mitigate issues at design, while generating security tests and documentation. That approach should be a strong argument to an educated leadership.

How Do I Overcome Resistance from the Rest of the Product Team?

Q: Management thinks threat modeling is a great idea. They have been shown, and understand, the value of performing this critical activity early in the life cycle. But I am encountering resistance from my fellow product teammates. What can I do to overcome this resistance?

A: First, you need to understand the source of their resistance. Talk to other developers and understand their pain points. It could be that they don't feel that they have the necessary experience; perhaps they are afraid of missing something important and being blamed afterwards. Perhaps the methodology proposed doesn't match their overall development methodology. Or perhaps they are overwhelmed with other requirements and feel they simply don't have the time to address one more requirement.

Act on three fronts:

Remove the blame
Threat modeling should be a blameless journey of exploration over a system's design. Nobody consciously makes a decision that leads to a flaw (unless they are a "malicious insider," of course). Doing this kind of work requires a "Take the win, or learn" mindset.

Adapt the approach
You may hear some common complaints: "It is too heavy," "It will slow us down," "We can write code or we can document the design; what will it be?" "We don't know enough about security," etc., if the team is not enthusiastic about the methodology used. See if you can identify a different methodology that the team can find (or be persuaded to be) acceptable. Understand that no methodology out there may fit your need as is. Don't be afraid to start small and grow as the practice gets better acceptance—remember how we mentioned the process should be evolutionary? The process should also evolve as it is better accepted in addition to the depth of analysis or "goodness" of the findings.

Bring in the expert
Especially when doing a first threat model of an existing, possibly complex system, the task is daunting by the sheer amount of possibilities. Having an expert threat modeler consult or at least deliver a presentation or demonstration to the team can make a huge difference in pointing them in the right direction. Remind the team that the expert's role is not to criticize the design, but to help make it more robust, resilient, and secure by facilitating the conversation around the design, and providing input and guidance to the team.

Remember, it is better to start small and have something in place than to go big and lose the opportunity of adding the practice to the secure development life cycle in your organization.

How Do We Overcome the Sense of (or Actual) Failure at Threat Modeling?

Q: The team is on-board, and management is supportive, but we feel like we are failing at threat modeling. How can we know if we are really failing or if this is just panic or uncertainty setting in? What can we do in either case to be successful with confidence?

A: If you have the backing of management and the team is on board, you already have the basic ingredients to build a successful threat modeling practice. But we acknowledge that this is by far not enough. Let's start by defining what *success* means in this context. Ask yourself a few questions, and think carefully about the answers:

Do you

> Feel like you are able to create a system model with its critical aspects of your system with all its major pieces in place?
>
> Have the agreement of the team that the system model (aka the abstraction of the system) corresponds to the actual system as designed or implemented?

Are you able to

> Point out where the crown jewels—the important assets, resources, and data of the system—live, and how they are protected from attack?
>
> Identify single points of failure, external dependencies, and "things that seem out of place"?

As shown in Figure 6-1, if your answer is "no" to any of the questions posed earlier, then you are feeling failure even before your threat analysis takes place. Instead, you should look more closely at how you approach the task of *system modeling*.

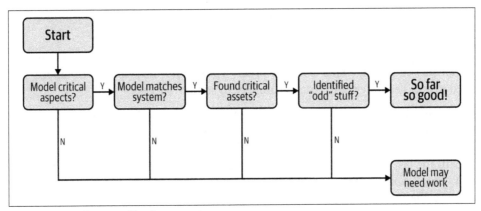

Figure 6-1. Ask yourself a few questions

Many times, collecting the information and getting everyone to agree that what you have put into the system model represents of the actual system under consideration is more difficult than identifying threats against it. Remember when we mentioned the eureka moment, when you find out that the implementation doesn't match the documented design? If this is the case, perhaps it is time to get the whole team together to update the abstraction of the system, rather than continuing the threat modeling exercise. Be careful to avoid making this about GIGO when discussing the root cause of the challenges in your team at this point; confusion or incompleteness in the system model is not the same as intentionally misleading or junk data. Build confidence in the team performing this exercise by pointing out discrepancies and get the team to collectively take action to identify where things went wrong, identify the necessary changes in the model to eliminate the discrepancies, and proceed with confidence, knowing that you have a solid, representative model to work from.

If your answer is "yes" to the questions asked previously, then you are building effective system models, but the analysis of the abstractions to identify threats may be an area of concern. Each team member should ask themselves, or collectively as a team, the following:

1. Is the threat modeling exercise generating valid findings?

2. Are you learning anything from the information collected that you didn't know before about your system?

3. Are you able to correct any flaws already identified?

Again it bears saying—it is *that* important—threat modeling is an evolutionary process (refer to Chapter 5 to see the idea in practice). Rather than aiming for boiling the ocean and trying to get everything right the first time, especially for a team that is new to the practice, you should adopt a methodology that permits periodic and constant bursts of evaluation and discovery, so that you are constantly learning and identifying flaws.

If you are able to answer "yes" to this latest set of questions, you are not failing. You are already extracting value from the process! If you still have a *sense* of failure, you need to build confidence in your capabilities to achieve success.

Confidence here comes from experience and a feeling of value; recognize when the team's findings are impactful. Identify the feedback loop—has there been a reduction in quality issues from the QA team? Has the security scanner picked up fewer findings in the last run? Has there been a change in the number of submissions against your bug bounty program? Take the data from downstream functions and relate them to the results of the threat modeling exercise and be confident that the result you are already achieving is having a meaningful impact on the overall health and security of the system. Completeness is not necessary for success, so don't be concerned at this point with perfection.

When thinking about what might have gone wrong that led to the challenge with the system model (i.e., abstraction), consider a few common areas where teams get tripped up:

- Not having the right people attend the creation of the system abstraction results in hearsay, misremembering, or misunderstanding of the design. Recheck who is contributing to the model and either bring others with direct knowledge[1] of the system design, or conduct interviews with people in the know to build firsthand experience by attendees.

- Unclear or ambiguous requirements can lead to assumptions or confusion in design—this would be an exception to the preceding "no GIGO" rule, and is something you should look at closely. If the design team is not able to reach a correct realization of the system because of confusion caused by the requirements, success is nearly impossible. *But* don't shift or assign blame to the product managers or other stakeholders who are responsible for the requirement definition; engineering, as a stakeholder in the requirement elicitation process, has a responsibility to identify areas for improvement, and to support the creation of requirements that can lead to correctness in the ultimate design. Use the "failure" to achieve success in threat modeling as a way to identify quality rules for requirements that will support designability in the future. Build confidence by showing that the results of threat modeling can be leveraged upstream in addition to downstream in the life cycle.

---

1 Assuming, of course, those individuals are still available.

- When dealing with third-party components, uncertainty or confusion around capabilities in hardware or software may result in poor assumptions of capability in the resulting system design. Ensure that the system abstraction has correct information based on the features and constraints from the system components that are involved. Identify weak points based on the abstraction details. Build confidence by having team members share this knowledge back out to other team members (such as the Quality or Build teams). If confusion exists at the designer or developer level, other members of the project likely are confused, and knowledge sharing is a good way to demonstrate competence and show value in the activity that leads to the construction of the abstraction and information about the system. It may also open lines of communication that will provide additional information to the system-modeling participants and lead to more-effective threat modeling exercises.

If you feel that despite doing everything noted here, your threat modeling is still failing to generate valid findings, then perhaps it is time to bring in an expert to jump-start the process by educating the team on possible flaws and vulnerabilities that the team may not currently be identifying. The expert may also help you institute a training program that focuses on fundamentals rather than formulas (for example, why mixing externally provided data and SQL queries may be a bad idea rather than "use an object-relational mapper (ORM)."[2] This will enable your team to go deeper into the system's functionality and identify more tactical threats, as well as be able to include security in design by adding middle layers that "do away" with whole classes of threats. Your team will gain confidence in actions being valued; in some cases, the value may not be purely security related, and that is OK.

How Should I Choose a Threat Modeling Methodology from Many Similar Approaches?

Q: Among all the threat modeling methodologies explored, what is the common thread? What are the absolute needs of a Threat Model that can be identified in most, if not all, methodologies?

A: Have you ever met Tim Toady? He is more popularly known as TIMTOWTDY, or to new acquaintances, "there is more than one way to do it"—a guiding maxim of the Perl programming language. By now, you know it definitely applies to threat modeling, taking into consideration your environment, team, development methodology, and other factors we have explored in the previous chapters. But as varied as the options are, a set of common needs must be answered in order to end up with a proper, useful, and representative threat model:

---

2 M. Hoyos, "What Is an ORM and Why You Should Use It," Medium, December 2018, *https://oreil.ly/qWtbb*.

System modeling

The ability to translate the system into a descriptive representation that can be manipulated as a function of the characteristics and attributes of each component in the system

Risk identification

The ability to traverse the system model and identify the kinds of risks it is under, and how they can be actualized as vulnerabilities

Risk classification and ranking

A formal approach to understanding which threat is more urgent than the other, how so, and in which way they impact the system

Follow-up

A manner to reach the state where the threats identified are either solved or mitigated, or at least accepted as part of the risk appetite profile of the organization

Knowledge sharing

Every methodology by its nature facilitates communication among team members and stakeholders that has an impact beyond the immediate security needs

Data collection on results

A feedback mechanism to measure the quality of the findings in relationship to the effort to identify them; the average criticality of the findings; the areas and subjects where they appear the most—in order to drive education and planning, and ideally, mitigation by use of overarching secure design patterns, libraries, and tools

If you are able to find or develop a methodology that works for your development team *and* fulfills these objectives, you have found your way to do it. At the end of the day, if you have useful findings (which apply to your system; are identified, classified, and ranked; and mitigations have been identified), your team is learning and becoming security-minded, and your system is being well represented and analyzed, then you have fulfilled all the needs of threat modeling and reaped the benefits of a threat model.

How Should I Deliver "the Bad News"?

Q: So I have a threat model and the findings it generated. How do I organize them for presentation and follow-up? And what if I have to give everyone bad news?

A: Sometimes your threat model findings indicate that it is time to go back to the drawing board and fix fundamental design flaws with the system. You can "soften the blow" of bad news—negative results—with some basic recommendations:

- Maintain a clearly defined rating system that is understood by all stakeholders.

- Build believable and achievable attack scenarios that enable a reader with limited security background to understand how a flaw would be exploited in a vulnerability.

- Present findings in terms that can be consumed by different levels of stakeholders—management, QA, developers, and risk assessment professionals.

If appropriate for your audience, include a small business case describing the finding, such as shown here:

> Posing as an authenticated user, an attacker is able to inject malicious JavaScript code in the Comments field of our product feedback pages. When other users (authenticated or not) access these pages to read the posted feedback, that JavaScript code will run in the context of their local browsers and be able to extract sensitive information like session identifiers and in some extreme cases credentials.

The information could be written in a different way, with more technical lingo that developers would immediately understand, such as, "you have a cross-site scripting flaw in your Comments field." That would be more concise, but would be lost to any non-security-minded reader. In the same way, you could add the CVSSv3 score as a measure of criticality (it is not, but for the purposes of this discussion, let's roll with the currently accepted industry standard) and add that the risk is "CVSS:3.0/AV:N/AC:L/PR:N/UI:R/S:U/C:H/I:N/A:N 6.5 Medium." That might throw off a risk professional who is looking for a categorization of impact times likelihood.

Delivering bad news is never pleasant, but clear presentation can go a long way toward promoting positive changes. Expose facts clearly, and include any assumptions that the finding may be relying upon, to make it easier for all the stakeholders to understand the need for changes and fixes. Using the correct language and representation for each one of the target stakeholders will guarantee that there is no ambiguity and that everyone has the data they need to drive their decision processes.

What Actions Should I Take for Accepted Findings?

Q: Once I have findings documented and ranked, it is time to establish a timeline for remediation. How do I know what to fix and when, and how long do I have until it needs to be fixed?

A: This will vary among organizations, and even among different environments; use your organization's risk-ranking system and risk-acceptance policy to address this choice. Consider the example of a critical vulnerability in a web-based system with a large number of users; this type of issue may be prioritized over a critical vulnerability targeting a desktop client that cannot be reached from outside the local network (because of the level of risk that differs from the two scenarios). The important thing to keep in mind is consistency. For every given criticality rank, set a policy, or a service-level objective, for the time allowed to address the issue. If you have an external commitment to resolve defects within a certain time period (e.g., "every externally reported critical vulnerability will be fixed in three business days"), use the same period for internally identified vulnerabilities. Allow exceptions only in those cases where they are truly necessary, lest you create a culture where "nonnegotiables" are suddenly flexible.

Valid examples of exceptions could be a design flaw identified in the very core of an application, which would necessitate major change to most components of the system; in those cases, it might be necessary to indirectly mitigate the impact by adding more "bumps in the road" to exploitation rather than stopping everything until the flaw is corrected. Conversely, an example of an invalid exception would be "we don't have the time right now." If you think time is short *right now*, imagine how much more rushed things will be when the vulnerability gets popped, and you have to solve things *right now* later. If you can make a valid case for the criticality of a particular finding, it should be a corollary to extend that to the need to fix the finding inside of a given time commitment. Otherwise, you are just creating documented security debt, to be solved "at a later date."

Treat findings as bugs, but maintain an extra layer of information. By keeping your findings in a defect-tracking system, clearly labeled as originating from the threat model, you'll be able to keep a running history of their mitigation and also to look back in time and extract enough information to better understand your performance and that of your teams. Add metadata that helps you categorize the findings so you can look for patterns. For example, if it turns out that most defects are labeled as threat-model-sourced authorization issues, then perhaps it is time to slow down, bring everyone to the table, and discuss the principles of authorization, and consider committing to a design pattern that centralizes all authorization requests among all parts of the system. This can lead to the establishment of a standard "this is how we do authorization decisions for our product," which then becomes a guideline for development. New additions to the team receive that as an accepted standard, and over time authorization issues will trickle down and disappear (or morph into different authorization issues to be solved).

It is also important to consider that different roles will be interested in different views of the same finding: quality assurance and developers will want as much detail as possible, while management may want only a running tab (hopefully declining!) of the findings identified, and product owners and program managers may be more interested in the emerging patterns among the distinct findings. It is important to be able to automate the production of these views as much as possible, by storing the details of findings in a way that permits querying. And, of course—all of this data must be behind strict access control.

Did I Miss Something?

Q: Through penetration testing exercises, bug bounties, and real security incidents, I keep finding things that are design-level issues—did I miss something during the threat model?

A: Probably. And that's OK. Threat models are far from the only source of findings. Penetration testing, quality assurance that is focused on security issues, and (recently) bug bounties are all sources of issues that necessitate the same ranking and mitigation. But there is always the question—if threat modeling is so great, why did it not identify the problems that these other activities found, after they were already part of the product?

There is a distinct difference between the *threat model* and its *findings*. A threat model should not be a point-in-time activity; it is a living document that changes with the system abstraction. Findings that are discovered by the threat model present an opportunity for improvement. To facilitate communication and understanding of the findings among versions and perhaps among different product teams, we recommend you follow a consistent format that reduces the amount of effort when revisiting the threat model, passing responsibility of threat models between people, and/or when people move to other teams.

Most important, a complete threat model needs to be classified as sensitive and treated accordingly after completed, since it contains practical blueprints about how to attack the system.

Threat modeling as a process is evolutionary. Today's threat model needs to be better than yesterday's, and tomorrow's needs to be even better. For that to occur, team members need to be constantly learning, and the findings after the threat model is complete are a great source of new areas where the team needs to look harder when threat modeling the next time. It is important to revisit your practice every few months and try to identify those areas that need less attention (because the organization has dealt with them appropriately, or at least learned how to) and new threat areas that need more attention (either because they have been identified as weak areas for the organization or because researchers have recently discovered them—or because you previously thought they were out of scope, or part of the system's security debt, in earlier rounds of threat modeling).

Take the hit and learn; then go back to the beginning and start all over again.

Summary and Closing

Our expectation is that these FAQs give you enough information and background to help you lead relevant discussions with other stakeholders. And through those discussions, you can identify the most frequent impediments to starting a threat modeling practice, and can quickly deal with "but what about" questions.

We hope you have gotten some useful advice and suggestions while reading this book. We close these pages with the feeling that if a text like this had been around years ago when we embarked on our threat modeling journey, it would have helped us. Other texts out there look at secure design and threat modeling with more focused, deeper approaches to specific methodologies and design patterns, and we wholeheartedly recommend that you use those texts.

We wish you an interesting and rewarding beginning, or continuation, of your threat modeling journey. In the words of Adam Shostack (*https://oreil.ly/qEg2V*): "The more I learn about threat modeling,[…]"—we work with threat models constantly, write articles, publish books, create methodologies, and present talks, and we are all still constantly learning. We look forward to your future contributions to the field.

Further Reading

Here are some prime recommendations for everyone interested in the field:

- Adam Shostack's blog, "Adam Shostack & Friends" (*https://oreil.ly/n8axu*)
- *Securing Systems: Applied Security Architecture and Threat Models* by Brook S.E. Schoenfield (CRC Press)
- *Threat Modeling: Designing for Security* by Adam Shostack (Wiley)

The following are some methodology-specific recommendations for those with more particular needs in their approaches:

- *Designing Usable and Secure Software with IRIS and CAIRIS* by Shamal Faily (Springer)
- *Risk Centric Threat Modeling: Process for Attack Simulations and Threat Analysis* by Tony UcedaVélez and Marco M. Morana (Wiley)

A Worked Example

We believe that we have given you a deep understanding of the process of threat modeling from building a system model, eliciting information about the system, and analyzing the abstraction for potential vulnerabilities and threats. Here, we walk you through an example in order to solidify your understanding.

 Since this is a static document that lacks the level of interactivity threat modeling usually requires, the following process steps are condensed to "set the stage" followed by "giving away the ending" (no spoilers here!). From this approach, you should glean how you might approach your own threat modeling exercise based on whichever methodology you may choose.

High-Level Process Steps

As a reminder from Chapter 2, here are the high-level threat modeling steps that we will follow in this sample:

1. Identify objects in the system under consideration.

2. Identify flows between those objects.

3. Identify assets of interest.

4. Determine the potential for impact on assets.

5. Identify threats.

6. Determine exploitability.

Following identification of threats would be filing defects, working out mitigations, and coordinating with the system development teams to get mitigations in place; we won't go into these steps in this sample, as that is organization-specific and we are not trying to change those aspects of your team (especially if those things work reasonably well for you now).

Approaching Your First System Model

The basic process for modeling starts by identifying the major building blocks in the system—these could be applications, servers, databases, data stores, or other things. Then identify the connections to each major building block:

- Does the application support an API or a user interface?
- Does the server listen on any ports? If so, over what protocol?
- What talks to the database, and whatever communicates to it, does it only read data, or does it write data too?
- How does the database control access?

Keep following threads of conversation and iterate through every entity at this context layer in the system model until you have completed all necessary connections, interfaces, protocols, and data streams.

Next, choose one of the entities—usually an application or server element—that may contain additional details you need to uncover in order to identify areas for concern, and break it down further. Focus on the entry and exit points to/from the application, and the communication channels that carry data and other messages between the component you are focusing on and other components or entities; be sure to identify the protocols and type and sensitivity of data passed across the channels.

 Update your system model with annotations based on the information you identify during engagement with your team.

During your threat modeling exercise, you will need to leverage your judgment and knowledge of security principles and technology to gather information to support vulnerability and threat identification.

Before you begin, select a threat modeling methodology and define the symbol set you intend to use if your selected methodology expects a graphical model. For this sample exercise, we will use a data flow diagram (DFD) as our primary modeling approach, and we'll include the optional initiator mark; we will not use the optional interface symbol or the trust boundary symbol in this example.

Leading a Threat Modeling Exercise

As the leader of the modeling exercise, make sure to include the right stakeholders. Invite the lead architect, if one exists, to the session, as well as other designers and the development lead(s). You should also consider inviting the QA lead. Encourage all members of the project team to provide their input to the construction of the model, although as a practical matter, we recommend keeping the attendee list to a manageable set to maximize the time and attention of those who do attend.

If this is the first time you or your development team are creating a system model, start slowly. Explain the goals or expected outcomes of the exercise to the team. You should also indicate how long you expect the exercise to take, and the process that you will follow, as well as your role in the exercise and the role of each stakeholder. In the unlikely event that team members are not all familiar with each other, go around the room (physically or virtually) to make introductions before you begin the session.

You should also decide who is responsible for any drawing required during the session. We recommend you do the drawing yourself because it puts you in the center of the conversation at all times and provides attendees an opportunity to focus on the task at hand.

A few points are worth remembering as you explore the system:

Timing of the exercise is important
> Too soon, and the design will not be formed sufficiently, and there will be a lot of churn as designers with differing viewpoints challenge one another and take the discussion off on tangents. Too late, and the design will be set, and any issues identified during threat analysis may not be resolved in a timely fashion, making your meeting a documentation exercise rather than an analysis for threats.

Different stakeholders will see things differently
> We have found it common, especially as the attendee count increases, that stakeholders are not always on the same page when it comes to how the system was actually designed or implemented; you will need to be able to guide the conversation to identify the correct path for the design. You may also need to moderate the discussion to avoid rabbit holes and circling conversation threads. Also be wary of sidebar conversations as they provide an unnecessary and time-consuming distraction. This also leads to eureka moments, where the expectation from the design and the reality of the implementation clash, and the team is able to identify those spots where constraints modified the initial design without control.

Loose ends are OK

As we mentioned previously, while you may strive for perfection, be comfortable with missing information. Just make sure to avoid or minimize knowingly *incorrect* information. It is better to have a data flow or element in the model that is filled with question marks than it is to have everything complete but some known inaccuracies. Garbage in, garbage out; in this case, the inaccuracies will result in poor analysis, which may mean false findings, or worse, a lack of findings in a potentially critical region of the system.

A Sample Exercise: Creating a System Model

For this sample exercise, we've chosen to demonstrate the process of a theoretical industrial control system. Here is a basic description and simple details of the system, from a product owner:

> This system is an industrial control system for pressure relief valves; the product is code-named Solar Flare. It consists of a device to control a valve, and a sensor to read pressure levels in the pipe approaching the valve. This is a "smart" valve, so it takes direction from the control plane to decide when to open the valve and how long to keep it open. The valve and sensor communicate to the control plane, which is running on a cloud service we host in a public cloud provider, and which contains a database for historical data trending and threshold settings and a device "shadow." The control plane exposes a device control protocol channel to the device for data collection and device command and control.

From this basic description, you probably have a couple of ideas as to where problems may exist, and probably many more questions you want to ask. Try to avoid diving into "solution space" right away, and as part of facilitation of the modeling exercise, stress that any questions that are asked are to gather more specific information, not to make judgment calls at this point, although you may capture concerns in preparation for later phases (i.e., in a "parking lot"). While you may see obvious areas for concern, you should want (and to some extent *need*) the team you are working with to want to be collaborative and open to get the best possible details from them to describe this system.

As a guide for readers who may be unfamiliar with the acronyms used in this sample, here are some quick definitions:

UART

Universal asynchronous receiver/transmitter

RS-232

A serial communication protocol

GPIO

General-purpose input/output

MQTT

Message Queuing Telemetry Transport

RTOS

Real-time operating system

Identifying Components, Flows, and Assets

At this point in the exercise, you have a basic description of the system—what it is, what it should be doing, and what is in (and potentially what is not in) scope. The next step is easy; all you have to do is ~~interrogate~~ work with your team to understand the specifics of the system and its components to build out the model and identify assets worth protecting.

Since this exercise is noninteractive, we'll save you the pressure and awkward conversations and provide you the information you might have collected:

- This system contains the valve control device, a valve unit, a remote control service, and a pressure sensor.
  - The valve control device is called the Valve Controller and Sensor Array Unit.
    - The device is connected to the sensor and valve units by serial communications via a UART, and GPIO lines, respectively.
    - The device has IPv4 networking capabilities to a remote control service.
    - The device initiates communications to the remote control service and to the valve module, but communication for each is bidirectional.
  - The private cloud-based remote control service has data analytics capabilities.
    - The control service gets data from the Valve Controller and Sensor Array Unit, and using this data makes a decision on when to open or close the connected valve.
  - The valve unit is a mechanical valve with an attached electronically controlled pneumatic actuator.
  - The sensor measures pressure in the pipe before the valve.

Based on this information, a drawing of the system components might look something like Figure A-1.

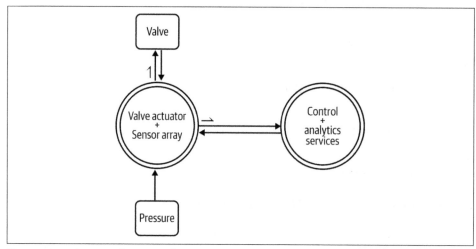

Figure A-1. Context drawing of system

 Don't worry if you are not an artist. No one will fault you for any drawing when you find valuable security or privacy flaws. In our experience, hand drawings help break the ice when meeting with development teams.

Starting from the information collected previously, you will want to dive deeper into the specifics of each component and flow to gain a refined understanding of the system and its characteristics. You can do this with directed questions on the properties of each entity you have within the system model. You should refer to Chapter 1 for some questions you might ask for each type of object; also see the subject list in Chapter 5 for more ideas.

Here is the information you might end up with after these follow-up conversations:

- The device uses an ARM processor and runs an RTOS and services written in C for coordinating actions.
  - Data messages to and control message from the remote service are over MQTT (a common IoT message queue), and are handled by the Control Proxy service.
  - The Cloud Proxy service maintains a record of device state in a "shadow," and coordinates any changes locally and on the remote control service.
  - The Sensor Reader service reads data from the sensor over a UART comm line and updates the on-board shadow.
  - The Valve Control service gets valve state over GPIO (in) and keeps the device shadow up to date with this information. It also writes over GPIO (out) to the valve to trigger an open or closed state. Finally, the service will trigger the valve to open or closed based on a state change in the device shadow.
- The sensor is looking at pressure in the line ahead of the valve, measured in pounds per square inch (psi); the data is sent to the valve actuator control device via a serial (RS-232) line.
- The actuator can receive a signal to activate (open) the valve; the default state when not receiving a signal is to deactivate (close) the valve.
  - The actuator open/closed state is output over another set of GPIO lines, which is then read by the Valve Control service on the device.
- The control service has two main functions—Shadow service and Decision Support service—and is written in Go (*https://golang.org*).
  - The Shadow service maintains a copy of the connected device state and can collect data from the device over the MQTT channel, storing the data first in the device shadow, then in the database, which is CockroachDB (*https://oreil.ly/BybER*).
  - The Decision Support service analyzes data in the database to determine when to open or close the valve; it updates the device shadow with the device state based on these calculations.

With this additional information about the components of the system, you might have drawings as shown in Figures A-2 and A-3.

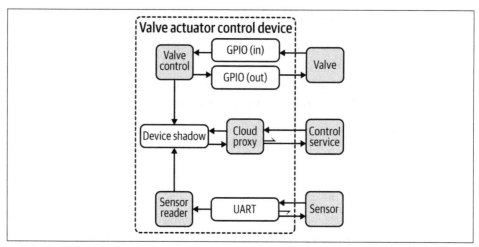

Figure A-2. Level 1 drawing of valve control device

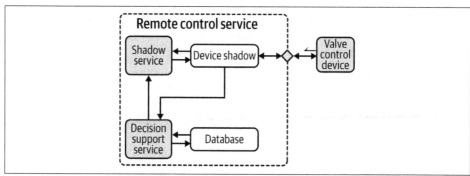

Figure A-3. Level 1 drawing of remote control service

Lastly, you will need to identify assets of value and the security (or privacy) requirements that exist for the assets identified. Some of the assets in this sample system may be obvious; others might be identified after conversation with the team.

Following are the assets of note for this sample system, and the security requirements for each. Note that privacy is not a concern in this sample because of the nature of the system (an industrial control application). Also note that the requirements are presented in semi-prioritized order, again based on the application's purpose in this sample:

Sensor data
Availability is crucial to the decision-making process, but integrity is important as well; the sensor connection is physically verifiable.

Valve state data
Similar to sensor data.

Valve actuation signal
Availability is the critical property.

Device shadow
Data in the device shadow needs to be correct (integrity) and up-to-date (available).

Device shadow data (in transit)
Data being transferred between the device and control service needs to be not tampered with (integrity) and optionally confidential.

Analytics database
Data in the database needs to have integrity; because the database is in a public cloud environment, it needs to be protected from being read by other tenants, including the public cloud provider (confidentiality).

Valve control service
The service needs to operate correctly (integrity) and also in a timely way (availability).

Sensor Reader service
The service needs to interpret the sensor data correctly (integrity).

Cloud proxy service
The service needs to operate correctly and communicate with the correct remote control server (integrity, availability).

Shadow service
The service needs to operate correctly (integrity) and be available (availability).

Decision Support service
The service needs to operate correctly (integrity) and also in a timely manner (availability).

Identifying System Weaknesses and Vulnerabilities

Using the information you have collected thus far, you now should be on the lookout for potential areas of concern against the assets in your system. In particular, that means looking for exploitable weaknesses that could impact one of the identified assets (and one of the security requirements for each asset).

Here are some potential weaknesses for you to consider in this sample:

1. Sensor data could be intercepted and modified, but this would require physical access to the serial cable or connectors.

    a. The sensor data format affords no integrity protection.

    b. The sensor data communication line has no redundancy in the case of a breakage.

    c. The sensor does not authenticate to the device controller, but is physically wired to the device controller so it can be visually inspected for authenticity and for tampering.

2. Valve state data could be intercepted and modified, but this would require physical access to the GPIO lines.

    a. The valve state data format affords no integrity protection.

    b. The valve state data communication line has no redundancy in the case of a breakage.

    c. The valve module is not authenticated by the device controller, but is physically wired to the device controller so it can be visually inspected for authenticity and for tampering.

3. The valve actuation signal could be prevented from reaching the valve if the GPIO line was severed (requires physical access to GPIO).

4. The device shadow (device side) could be destroyed if power is lost to the controller device.

    a. The device shadow data is held in memory on the device controller under control of a service written in a non-memory-safe language.

    b. The device shadow is defined as a structure with fixed memory size.

5. The analytics database is accessible to anyone with access to the cloud account.

    a. The database does not support encryption for data.

    b. The database is hosted on a storage node with built-in encryption.

6. The Valve Control service is given a high event priority.

7. The Sensor Reader service is given a high event priority.

8. The Cloud Proxy service could send device shadow data to the wrong cloud service.

    a. MQTT as a protocol has no protection for integrity or confidentiality.

    b. The transport protocol is reliable.

Additionally, the MQTT data in transit could be intercepted and modified by anyone with access to the network connection between the device controller and the cloud service.

 Reminder: for demonstration purposes, this is not a complete list of all possible impacts to the system's assets. Instead, we are trying to give you a good representation of what you might discover and show how to close out the threat modeling exercise.

Identifying Threats

Based on all the information you have identified from the system modeling exercise, the following threats are revealed:

1. A malicious actor can spoof the remote control server to trick the valve actuator control device into sending its data to a system under control of the adversary; this requires being on the same subnet as the valve actuator control device, or compromising or having access to the cloud account.

2. A malicious actor can spoof the remote control server to trick the valve actuator control device into performing incorrect actions (e.g., opening the valve at the incorrect time, or failing to open the valve at the correct time); this requires being on the same subnet as the valve actuator control device, or compromising or having access to the cloud account.

3. A malicious actor can prevent the pressure sensor data from reaching the valve actuator control device or modify the reported values; this requires physical access to the device or sensor.

4. A malicious actor can prevent the valve actuation signal from reaching the valve, resulting in an unexpected change in the pressure before or after the valve.

5. A malicious actor can prevent valve state information from reaching the valve actuator control device, potentially impacting how the Decision Support service operates (resulting in future incorrect actions to open or close the valve).

Determining Exploitability

This list of five threats seem pretty serious, but which should be fixed first? Here is where things get a little fuzzy. There is a difference between *severity* and *risk*. When calculating exploitability, which is useful for prioritization of identified vulnerabilities and threats, we can use a tool like the Common Vulnerability Scoring System (CVSS) to generate a score. As a refresher, the following factors go into the CVSS score:

- AV: Attack vector

- AC: Attack complexity

- PR: Privileges required

- UI: User interaction (required)

- SC: Scope change

- C: Confidentiality

- I: Integrity

- A: Availability

Some of the threats have other qualitative-based severity values, which we will call out when they occur.

Threats 1 and 2 involve a malicious actor spoofing the cloud service endpoint, which is possible because of the MQTT channel not using a secure protocol. As with many threats, there may be multiple ways to exploit the vulnerability and cause a negative impact.

The CVSS v3.1 factors for one exploitation path of this threat—where the attacker has a foothold on the local subnet of the valve actuator control device—are:

- AV: Adjacent network

- AC: Low

- PR: None

- UI: None

- SC: None

- C: High

- I: High

- A: High

The resulting CVSS v3.1 score, rating, and vector are 8.8/High (CVSS:3.1/AV:A/ AC:L/PR:N/UI:N/S:U/C:H/I:H/A:H).

Alternatively, an attacker with account access can modify the entry point for the remote control service to cause it to perform incorrectly (from the perspective of the valve actuator control device at least). In this case, here are the factors:

- AV: Network
- AC: High
- PR: High
- UI: None
- SC: Yes
- C: High
- I: High
- A: High

The resulting CVSS v3.1 score, rating, and vector are 8.0/High (CVSS:3.1/AV:N/AC:H/PR:H/UI:N/S:C/C:H/I:H/A:H).

You should continue rating threats 3, 4, and 5 as an exercise on your own.

Wrapping Things Up

At this point in the threat modeling activity, you will have a good understanding of the potential severity of the identified issues, and based on the characteristics of the system under consideration, an estimation of risk could be performed. As you can imagine, some of the threats will be easier and less costly to fix, or mitigate the impact from, than others.

Adding mutual TLS to the MQTT communication channel will mitigate threats 1 and 2, which are the most severe threats (when using CVSS v3.1 to rate the severity).

The Threat Modeling Manifesto

Let's begin by defining a subset in the security and privacy communities composed of people with what we could call a "meta-interest" in threat modeling. These people research methods in an academic setting, perform threat modeling as professionals in companies or as consultants, speak on the subject at industry conferences, and evangelize threat modeling regularly. These individuals believe and from experience know that threat modeling is a worthy practice in developing more secure systems.

This collection of individuals is the threat modeling community. It has always been vocal and prolific, but since 2017 it started seeing interest in threat modeling rise among companies and product development teams. In 2019–2020, a feeling started to permeate among the threat modeling community that it was time to cast off the common belief that threat modeling is an "art" practiced by a few experts and start considering it a *discipline* that can be taught (or, as Chris Romeo aptly puts it (*https://oreil.ly/4lVGI*), "better caught than taught"). Like other disciplines, threat modeling can be researched, measured, explained, tested, improved, questioned, and discussed; all the processes that make for a de facto discipline.

We have cited many members of the threat modeling community, and shared our individual and collective experiences, to give you the background you need to move forward. Throughout the book, we were careful to point out where our personal beliefs and experience came into play.

In the middle of 2020 DC,[1] many well-known individuals in the threat modeling community whom we came to know and respect as part of prior collaborations, came together to create the *Threat Modeling Manifesto*. We are honored to be part of this group and to be the first in print to share this resource and the background behind it.

---

1 "During COVID-19."

Not by coincidence, you'll recognize many of the values and principles as we have discussed them in depth in this book.

Method and Purpose

These people wanted to put the house in order so that this demystification of threat modeling could happen on a strong foundation. These individual authors collectively have dozens of years of experience teaching, doing, and researching threat modeling. We (the authors of the Manifesto, from here on, unless noted differently) found that by taking inspiration from the successful previous experience of the Agile Manifesto (*https://agilemanifesto.org*), we could perhaps distill that experience in a way that others would find valuable and that would serve as a foundation for future improvement. In this way, the Threat Modeling Manifesto is built in three parts:

1. A definition and scope
2. Threat modeling values
3. Threat modeling principles

Why start with a definition and scope? Don't we all know what threat modeling is? Well, we do. And now you do too. But…in the course of our initial discussions, it became clear that at times we behaved like the blind men in the parable "The Blind Men and an Elephant" (*https://oreil.ly/McFdH*) (remember Chapter 3? It is a useful analogue!). While we all "know" what threat modeling is, by virtue of our experience and individual approaches, sometimes different aspects of it presented themselves as more important, central, or defining than others. Some of us gave more centrality to eliciting threats, others to creating realistic models, others yet to the meta-approach of how to do the whole thing.

By converging (note we are not saying *agreeing*!) on a minimal definition we were able to have a conversation around all these shared and individual opinions and come down to the bare metal of what threat modeling actually may be. From there, we were able to build.

The values appear in the format "We value *x* over *y*." This is not to say that *x* is intrinsically better than *y*, or that *y* should be avoided, always. It means that over the period of our collected experience, we have observed that *x* usually brings better results than *y*. At times *y* will be perfectly acceptable, and even *z* will surface as a different characteristic. But by and large, we have agreed that *x* is more desirable than *y*. The principles aim to explain the values in light of the definition.

We (Matt and Izar!) are grateful to the other members of the Threat Modeling Manifesto group for this experience of collaboration, learning, and discussion. Without further ado, we are proud to present the Threat Modeling Manifesto.

The Threat Modeling Manifesto

What Is Threat Modeling?

Threat modeling is analyzing representations of a system to highlight concerns about security and privacy characteristics. At the highest levels, when we threat model, we ask four key questions:[2]

1. What are we working on?
2. What can go wrong?
3. What are we going to do about it?
4. Did we do a good enough job?

Why Threat Model?

When you perform threat modeling, you begin to recognize what can go wrong in a system. It also allows you to pinpoint design and implementation issues that require mitigation, whether it is early in or throughout the lifetime of the system. The output of the threat model, which are known as threats, informs decisions that you might make in subsequent design, development, testing, and post-deployment phases.

Who Should Threat Model?

You. Everyone. Anyone who is concerned about the privacy, safety, and security of their system.

How Should I Use the Threat Modeling Manifesto?

Use the Manifesto as a guide to develop or refine a methodology that best fits your needs. We believe that following the guidance in the Manifesto will result in more effective and more productive threat modeling. In turn, this will help you to successfully develop more secure applications, systems, and organizations and protect them from threats to your data and services. The Manifesto contains ideas, but is not a how-to, and is methodology-agnostic.

The Threat Modeling Manifesto follows a similar format to that of the Agile Manifesto[3] by identifying the two following guidelines:

---

2 "Shostack's 4 Question Frame for Threat Modeling" (*https://oreil.ly/NlzOH*) by Adam Shostack, a member of the Threat Modeling Manifesto group.

3 The Manifesto for Agile Software Development created in 2001 identifies software development values and principles, some of which align with this Threat Modeling Manifesto.

- **Values:** A value in threat modeling is something that has relative worth, merit, or importance. That is, while there is value in the items on the right, we value the items on the left more.
- **Principles:** A principle describes the fundamental truths of threat modeling. There are three types of principles: (i) fundamental, primary, or general truths that enable successful threat modeling, (ii) patterns that are highly recommended, and (iii) anti-patterns that should be avoided.

Values

We have come to value:

- A culture of finding and fixing design issues over checkbox compliance.
- People and collaboration over processes, methodologies, and tools.
- A journey of understanding over a security or privacy snapshot.
- Doing threat modeling over talking about it.
- Continuous refinement over a single delivery.

Principles

We follow these principles:

- The best use of threat modeling is to improve the security and privacy of a system through early and frequent analysis.
- Threat modeling must align with an organization's development practices and follow design changes in iterations that are each scoped to manageable portions of the system.
- The outcomes of threat modeling are meaningful when they are of value to stakeholders.
- Dialog is key to establishing the common understandings that lead to value, while documents record those understandings, and enable measurement.

These patterns benefit threat modeling:

- **Systematic Approach:** Achieve thoroughness and reproducibility by applying security and privacy knowledge in a structured manner.
- **Theory into Practice:** Use successfully field-tested techniques aligned to local needs, and that are informed by the latest thinking on the benefits and limits of those techniques.
- **Informed Creativity:** Allow for creativity by including both craft and science.

- **Varied Viewpoints:** Assemble a diverse team with appropriate subject matter experts and cross-functional collaboration.
- **Useful Toolkit:** Support your approach with tools that allow you to increase your productivity, enhance your workflows, enable repeatability, and provide measurability.

These anti-patterns inhibit threat modeling:

- **Perfect Representation:** It is better to create multiple threat modeling representations because there is no single ideal view, and additional representations may illuminate different problems.
- **Hero Threat Modeler:** Threat modeling does not depend on one's innate ability or unique mindset; everyone can and should do it.
- **Admiration for the Problem:** Go beyond just analyzing the problem; reach for practical and relevant solutions.
- **Tendency to Overfocus:** Do not lose sight of the big picture, as parts of a model may be interdependent. Avoid exaggerating attention on adversaries, assets, or techniques.

About

Our intention for the Threat Modeling Manifesto is to share a distilled version of our collective threat modeling knowledge in a way that should inform, educate, and inspire other practitioners to adopt threat modeling as well as improve security and privacy during development.

We developed this Manifesto after years of experience thinking about, performing, teaching, and developing the practice of, Threat Modeling. We have diverse backgrounds as industry professionals, academics, authors, hands-on experts, and presenters. We bring together varied perspectives on threat modeling. Our ongoing conversations, which focus on the conditions and approaches that lead to the best results in threat modeling, as well as how to correct when we fail, continue to shape our ideas.

Authors

The working group of the Threat Modeling Manifesto consists of individuals with years of experience threat modeling for security or privacy:

- Zoe Braiterman, @zbraiterman
- Adam Shostack, @adamshostack
- Jonathan Marcil, @jonathanmarcil

- Stephen de Vries, @stephendv
- Irene Michlin, @IreneMichlin
- Kim Wuyts, @wuytski
- Robert Hurlbut, @RobertHurlbut
- Brook S.E. Schoenfield, @BrkSchoenfield
- Fraser Scott, @zeroXten
- Matthew Coles, @coles_matthewj
- Chris Romeo, @edgeroute
- Alyssa Miller, @AlyssaM_InfoSec
- Izar Tarandach, @izar_t
- Avi Douglen, @sec_tigger
- Marc French, @appsecdude

The working group would like to thank Loren Kohnfelder and Sheila Kamath for their technical edit review and expert feedback on the document content and structure.

Index

threat JSON structure, 124
threats revealed, 123

Q

questions commonly asked
    bad threat model findings, 170, 173
    failure looms, 166-169
    further reading, 174
    leadership brought on-board, 163
    methodology selection, 169
    product team resistance, 165
    remediation actions, 171

R

RACI (responsible, accountable, consulted, informed) diagram in PASTA, 64
RCE (remote code execution), 22
remediations, 171
resources
    attacker identification and characterization, 24, 40, 68
    author contact, xiv
    Autodesk Secure Developer Checklist, 152
    book web page, xv
    Building Security in Maturity Model (BSIMM), 164
    CAPEC, 65, 66, 68
    CAPEC Mechanisms of Attack, 114
    community online, 91
    Continuous Threat Modeling Handbook, 139
    CVE, 63
    CWE, 65, 68
    CWE Architectural Concepts list, 114
    further reading, 174
    games running list online, 86
    LINDDUN tutorials, 75
    MITRE ATT&CK framework, 24, 40, 68
    pytm, 118
    Risk Centric Threat Modeling book, 58
    SAFECode, 164
    Threat Modeling Designing for Security book, 57
    ThreatPlaybook, 100
    Threatspec, 98, 99
    weakness taxonomy, xxviii
risk
    calculating, xxx
        DREAD, xxxii

FAIR method, xxxiii, 83
    definition, xxx
    PASTA risk analysis, 63
    risk appetite, 24
    risk register for leadership education, 164
    security basic concepts, xxviii
    security posture, xxv
    severity versus, 185
    SPARTA risk analysis, 83
    Trike risk model, 74
Risk Centric Threat Modeling (book; UcedaVélez and Morana), 58, 174
risk management and defense in depth, xxxix
risk-centric methodology PASTA, 58
Roberts, John, 139
Robot Framework Libraries, 100
role-based access control (RBAC), xxxvi
Romeo, Chris
    threat modeling as discipline, 189
    Threat Modeling Manifesto author, 194

S

SAFECode, 164
safety definition, xxxv
Saitta, Paul, 71
Saltzer, Jerome, xxxvii
scalability
    automation needed for threat modeling, 112
    evolutionary threat models, 139
    methodology grading parameter, 48
    security consultants challenging, 99
Scandariato, Riccardo, 75, 90
Schneider, Christian, 126
Schoenfield, Allison, 139, 161
Schoenfield, Brook S. E.
    observing mutual distrust, xxxviii
    security contracts, xxxix
Schoenfield, Brook S.E.
    Secrets of a Cyber Security Architect book, 141
    Securing Systems book, 174
    STRIDE per Element warning, 56
    STRIDE warning, 55
    threat model report as living document, 140, 141
    threat modeling during development, 160
    Threat Modeling Manifesto author, 194
    threat models up to date, 6
Schroeder, Michael, xxxvii

About the Authors

Izar Tarandach is a senior security architect at Bridgewater Associates. Previously he was lead product security architect at Autodesk and the security architect for enterprise hybrid cloud at Dell EMC, following a long stint in the Dell EMC Product Security Office as a security advisor. He's a core contributor to SAFECode and a founding contributor to the IEEE Center for Security Design. Izar was an instructor in digital forensics at Boston University and in secure development at the University of Oregon.

Matthew Coles is a leader and security architect for product security programs in companies such as EMC, Analog Devices, and Bose, where he applies his over 15 years of product security and systems engineering experience to build security into the products and personalized experiences for customers worldwide. Matt has been involved in community security initiatives including the CWE/SANS Top 25 list and was an instructor in software security at Northeastern University.

Colophon

The animal on the cover of *Threat Modeling* is the red scorpionfish (*Scorpaena scrofa*). This fish is found in the eastern Atlantic Ocean and the Mediterranean Sea.

The red scorpionfish can grow to a maximum length of 20 inches, and can reach a maximum weight of almost seven pounds. Their coloring—which ranges from dark red to pale pink, and shades of beige and white—helps them blend into their environment. They breed in the early summer months, and their eggs float to the surface to hatch.

These fish have many envenomed defensive spines in their fins; a channel in the middle of the spine delivers the venom from glands at the base into the fish's antagonist. A nocturnal hunter, red scorpionfish at night swim along the sea floor, feeding on other fish as well as crabs and mollusks.

Red scorpionfish are sought by commercial fishing trawlers. This fish is prized as an ingredient in the traditional Provencal recipe for bouillabaisse (French recipes refer to this fish as *rascasse* or *scorpion de mer*).

Despite commercial pressures, red scorpionfish are listed by the IUCN as being of Least Concern. Many of the animals on O'Reilly covers are endangered; all of them are important to the world.

The cover illustration by Karen Montgomery, based on a black and white engraving from *Wood's Illustrated Natural History* (1854). The cover fonts are Gilroy and Guardian Sans. The text font is Adobe Minion Pro; the heading font is Adobe Myriad Condensed; and the code font is Dalton Maag's Ubuntu Mono.

Milton Keynes UK
Ingram Content Group UK Ltd.
UKHW010950010924
447702UK00008B/12